DEVELOPER TESTING

DEVELOPER TESTING

BUILDING QUALITY INTO SOFTWARE

ALEXANDER TARLINDER

✦Addison-Wesley

Boston • Columbus • Indianapolis • New York • San Francisco • Amsterdam • Cape Town
Dubai • London • Madrid • Milan • Munich • Paris • Montreal • Toronto • Delhi • Mexico City
São Paulo • Sydney • Hong Kong • Seoul • Singapore • Taipei • Tokyo

Library of Congress Control Number: 2016944434

ISBN-13: 978-0-13-429106-2
ISBN-10: 0-13-429106-9
Text printed in the United States on recycled paper at RR Donnelley in Crawfordsville, Indiana.
1   16

To my grandfather Romuald, who taught me about books.

CONTENTS

FOREWORD BY JEFF LANGR

Ten years ago, I became the manager and tech lead for a small development team at a local, small start-up after spending some months developing for them. The software was an almost prototypically mired mess of convoluted logic and difficult defects. On taking the leadership role, I began to promote ideas of test-driven development (TDD) in an attempt to improve the code quality. Most of the developers were at least willing to listen, and a couple eventually embraced TDD.

One developer, however, quit two days later without saying a word to me. I was told that he said something to the effect that "I'm never going to write a test, that's not my job as a programmer." I was initially concerned that I'd been too eager (though I'd never insisted on anything, just attempted to educate). I no longer felt guilty after seeing the absolute nightmare that was his code, though.

Somewhat later, one of the testers complained to me about another developer—a consultant with many years of experience—who continually submitted defect-riddled code to our QA team. "It's my job to write the code; it's their job to find the problems with it." No amount of discussion was going to convince this gentleman that he needed to make any effort to test his code.

Still later and on the same codebase, I ended up shipping an embarrassing defect that the testers failed to catch—despite my efforts to ensure that the units were well tested. A bit of change to some server code and an overlooked flipping of a boolean value meant that the client—a high-security chat application—no longer rang the bell on an incoming message. We didn't have comprehensive enough end-to-end tests needed to catch the problem.

Developer tests are tools. They're not there to make your manager happy—if that's all they were, I, too, would find a way to skip out on creating them. Tests are tools that give you the confidence to ship, whether to an end customer or to the QA team.

Thankfully, 10 years on, most developers have learned that it's indeed their job to test their own code. Few of you will embark on an interview where some form of developer testing isn't discussed. Expectations are that you're a software development professional, and part of being a professional is crafting a high-quality product. Ten years on, I'd squash any notions of hiring someone who thought they didn't have to test their own code.

Developer testing is no longer as simple as "just do TDD," or "write some integration tests," however. There are many aspects of testing that a true developer must embrace in order to deliver correct, high-quality software. And while you can find a good book on TDD or a good book on combinatorial testing, *Developer Testing:*

Building Quality into Software overviews the essentials in one place. Alexander surveys the world of testing to clarify the numerous kinds of developer tests, weighing in on the relative merits of each and providing you with indispensable tips for success.

In *Developer Testing*, Alexander first presents a case for the kinds of tests you need to focus on. He discusses overlooked but useful concepts such as programming by contract. He teaches what it takes to design code that can easily be tested. And he emphasizes two of my favorite goals: constructing highly readable specification-based tests that retain high documentation value, and eliminating the various flavors of duplication—one of the biggest enemies to quality systems. He wraps up the topic of unit testing with a pragmatic, balanced approach to TDD, presenting both classical and mockist TDD techniques.

But wait! There's more: In Chapter 18, "Beyond Unit Testing," Alexander provides as extensive a discussion as you could expect in one chapter on the murky world of developer tests that fall outside the range of unit tests. Designing these tests to be stable, useful, and sustainable is quite the challenge. *Developer Testing* doesn't disappoint, again supplying abundant hard-earned wisdom on how to best tackle the topic.

I enjoyed working through *Developer Testing* and found that it got even better as it went along, as Alexander worked through the meaty coding parts. It's hard to come up with good examples that keep the reader engaged and frustration free, and Alexander succeeds masterfully with his examples. I think you'll enjoy the book too, and you'll also thank yourself for getting a foundation of the testing skills that are critical to your continued career growth.

FOREWORD BY LISA CRISPIN

The subtitle says it all—"Building Quality into Software." We've always known that we can't test quality in by testing after coding is "done." Quality has to be baked in. To do that, the entire delivery team, including developers, has to start building each feature by thinking about how to test it. In successful teams, every team member has an agile testing mind-set. They work with the delivery and customer teams to understand what the customers need to be successful. They focus on preventing, rather than finding, defects. They find the simplest solutions that provide the right value.

In my experience, even teams with experienced professional testers need developers who understand testing. They need to be able to talk with designers, product experts, testers, and other team members to learn what each feature should do. They need to design testable code. They need to know how to use tests to guide coding, from the unit level on up. They need to know how to design test code as well as—or even better than—production code, because that test code is our living documentation and our safety net. They need to know how to explore each feature they develop to learn whether it delivers the right value to customers.

I've encountered a lot of teams where developers are paid to write production code and pushed to meet deadlines. Their managers consider any time spent testing to be a waste. If these organizations have testers at all, they're considered to be less valuable contributors, and the bugs they find are logged in a defect tracking system and ignored. These teams build a mass of code that nobody understands and that is difficult to change without something breaking. Over time they generally grind to a halt under the weight of their technical debt.

I've been fortunate over the years to work with several developers who really "get" testing. They eagerly engage in conversations with business experts, designers, testers, analysts, data specialists, and others to create a shared understanding of how each feature should behave. They're comfortable pairing with testers and happily test their own work even before it's delivered to a test environment. These are happy teams that deliver solid, valuable features to their customers frequently. They can change direction quickly to accommodate new business priorities.

Testing's a vast subject, and we're all busy, so where do you start? This book delivers key testing principles and practices to help you and your team deliver the quality your customers need, in a format that lets you pick up ideas quickly. You'll learn the language of testing so you can collaborate effectively with testers, customers, and other delivery team members. Most importantly (at least to me), you'll enjoy your work a lot more and be proud of the product you help to build.

PREFACE

I started writing this book four years ago with a very clear mental image of what I wanted it to be and who my readers were going to be. Four years is quite a while, and I've had to revise some of my ideas and assumptions, both in response to other work in the field and because of deepening understanding of the subject. The biggest thing that has happened during the course of those years is that the topic has become less controversial. Several recent books adopt a stance similar to this one, and there's some reassuring overlap, which I interpret as being on the right track.

Why I Wrote This Book

I wrote this book because this was the book I should have read a decade ago! Ten years is a long time, but believe it or not, I still need this book today—although for other reasons.

Roughly 10 years ago I embarked on a journey to understand software quality. I wasn't aware of it back then; I just knew that the code that I and my colleagues wrote was full of bugs and made us sad and the customers unhappy. I was convinced that having testers execute manual routines on our software wouldn't significantly increase its quality—and time has proven me right! So I started reading everything I could find about software craftsmanship and testing, which led to two major observations.

First, to my surprise, these topics were often totally separated back then! Books about writing software seldom spoke of verifying it. Maybe they mentioned one or two testing techniques, but they tended to skip the theory part and the conceptual frameworks needed for understanding how to work systematically with testing in different contexts. That was my impression at least. On the other hand, books on testing often tended to take off in the direction of a testing process. Books on test-driven development focused on test-driven development. This applied to blogs and other online material too.

Second, writing testable code was harder than it initially appeared, not to mention turning old legacy monoliths into something that could be tested. To get a feeling for it, I had to dive deep into the areas of software craftsmanship, refactoring, legacy code, test-driven development, and unit testing. It took a lot of deliberate practice and study.

Based on these observations and my accumulated experience, I set some goals for a book project:

- Make the foundations of software testing easily accessible to developers, so that they can make informed choices about the kind and level of verification that would be the most appropriate for code they're about to ship. In my experience, many developers don't read books or blogs on testing, yet they keep asking themselves: When have I tested this enough? How many tests do I need to write? What should my test verify? I wanted these to become no-brainers.

- Demonstrate how a testing mind-set and the use of testing techniques can enrich the daily routines of software development and show how they can become a developer's second nature.

- Create a single, good enough body of knowledge on techniques for writing testable code. I realized that such a work would be far from comprehensible, especially if kept concise, but I wanted to create something that was complete enough to save the readers from plowing through thousands of pages of books and online material. I wanted to provide a "map of the territory," if you will.

This is why I should have had a book written with these goals in mind a decade ago, but why today? Hasn't the world changed? Hasn't there been any progress in the industry? And here comes the truly interesting part: this book is just as applicable today as it would have been 10 years ago. One reason is that it's relatively technology agnostic. Admittedly it is quite committed to object-oriented programming, although large parts hold true for procedural programming, and some contents apply to functional programming as well. Another reason is that progress in the field it covers hasn't been as impressive as in many others. True, today, many developers have grasped the basics of testing, and few, if any, new popular frameworks and libraries are created without testability in mind. Still, I'd argue that it's orders of magnitude easier to find a developer who's a master in writing isomorphic JavaScript applications backed by NoSQL databases running in the cloud than to find a developer who's really good at unit testing, refactoring, and, above all, who can remain calm when the going gets tough and keep applying developer testing practices in times of pressure from managers and stressed-out peers.

Being a consultant specializing in software development, training, and mentoring, I've had the privilege to work on several software development teams and to observe other teams in action. Based on these experiences, I'd say that teams and developers follow pretty much the same learning curve when it comes to quality assurance. This book is written with such a learning curve in mind, and I've done my best to help the reader overcome it and progress as fast as possible.

Target Audience

This is a book for developers who want to write better code and who want to avoid creating bugs. It's about achieving quality in software by acknowledging testability as a primary quality attribute and adapting the development style thereafter. Readers of this book *want* to become better developers and want to understand more about software testing, but they have neither the time nor support from their peers, not to mention from their organizations.

This is not a book for beginners. It *does* explain many foundations and basic techniques, but it assumes that the reader knows how to work his development environment and build system and is no stranger to continuous integration and related tooling, like static analysis or code coverage tools. To get the most out of this book, the reader should have at least three years of experience creating software professionally. Such readers will find the book's dialogues familiar and should be able to relate to the code samples, which are all based on real code, not ideal code.

I also expect the reader to work. Even though my ambition is to make lots of information readily available, I leave the knowledge integration part to the reader. This is not a cookbook.

About the Examples

This book contains a lot of source code. Still, my intention was never to write a programming book. I want this to be a book on principles and practices, and as such, it's natural that the code examples be written in different languages. Although I'm trying to stay true to the idioms and structure used in the various languages, I also don't want to lose the reader in fancy details specific to a single language or framework; that is, I try to keep the examples generic enough so that they can be read by anyone with a reasonable level of programming experience. At times, though, I've found this stance problematic. Some frameworks and languages are just better suited for certain constructs. At other times, I couldn't decide, and I put an alternative implementation in the appendix. The source code for the examples in the book and other related code are available on the book's companion website—http://developertesting.rocks.

How to Read This Book

This book has been written with a very specific reader in mind: the pressed-for-time developer who needs practical information about a certain topic without having to read tons of articles, blogs, or books. Therefore, the underlying idea is that each chapter should take no more than one hour to read, preferably less. Ideally, the reader should be able to finish a chapter while commuting to work. As a consequence, the chapters are quite independent and can be read in isolation. However, starting with the first four chapters is recommended, as they lay a common ground for the rest of the material.

Here's a quick overview of the chapters:

- **Chapter 1: Developer Testing**—Explains that developers are engaged in a lot of testing activities and that they verify that their programs work, regardless of whether they call it testing or not. Developer testing is defined here.

- **Chapter 2: Testing Objectives, Styles, and Roles**—Describes different approaches to testing. The difference between testing to critique and testing to support is explained. The second half of the chapter is dedicated to describing traditional testing, agile testing, and different versions of behavior-driven development. Developer testing is placed on this map in the category of supporting testing that thrives in an agile context.

- **Chapter 3: The Testing Vocabulary**—This chapter can be seen as one big glossary. It explains the terms used in the testing community and presents some commonly used models like the matrix of test levels and test types and the agile testing quadrants. All terms are explained from a developer's point of view, and ambiguities and different interpretations of some of them are acknowledged rather than resolved.

- **Chapter 4: Testability from a Developer's Perspective**—Why should the developer care about testability? Here the case for testable software and its benefits is made. The quality attribute *testability* is broken down into observability, controllability, and smallness and explained further.

- **Chapter 5: Programming by Contract**—This chapter explains the benefits of keeping *programming by contract* in mind when developing, regardless of whether tests are being written or not. This technique formalizes responsibilities between calling code and called code, which is an important aspect of writing testable software. It also introduces the concept of assertions, which reside at the core of all testing frameworks.

- **Chapter 6: Drivers of Testability**—Some constructs in code have great impact on testability. Therefore, being able to recognize and name them is critical. This chapter explains direct and indirect input/output, state, temporal coupling, and domain-to-range ratio.

- **Chapter 7: Unit Testing**—This chapter starts by describing the fundamentals of xUnit-based testing frameworks. However, it soon moves on to more advanced topics like structuring and naming tests, proper use of assertions, constraint-based assertions, and some other technicalities of unit testing.

- **Chapter 8: Specification-based Testing Techniques**—Here the testing domain is prevalent. Fundamental testing techniques are explained from the point of view of the developer. Knowing them is essential to being able to answer the question: "How many tests do I need to write?"

- **Chapter 9: Dependencies**—Dependencies between classes, components, layers, or tiers all affect testability in different ways. This chapter is dedicated to explaining the different kinds and how to deal with them.

- **Chapter 10: Data-driven and Combinatorial Testing**—This chapter explains how to handle cases where seemingly many similar-looking tests are needed. It introduces parameterized tests and theories, which both solve this problem. It also explains generative testing, which is about taking test parameterization even further. Finally, it describes techniques used by testers to deal with combinatorial explosions of test cases.

- **Chapter 11: Almost Unit Tests**—This book relies on a definition of unit tests that disqualifies some tests that look and run almost as fast as unit tests from actually being called by that name. To emphasize the distinction, they're called "fast medium tests". They typically involve setting up a lightweight server of some kind, like a servlet container, mail server, or in-memory database. Such tests are described in this chapter.

- **Chapter 12: Test Doubles**—This chapter introduces typical test doubles like stubs, mocks, fakes, and dummies, but without using any mocking frameworks. The point is to understand test doubles without having to learn yet another framework. This chapter also describes the difference between state-based and interaction-based testing.

- **Chapter 13: Mocking Frameworks**—Here it gets very practical, as the mocking frameworks Moq, Mockito, and the test double facilities of Spock are used to create test doubles for different needs and situations—especially stubs and mocks. This chapter also includes pitfalls and antipatterns related to the use of mocking frameworks.

- **Chapter 14: Test-driven Development—Classic Style**—Here, classic test-driven development is introduced through a longer example. The example is used to illustrate the various details of the technique, such as the order in which to write tests and strategies for making them pass.

- **Chapter 15: Test-driven Development—Mockist Style**—There's more than one way to do test-driven development. In this chapter, an alternative way is described. It's applicable in cases where test driving the design of the system is more important than test driving the implementation of a single class or component.

- **Chapter 16: Duplication**—This chapter explains why code duplication is bad for testability, but sometimes a necessary evil to achieve independence and throughput. Two main categories of duplication are introduced and dissected: mechanical duplication and duplication of knowledge.

- **Chapter 17: Working with Test Code**—This chapter contains suggestions on what to do before resorting to comments in test code and when to delete tests.

- **Chapter 18: Beyond Unit Testing**—Unit testing is the foundation of developer testing, but it's just *one* piece of the puzzle. Software systems of today are often complex and require testing at various levels of abstraction and granularity. This is where integration, system, and end-to-end tests come in. This chapter introduces such tests through a series of examples and discusses their characteristics.

- **Chapter 19: Test Ideas and Heuristics**—This final chapter, on the border of being an appendix, summarizes various test heuristics and ideas from the book.

Register your copy of *Developer Testing* at informit.com for convenient access to downloads, updates, and corrections as they become available. To start the registration process, go to informit.com and log in or create an account. Enter the product ISBN (9780134291062) and click Submit. Once the process is complete, you will find any available bonus content under "Registered Products."

ACKNOWLEDGMENTS

Writing a book is a team effort. The author is the one who writes the text and spends the most time with it, but many people make their contributions. This book is no exception. My first thanks go to Joakim Tengstrand, an expert in software development with a unique perspective on things, but above all, my friend. He's been giving me continual and insightful feedback from very early stages of writing to the very end.

Another person who needs a special mention is Stephen Vance. He helped me by doing a very exhaustive second-pass technical review. Not only did he offer extensive and very helpful feedback, he also found many, if not all, places where I tried to make things easy for myself. In addition, he helped me broaden the book by offering alternatives and perspectives.

As a matter of fact, this entire book wouldn't exist in its present form without Lisa Crispin's help. She's helped me to get it published, and she has supported me whenever I needed it throughout the entire process. I'm honored to have her write one of the forewords. Speaking of which, Jeff Langr also deserves my deepest gratitude for writing a foreword as well and for motivating me to rewrite an important section that I had been postponing forever. Mike Cohn, whom I've never had the pleasure of meeting, has accepted this book into his series. I can't even express how grateful I am and what it means to me. Thanks!

While on the topic of publication, I really need to thank Chris Guzikowski at Addison-Wesley. He's been very professional throughout the process and, above all, supportive beyond all limits. I don't know how many e-mails I started with something akin to: "Thanks for your patience! There's this thing I need to do before handing in the manuscript . . ." During the process of finalizing the book, I've had the pleasure to work with very professional and accommodating people, who really made the end of the journey interesting, challenging, and quite fun. Many thanks to Chris Zahn, Lisa McCoy, Julie Nahil, and Rachel Paul.

My reviewers, Mikael Brodd, Max Wenzin, and Mats Henricson, have done a huge job going through the text while doing the first-pass technical review.

Carlos Blé deserves special thanks for taking me through a TDD session that ended up producing a solution quite different from the one in the chapter on TDD. It sure gave me some things to think about, and it eventually led to a rewrite of the entire chapter. Ben Kelly has helped me enormously in getting the details of the testing terminology right, and he didn't let me escape with dividing some work between developers and testers. Dan North has helped me get the details straight about BDD and ATDD. Frank Appel has helped me around the topic of unit testing and related material. His well-grounded and thorough comments really made me stop and think at times. Many thanks. Alex Moore-Niemi has widened the book's scope by providing a sidebar on types, a topic with which I'm only superficially familiar.

I'd also like to extend my thanks to Al Bagdonas, my first-pass proofreader and copy editor for his dedication to this project.

In addition, I'd like to thank other people who have helped me along the way or served as inspiration: Per Lundholm, Kristoffer Skjutare, Fredrik Lindgren, Yassal Sundman, Olle Hallin, Jörgen Damberg, Lasse Koskela, Bobby Singh Sanghera, Gojko Adzic, and Peter Franzen.

Last, but not least, I'm joining the scores of authors who thank their wives and families. Writing a book is an endeavor that requires a lot of passion, dedication, and above all, time away from the family. Teresia, thanks for your patience and support.

About the Author

Alexander Tarlinder wrote his first computer program around the age of 10, sometime in the early nineties. It was a simple, text-based role-playing game for the Commodore 64. It had lots of GOTO statements and an abundance of duplicated code. Still, to him, this was the most fantastic piece of software ever conceived, and an entry point to his future career.

Twenty-five years later, Alexander still writes code and remains a developer at heart. Today, his professional career stretches over 15 years, a time during which he shouldered a variety of roles: developer, architect, project manager, Scrum-Master, tester, and agile coach. In all these roles, he has gravitated toward sustainable pace, craftsmanship, and attention to quality, and he eventually got test infected around 2005. In a way, this was inevitable, because many of his projects involved programming money somehow (in the banking and gaming industry), and he always felt that he could do more to ensure the quality of his code before handing it over to someone else.

Presently, Alexander seeks roles that allow him to influence the implementation process on a larger scale. He combines development projects with training and coaching, and he shares technical and nontechnical aspects of developer testing and quality assurance in conferences and local user groups meetings.

Chapter 1

DEVELOPER TESTING

Working in cross-functional teams has broadened the responsibilities of software professionals. Few have the dubious luxury of performing the same narrow tasks day after day without having to care about what the team delivers as a whole. This makes the daily work both more dynamic and interesting, but it also requires that each person be prepared to work in areas that may have "belonged" to a different role in the past. For developers, this manifests itself as taking ownership of the quality of the produced code, instead of expecting that someone else will test it. This is by no means anything new, but frequent deliveries, maybe as frequent as several times a day, accentuate the need for development practices that strive to eliminate the defects even before they are introduced. Because quality cannot be *tested* in, it has to be *built in*, and this path leads through the field of testing.

Developers Test

Developers have and will always test their software. Imagine the beginners writing their first "Hello, World" program. No doubt they will execute it to verify that it actually outputs the everlasting words that have been echoed decade after decade by thousands of programmers around the globe (see Figure 1.1).

Developers don't need to be testing experts. Some types of testing require specific skills or some distance from the tested software in order to mitigate any bias its creators may be subject to. This is why testing is a separate area of expertise.

Before embarking further into the field, let's pause for a moment and get the meaning of the word "developer" clarified. In some teams, most notably the ones doing Scrum, all members of the development team are developers, and they specialize in programming, testing, interface design, or architecture (Sutherland & Schwaber 2013). In this book the word "developer" refers to a person whose primary responsibility is to write source code.

Regardless of whether all testing is done within the team or by someone from outside, the output of the developers should be *working* software, not just something that compiles. To either fulfill the quality standards set by the team or to avoid that whoever does the final testing gets handed software of inferior quality, developers must ensure the correctness of their code. In order to do that, they have to write their code in a way that makes verification possible. Enter developer testing!

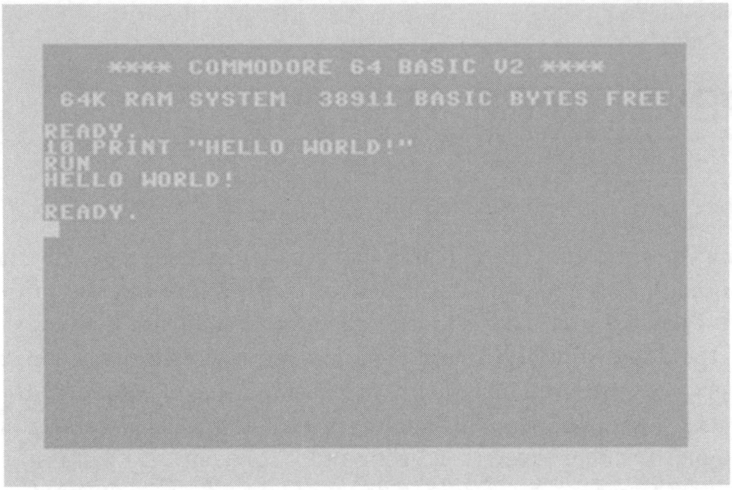

FIGURE 1.1 Ad hoc testing of a well-known program running in a nostalgic environment.

Developer Testing Activities

How much testing-related work does a developer do on a daily basis? In the next chapter we'll see that defining testing isn't entirely trivial. In this chapter we'll stay a bit informal, make some simplifications, and ignore some dimensions. For now, let's think of testing as an activity performed to ensure correctness and quality of software. When adopting this perspective, quite a few activities can be viewed in the light of developer testing.

Unit Testing

Developers write unit tests. It's their easiest, fastest, and most consistent way to verify their assumptions about the code they produce. Either they do it before writing the code to drive its design, or they do it after having written the code to verify that it works as expected. In the first case, the testing and verification aspect may not be as apparent as in the second. Nevertheless, unit tests are 100 percent developer-owned.

Integration Testing

In this chapter, the exact definition of the term "integration test" will remain a bit vague (it'll be defined in Chapter 3, "The Testing Vocabulary"). For now, let's just acknowledge that some tests are more complex than unit tests and benefit from being written by developers. Such tests require more sophisticated setup and may execute significantly slower. Running them manually would be both hard, because of their coupling to the source code and implementation details, and impractical because of their sheer number.

Maintenance

That the majority of a system's life cycle is about maintenance isn't a closely guarded secret in the industry. It's a well-known fact. Once a piece of software has been rolled out into production, it goes into maintenance, which falls into either of two categories:

- **Maintenance of a system under development**—The system is already running in production while new features are being added to it.

  Adding features to collectively owned code that's constantly in flux can be quite tricky. Parts of the codebase are being refactored, and others are being extended. The final result will hopefully be verified somehow, but no sooner than when most of the functionality is implemented. In the meantime, the code must be intact enough to allow the entire team to work on it. Guaranteeing that the software will remain in working condition in the flurry of collective ownership and maintenance is developer work.

- **Patching and bug fixing**—The system has been stable for quite a while and requires relatively little intervention, but once in a while a defect pops up and a bug fix is required.

  Changes are introduced carefully, and their scope is limited to addressing the defect, while leaving everything else intact. A well-proven technique for fixing bugs is restraining oneself from rushing ahead to implement a fix, and first writing a test that'll fail because of the bug's presence. In the absence of the bug, that test would pass. Once the test is in place, the bug is fixed. If the fix is correct, the test passes. That test is now in the codebase and ensures the presence and correctness of the fix. This is also developer work.

Both types of maintenance require that the code be written with testability in mind. The opposite—code that turns all attempts to change it into a mixture of one part guessing game and one part nightmare—is called *legacy code*. Michael Feathers, the author of *Working Effectively with Legacy Code*, defines legacy code as code without tests.

A safe way of working with legacy code is adding tests to it retroactively to pin down its behavior before making any changes. Such tests are called *characterization tests* (Feathers 2004). Doing this is time consuming, sometimes hard, and not always a very exciting activity, but the alternative is reading the code carefully before making any changes and wishing that nothing breaks.[1]

Adding the missing tests and making the actual changes fall on the developers.

Continuous Integration

Continuous integration (CI) is the practice of integrating frequently and always keeping the main build stable (Duvall, Matyas & Glover 2007). There are two sides to this practice—the technical side and the social side. The technical side of continuous integration is made up of the process and infrastructure needed to achieve an automated stable build:

- Before committing anything to the version control system, the developer fetches the latest version of the code, merges it with his local changes, and runs the test suite on his machine—unit tests in practice.

- If all tests pass, the developer commits the new code to the version control system. The build server picks up the changes, fetches the latest version of the code, compiles it, and runs its unit tests. This is bare-bones CI, practiced by teams that have just started out.[2]

- Long-running tests and analysis of the code (for example, code coverage or coding convention violations) are run either nightly or as often as the load on the CI server(s) permits.

The social dimension is about following the practices to the letter by actually running the tests locally before committing, by committing frequently, and, above all, by reacting to broken builds and fixing them immediately before committing any other work. This requires discipline and a dedicated team pulling in the same direction. Getting this right is often harder than setting up the infrastructure and automation.

---

1. Actually, legacy code can be attacked by pair programming or working with reviews or formal code inspections. However, they are only as good as the moment they are performed in. Tests live longer and can be run over and over again.
2. Continuous integration can get arbitrarily complex depending on the type of system and the expertise of the team. Experienced teams include deployment of a new version of the system and end-to-end tests that require the system to be up and running in their CI build. This is where continuous integration starts becoming continuous delivery (CD). For a more in-depth description of continuous delivery, see Humble and Farley (2010).

So where do developers come in? They're the ones writing and running the tests before committing, and they're the ones fixing the build if it breaks. More often than not, they'll be the ones to set up the CI server, especially when they need to run the unit and integration tests.

Test Automation

In many cases, test automation is a developer activity. Only time and imagination set the bounds for what kind of work we can automate: test data and environment generation, scripted execution, or automated checking, to name a few examples.

Acceptance test-driven development is also a good example, because it boils down to authoring a test that's readable to nontechnical users, implementable by developers, and executable by a dedicated framework. There are different opinions on exactly who should write the test, using what format and what tool. However, from the developer's point of view, these differences can be thought of as minor. In the end, it's the developer's job to provide the infrastructure that will execute the tests. In many cases it's quite a body of code. The same goes for the other aforementioned automation activities.

What Developers Usually *Don't* Do

The examples in the previous section don't mention usability testing, security testing, and performance testing. These are all important types of testing, but they tend to require skills that are quite separate from a developer's. In practice, we can expect the professional developer to have read some user interface design guidelines; to know about file traversal vulnerabilities, SQL injections, buffer overflows, and cross-site scripting; and to be familiar with the time complexity of the most popular algorithms.

Then there's exploratory testing, which can be performed by developers in a cross-functional team. My experience is that this can work well, especially if they refrain from running exploratory sessions on functionality they have implemented themselves and focus on helping their colleagues instead. Again, this is a good thing, but it's not what this book is about.

Finally, there are the activities associated with the (in)famous "tester mind-set." It's safe to say that developers usually don't spend their working hours coming up with the really nasty test cases. Neither do they focus on fault injections, creating race conditions, or messing with their software's state in other ways if there are professional testers on the team.

Nasty Test Cases

What's a nasty test case? It's a test case that attempts to do something unusual and unexpected, especially from a developer's point of view. In my experience, testing for I/O-related errors makes a good example. How often do developers test code that writes to a file or stores data in a database for the possibility of the disk being full? These days many languages handle this quite gracefully with exceptions. Superficially tested applications tend to handle such exceptions quite poorly. In many cases they'll display a technical error message, like "I/O error," to the user. But wouldn't a user want a more specific error message, one that indicates that the system understands that the disk is full? A tester would certainly test for that and would probably create a small disk partition and fill it up, leaving just a few bytes of available space, before launching the application to see how it would respond. In some circumstances, this would be a critical test.

   In other circumstances, the same tester would show judgment and prioritize other tests, especially if disk I/O wasn't critical or there was little risk of the system running out of space. Anyhow, testers would most likely be more qualified to do such testing and make the trade-offs.

Due to the complexity of both professions, it's impossible to say exactly when developer work becomes tester work. That depends entirely on the context and on factors like application domain, complexity, legal regulations, or team composition. However, there are cases where it's quite clear that a developer's verification yields diminishing returns.

Defining Developer Testing

So far, I've given examples of testing activities that I consider to be the developer's responsibility. I've also drawn, albeit fuzzy, a line of demarcation between developer work and tester work. What remains is defining developer testing.

   Developer testing is an umbrella term for all test-related activities a developer engages in. This particular book is about building quality into the code (and in the longer run, the software), which narrows the scope. The relation to traditional testing is a defining trait of developer testing. Much of the material in this book is directly derived from and related to the basics of testing, which is why testing terminology and testing techniques keep appearing throughout the text.

   When working in various companies on different projects, I've noticed that developers who start taking an increasing responsibility for quality often follow a similar learning curve and ask the same questions. The following questions have helped me to refine the theory and practices underlying developer testing even further. Here are some of them:

- How much, if any, testing should developers do?
- What kind of testing will give the best return on investment for this particular system?
- Why is testability important, and how can it be achieved?
- Why does a method/class/component seem untestable, and how can it be made testable?
- What's "testable" code anyway?
- How "good" should test code be?
- When is a method/class/component sufficiently covered by tests?
- How should tests be named?
- When should a certain kind of test-double be used?
- What's the best way to break this particular kind of dependency?
- Who checks the arguments to a method? The caller or the callee?
- How should test code be structured to avoid duplication, and is all duplication bad?
- In test-driven development, what's the next test to write?
- How does one test-drive an enterprise system with many delegating layers?
- How does one avoid combinatorial explosions in test code and still feel confident?
- What factors determine the number of assertions in a test?
- Should tests target state or behavior?

In order to answer these questions, effective developers need to do their share of test-related work, and they need to develop specific skills to do it well.

Developer Testing and the Development Process

Developer testing as such is quite independent of the development process. Waterfall, ad hoc, agile—regardless of how the software is being developed, applying developer testing practices will result in better software. Having said that, the whole idea of blending development and testing practices into something big enough to fill a book came from my ambition to strengthen developers in cross-functional teams. Therefore, this book recurrently returns to the topic of collaboration between team members who are better at writing the code and team members who are better at testing it. It also assumes that there's an ambition to ship the software relatively frequently; that is, it doesn't have to function correctly upon one delivery—it must function correctly upon multiple deliveries, and it should be prepared for many more to come.

Summary

Developers perform activities related to verification and quality assurance more often than they may realize. In addition to running their code to check that it seems to behave correctly, they

- Write unit tests

- Write integration tests

- Perform maintenance

- Implement continuous integration

- Provide the infrastructure for test automation

Each of these activities will benefit from the developer having some fundamental testing knowledge and skills.

Developer testing is everything developers do to test their code, and this book describes helpful behaviors, activities, and tools related to building quality into the code.

Although developers can and should do as much as possible to ensure the correctness and quality of their software, some testing-related activities are still best performed by someone with a skill set slightly different from the developer's. Such activities include

- Performance testing

- Security testing

- Usability testing

- Testing the untypical and pathological cases

Nothing prevents the developer from doing any of these activities, but they aren't covered in this book.

Chapter 2

TESTING OBJECTIVES, STYLES, AND ROLES

Organizations may differ enormously in their views on testing and development and above all, in their opinions on how these two activities should be combined. In this chapter we'll take a quick look at what testing and quality assurance may look like in different settings and see how developer testing fits into the picture.

Testing and Checking

It's not uncommon to make a distinction between testing and checking to emphasize the difference between an activity that requires curiosity, flexibility, and the ability to draw conclusions and a tedious process that compares the outcome of performing some action to an expected result. In most cases, the latter is best left to a machine. Thus, a person using her skills and knowledge of software testing, the business domain, and any other relevant experience will obviously produce results different from a tool that somehow automates checking. James Bach and co-author Michael Bolton put it quite eloquently: "Testing is the process of evaluating a product by learning about it through exploration and experimentation, which includes to some degree: questioning, study, modeling, observation, inference, etc." (Bach 2013).

Tools can be used in numerous ways to aid in the process, but they'll operate within the boundaries of their functionality and programming. Admittedly, some tool-based techniques, like model-based testing or generative testing, may discover new defects on their first run, but generally tests performed by tools seldom uncover new bugs or produce new insights. They're better at finding regressions and verifying existing assumptions. Still, tests executed by tools beat a human tester in the discipline of repetitive and tedious verification—and what's even more important, they let developers express their assumptions about the code they write.

From the perspective of testing and checking, developer testing is largely about making developers write code with automated checks constantly in mind, so that testing time needn't be wasted on checking. In organizations where developers spend too little time testing and verifying their code, the testing activities, whatever they may be, often have to compensate for the inferior development process by focusing primarily on rudimentary checking.

Motivation Behind Developer Testing

Developer testing turns human checking into machine checking, thus, by definition, resulting in testable ("checkable") software and freeing up time for more interesting and intellectually demanding testing activities.

Testing Objectives

Another way to look at testing is to examine its underlying objectives. At the extremes, there are two fundamental approaches to testing: critiquing and supporting. They come with different objectives and different vocabularies. Few, if any, organizations operate in either extreme, but one of the perspectives usually dominates and gives rise to the processes and the in-house vocabulary.

Testing to Critique

Testing to critique means to test something that's finished and needs evaluating. Once the software to be tested exists, the objective of the testing is to obtain information about it. Such information can be used to answer questions like: "Does it deviate from the specification?" or "Are there any defects in it?" In many people's eyes, this is the archetype of testing: verifying that something works.

If the information gathering happens in a wider scope and targets areas beyond defects and deviations from the specification, questions like the following may be answered:

- Will the users be delighted by the software?

- Is the scope of the software reasonable?

- Has any functionality been forgotten?

- Does the software run fast enough? Or does it run slow, but in a way that isn't perceived as annoying by the user?

- Is the software compliant with legal regulations?

The vocabulary of testing to critique includes the *tester mind-set* and the *developer mind-set*, according to which developers want to build and testers want to break. After all, the majority of a tester's time and skill set is spent investigating how the product might fail, whereas the developer's energy is channeled into constructing it. As a consequence, developers may fall victims to viewing their code as an extension of themselves. If so, they will work very hard to prove that the code is correct, even though it's full of obvious bugs. If a bug is found, they're imperfect—they may suffer from cognitive dissonance, a psychologically inconvenient state, and try to reduce that dissonance by producing explanations as to why the software (i.e., themselves) isn't faulty (Weinberg 1998). A simpler way to put this is to say that they suffer from author bias, the inability to see faults in one's own creation. Common phrases like "nobody would ever do that," "works on my machine," and "I didn't even touch that bit of code" illustrate this quite well. This is why independent testing is in the critiquing testing vocabulary.

Reducing risk is also an important objective of critique-based testing. Defects in the software present varying degrees of risk, and by inspecting it critically, risks may be mitigated.

Testing to Support

Testing to support is about safety, sustainable pace, and the team's ability to work fast and without fear of introducing defects during development. Its purpose is to provide feedback and help the team achieve immediate and constant confidence in the software it produces. To gain such confidence, the team, and especially those whose primary responsibility is to be quality champions, will sometimes perform testing activities that critique. That said, their emphasis won't be on obtaining information based on supposedly completed software, but rather on obtaining information as quickly as possible in parallel with the ongoing implementation. So, although information gathering does take place and defects are being found, these activities are part of the team's quality feedback loop, which ultimately supports the whole team's development effort.

Test automation, test-driven development, and activities that aim at stabilizing the development process and introducing fail-safes also belong in the domain of support testing.

By now it should be obvious that developer testing, as described in this book, is testing meant to support.

Testing Styles

In some environments the style of testing is more noticeable than the underlying objectives. Certain testing styles are more coupled to specific processes than others.

Traditional Testing

Traditionally, testing is thought of as a verification phase occurring after a construction phase. First something gets built and then it's verified to make sure that it works. What "built" and "verified" mean and how much effort these phases require vary between industries and products.

This view often goes hand in hand with the building metaphor for systems and their architectures. It assumes that there's a master blueprint or specification to guide all aspects of the construction (see Figure 2.1). Given this assumption, it makes perfect sense to have a verification phase after the construction phase. Because a lot of effort has been put into creating the blueprint,[1] building the system should be only about following it. In that sense, traditional testing is an embodiment of testing to critique.

While theoretically guaranteeing independent testing and immunity to all forms of author bias, this setup comes with an inherent risk of fragmentation and convergence. Because of the clear division of labor, employing traditional testing may create an environment where developers and testers develop quite an adversarial view of each other. Therefore, it's not uncommon that developers and testers start using the blueprint in isolation from each other and with very little communication between the groups. While the developers try to implement it or create some kind of design document out of it, the testers start deriving test cases from it. Once all features are implemented, the resulting system is tested, and it comes as a surprise that the blueprint has diverged and that there's a mismatch between the produced software, the test cases, and the original intent.

Well-defined processes are crucial for traditional testing to work. One such process is the *fundamental test process*, which involves the following activities (ISTQB 2011):

- Test planning and control
- Test analysis and design
- Test implementation and execution
- Evaluating exit criteria and reporting
- Test closure activities

My experience is that organizations that structure their quality assurance as described earlier tend to do it in a way that decouples testing from development. Therefore, from the developer's point of view, the outcome of the aforementioned activities tends to result in written defect reports or tickets in a bug-tracking tool. This is a little disheartening, because the structure of the fundamental test process can actually reflect the way developers would go about writing and implementing their tests.

If you're a developer and you work in an organization that adheres to a process that resembles the fundamental test process, you're probably only expected to write unit tests. You may even write some integration tests disguised as unit tests. Most

---

1. Business analysts (BAs), architects, and customer representatives have spent many meeting hours in creating an exhaustive specification.

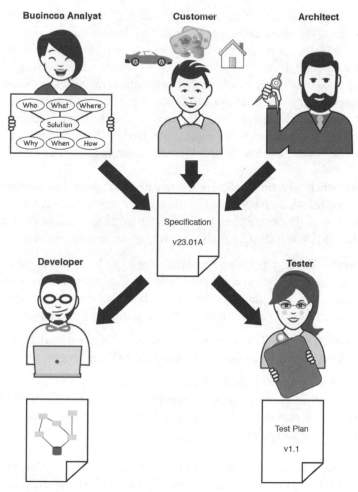

FIGURE 2.1   Traditional testing.

likely, that will be the extent of your verification activities, apart from reading bug reports created by a separate quality assurance (QA) group or department. I'd argue that nothing in the process says that it has to be this way, but my experience is that this is how it plays out.

Agile Testing

Agile testing is testing that enables agile development. In essence, it's about empowering the tester and increasing collaboration within the team and with external stakeholders (Gregory & Crispin 2008). In agile testing, the role of the tester is shifted from reactive to proactive. Instead of writing test cases, waiting for something to test, or executing manual tests, the tester becomes the team's quality champion and contributes to a successful release in any way she can. For example, by helping the customer or product owner to specify desired functionality, by making sure that testing activities are taken into account during planning and estimation meetings, by educating and assisting the developers in test design and test automation, or by pair programming or pair testing. Thus the tester's role blends with the developer's in the sense that both take part in the development process, but from different angles. Having testing experts on the development team provides several immediate advantages:

- **No testing crunch**—Testing activities are planned alongside development activities.[2] The team's delivery succeeds if, and only if, the software is implemented *and* tested. The mere presence of a tester tends to result in the team asking: "How do we test this?," which in turn leads to testable software.

- **No handovers**—Defect reports and bug-tracking tools become less significant, because the testers may report their findings directly to the developer who wrote the code. Such conversations not only lead to bugs being fixed, they also help in creating a common "language of quality" in the team.

- **Local testing expertise**—Testers increase the team's focus on quality and can teach developers testing techniques that may help in their programming.

- **Little or no mind-numbing work**—Developers and testers work on test automation together. Automating some repetitive tasks or tedious tests that have to be run over and over frees up testers to engage in more valuable and interesting work, like exploratory testing.

Everyone on an agile team is responsible for turning the functionality requested by the customer into software. However, testers are usually the ones who spend more time with the customer, because it's a natural part of their role to help clarify requirements and to design test cases, which may depend on intimate knowledge of business rules.

Adopting agile testing in the team affects the kinds of testing activities the developers engage in. The developer will collaborate with her tester colleague on automated acceptance tests and test automation in general. They also work together to cover areas like usability testing and security testing, especially if no one on the team is an expert in these areas. The tester may report bugs, especially toward the end of the iteration, but they won't come as anonymous tickets in a bug-tracking tool.

---

2. The wording is important here. In traditional testing, tests are supposed to be planned and created in parallel with the development. The difference is that collaboration, joint planning, and common success/completion criteria aren't emphasized.

Instead, developers will likely be notified about any errors they've introduced as soon as they're found.

Developers will still write unit tests, but they always have a colleague to ask about test design. Imagine always being able to ask: "How will you test this?" or "What else will you test?" Such an environment stimulates learning about testing and quality assurance.

In the Absence of Collaboration

Systems can be developed without many of the important questions being asked. However, the result will be incomplete, and cases outside the happy path may be handled in very creative (bad) ways. Developers are clever and try to infer requirements to their best ability. Either that, or they pick the solution that seems the most interesting.

Planning testing *early* and *collaboratively* within the team will help prevent this from happening, or at least reduce the likelihood.

BDD, ATDD, and Specification by Example

As part of their development process, mature agile teams tend to adopt a set of practices that help them build the right product. These practices go by different names, and historically there are some minor differences between them. *Behavior-driven development* (BDD, North 2006), *acceptance test-driven development* (ATDD, Pugh 2011), and *specification by example* (Adzic 2011) all address the problem of different stakeholders using different vocabularies, which in turn results in incorrect interpretation of requirements and discrepancies between code, tests, and customer expectations. In addition, Behavior-driven development offers advice on the actual design of the code, thus becoming a design technique.

All three practices incorporate the following elements to a lesser or greater extent: Before starting to implement a story, the team makes sure that everybody is on the same page. This is done by having it examined jointly by the customer (who may consult many other stakeholders outside the team), a tester, and a developer—and sometimes even the entire team. The participants of the conversation may vary, which is perfectly fine, as long as the story is covered from a business, quality, and technical perspective. Having different stakeholders discuss the story leads to a shared understanding (see Figure 2.2), adds new perspectives, and enables questions to be raised as soon as possible. Later down the road, it eliminates handovers.

Ordinarily, the conversations take place in workshops before or at the very beginning of the iteration, but nothing prevents them from happening whenever they're needed. A critical element of such conversations is that the language of the customer be retained and used, and that it be done all the time and by everybody. Such a language is often called *the ubiquitous language* (Evans 2003), and using it consistently and constantly allows tests, or sometimes[3] even source code, to be written in such a way that nontechnical stakeholders can verify them.

A ubiquitous language is one pillar of shared understanding; concrete examples are another. They replace the vague language often seen in specifications that make too much use of words like "shall," "must," and "should." The team will use the examples in its conversations, workshops, and planning meetings to uncover assumptions, corner cases, ambiguities, and inconsistencies that would remain hidden behind the high-level wording of a user story or requirements document.

Concrete examples are either written as textual scenarios:

```
Given that I'm a loyal customer
When my order exceeds $99
I get a free gift
```

Or in tabular form:

Purchases made so far	Purchase amount	Get gift
1	100.00	No
1	150.00	No
1	150.00	No
2	100.00	No
3	99.00	No
3	99.01	Yes
10	99.01	Yes
10	99.00	No

Here we see that a seemingly trivial story can contain magic words like "loyal customer" and "exceeds," which are easily clarified using actual values. In this case, customers are considered loyal if they've placed at least three orders in the past, and they qualify for gifts if they exceed the $99 threshold by as little as one cent.

Concrete examples can easily evolve into tests, which will serve to enforce the acceptance criteria. If the new functionality behaves as illustrated by the examples

---

3. One of my reviewers suggested that I get rid of this "sometimes." I wish that I could, but unfortunately, using a ubiquitous language and having a shared understanding don't prevent us from messing up the code. On the other hand, teams that have successfully embraced these practices are likely to have good coding practices as well.

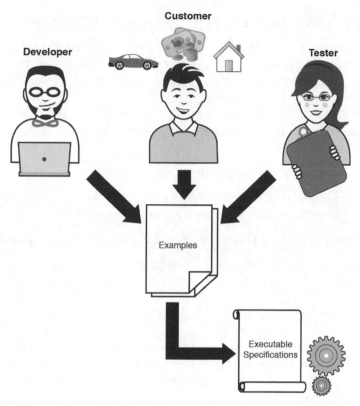

FIGURE 2.2 Building a shared understanding. Translation between different vocabularies is no longer necessary.

after having been implemented, it's most likely correct. Therefore, the next step is to turn the examples into executable specifications. This is done using tools like Fit-Nesse, Concordion, Cucumber, or SpecFlow, which all allow binding a textual arti-fact—a scenario or table—to executable code. The tests run from outside the system, or at least against the business layer, which is why they are often called *automated acceptance tests*. Their function is to provide a receipt of the new functionality being implemented, and they're written ahead of the production code.

Who's the Customer?

This is not a book on agile methodologies, so it makes some simplifications about a topic to which other books devote several chapters. In this book, the word "customer" simply refers to a stakeholder who wants certain functionality in the software. In Scrum, for instance, such stakeholders are represented by the Product Owner role.

Your Quality Assurance and Developer Testing

By now we've explored how some common ways of working with software quality mix and match with developer testing. The processes described so far have been rather generic, and you may feel that your reality is slightly different. Maybe your daily struggles are more along these lines:

- Nobody speaks of quality assurance, neither in terms of a "process," nor as something the team does.

- There are no people who are experts in testing.

- There are people who perform independent testing, but they're across the globe in a different time zone, and they communicate only by e-mail.

- There's no sense of pride and craftsmanship in the team or the organization.

- Everything should have been delivered "yesterday."

- The codebase is all legacy.

- You're a solo developer.

You know what? None of these factors really matter. If you're the only developer, or your team doesn't have any testers, or you're being rushed by others, or the system is old and crappy, *your* quality assurance process is the only one you have, and it will make or break your software.

Conversely, if your code will be tested by someone else, do you want that person to find obvious and plainly stupid bugs in it? Do you want to waste that person's time and your employer's money by turning trivial checks that are easily automated into manual test cases or subjects of an exploratory testing session? Probably not. For many developers, the harsh reality is that professional testers who know their craft are a rare commodity, which is why we don't want to waste their time and effort by creating software that's flawed by design and full of bugs that could easily have been avoided.

Every organization, team, and project is different, and provocative as it may sound, that shouldn't affect how the developers work. At the end of the day, it's *you* who'll make changes to the software and fix the bugs, irrespective of the quality assurance process. Therefore, it's in *your* interest that the software be both testable and tested.

Summary

There's a difference between *testing* and *checking*. The former assumes curiosity and creativity, whereas the latter is mechanical and can safely be delegated to a computer.

Testing can be performed either to *critique* or to *support*. The contents of the developer role and tester role are greatly affected by the organizational culture and beliefs about what the two roles are about and how they should contribute. In cross-functional teams, smaller companies, or agile-minded organizations, the developers will be more involved in quality assurance, either by collaborating with testers on a daily basis or by doing the verification and other QA activities themselves.

In larger companies or in companies that separate testing from development, the developer may be at the mercy of the QA or testing department. There will be test plans, and bugs will be called defects in a bug-tracking tool.

Most organizations will most likely adapt one of the following stances on testing:

- Traditional—Process-oriented, independent, formal

- Agile testing—Proactive, integrated, collaborative

Implementing behavior-driven development helps a team to collaboratively clarify requirements by using concrete examples, to know when a feature is truly implemented, and to create a living documentation. Regardless of a team's situation and access to professional testers, the fact remains that developers always have tested and always will test their software. After all, running the main method of a program or poking around in the user interface after making some changes is nothing but ad hoc testing. When the dust settles, it's the developers who reap the benefits of building in quality and verifying it continually.

Chapter 3
THE TESTING VOCABULARY

What do people mean when they say that software should be tested? What activities, performed when, and by whom do they refer to? The previous chapter described the objectives and styles of testing. This chapter will get more concrete and take on actual testing activities and the vocabulary of testing. Unfortunately, the language of testing is quite elusive and the terminology rather ambiguous at times. The use of terms and employment of techniques vary not only across different organizations, but chances are that as soon a new person enters your team, that person may attach a different meaning to some of the words that you use when you speak about testing and quality assurance.

This chapter is organized as a taxonomy of different types of testing and a dictionary of some terms frequently used by testers. As a developer, it's crucial to be well familiar with the nuances of this vocabulary. There's a high probability that it has affected the way your colleagues approach quality assurance, so you'd better know where the stuff in the walls comes from. This is especially true in organizations in which development and testing have been, or still are, disconnected.

In addition, knowing about various types of testing gives a developer a more solid understanding of the work needed to ensure correctness and other desirable properties of the software. Thus, it helps to decompose the mystical task of testing into very concrete activities, some of which are performed by developers, and some by team members with other specialties. Estimating testing activities gets easier and it becomes clear when the software is "good enough."

Putting this material together was challenging, because getting just one precise definition of a certain type of test is hard and maybe not even meaningful. The important fact to be aware of is that there are variations and differences. As you read this chapter, please keep this in mind: what's really important is that *you* **agree on the terminology in your organization**. Ideally, your team decides on how its testing is conducted and how it uses the vocabulary, after which it documents the results so that they're visible to everybody, like on a poster in the team's room. In a not so ideal world, an architect or test manager makes these decisions and writes them down in a document (where they'll likely never be found and read).

Errors, Defects, Failures

All developers sometimes make mistakes. These are known as *errors* in the language of testing. Errors lead to *defects* in the software. A more frequently used term for defect is *bug*,[1] named for the insect that got trapped in the bowels of prehistoric hardware. Defects/bugs may lead to software *failures*. Not all of them do, though. A defect in code that's never executed won't cause a failure. Conversely, environmental conditions, like moisture, overheating, magnetic fields, or other events, may do so. So can incorrect or unintended use or abuse of the software.

White Box and Black Box Testing

Testing takes on fundamentally different forms depending on whether or not we have access to the tested artifact's internals—most notably its source code. *White box testing* refers to testing where we do have access to the source code and are able to inspect it, either for verification or inspiration for new tests. *Black box testing* is the opposite. We only have access to the tested artifact's external interface, whatever that might be. When doing black box testing, there's no way to inspect the internal state. Instead, the result of the tests is observed in the artifact's output or by some other indirect means.

Because of how many companies organize their testing activities, testers tend to work from the black box angle, which means that they have to resort to techniques that don't assume they know everything about the system they're testing. Not only has this constraint given rise to various testing methods and techniques, but a black box approach imposes an emotional distance from the target of the test.

Black Box Development

This is a good place to halt the terminology tour and reflect on practices. Even when developers can inspect and access everything in the codebase, they should keep the black box approach in mind. Not only does it reduce coupling between test and production code, viewing the component or system as a black box helps when defining its contract and behavior. I strongly suggest that the following questions be raised for each method, class, component, or other artifact:

---

1. According to lore, Rear Admiral Grace Murray Hopper found a moth trapped in a relay of a Mark II computer.

- What is its interface to the outside world?
- What inputs does it take? (Have all allowed values been specified?)
- How does it communicate success or failure?
- How does it react to bad input? (Does it recover or crash?)
- Does it surprise by doing something unexpected or unusual?

Thinking in terms of contracts and behavior is both a fundamental and very usable design technique, and it leads to software that can readily be tested. Programming by contract and test-driven development, two techniques that will be introduced later in the book, both favor this kind of outside-in perspective.

Classifying Tests

There are numerous ways to test software. Depending on the type of information we want to discover about it and the kind of feedback we're interested in, a certain way of testing may be more appropriate than another. Tests are traditionally classified along two dimensions: *test level* and *test type* (see Figure 3.1). Combining them into a matrix provides a helpful visualization of the team's testing activities.

Test Levels

A test level can be thought of as expressing the proximity to the source code and the footprint of the test. As an example, unit tests are close to the source code and cover a few lines. On the contrary, acceptance tests aren't concerned about implementation details and may span over multiple systems and processes, thus having a very large footprint.

Unit Test

Unit testing refers to authoring fast, low-level tests that target a small part of the system (Fowler 2014). Because of their natural coupling to the code, they're written by developers and executed by unit testing frameworks.

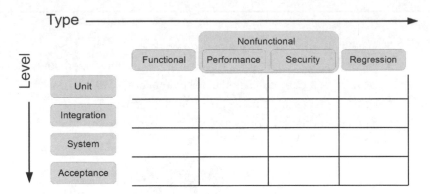

FIGURE 3.1   Test levels and types covered in this chapter.

This sounds simple enough, but the term comes with its gray areas: size and scope of a unit of work, collaborator isolation, and execution speed. Where the boundary of a unit is drawn depends on the programming language and type of system. A unit test may exercise a function or method, a class, or even a cluster of collaborating classes that provide some specific functionality. This description may seem fuzzy, but given some experience, it's easy to spot unit tests that don't make sense or are too complicated. Collaborator isolation, along with speed of execution, is subject to more intense debate. There are those who mandate that a unit test isolate all collaborators of the tested code. Others strive for a less ascetic approach and isolate only collaborators that, when invoked, would make the test fail because of unavailable or unreachable resources or external hosts. In either case, execution speed isn't an issue. Finally, some people argue that unit tests don't have to replace slower collaborators at all as long as the test is otherwise simple and to the point. This book uses a definition of unit testing that fits the second of the three aforementioned variants.

When doing research for this book, I found that some sources used the terms unit and component more or less interchangeably, in which case both referred to a rather small artifact that can be tested in isolation. To a developer, a unit and a component mean different things. As stated previously, a unit of work is a small chunk of functionality that can be tested in a meaningful way. Components have a more elusive definition, but the authors of *Continuous Delivery—Reliable Software Delivery through Build, Test, and Deployment Automation* nail it quite well: ". . . a reasonably large-scale code structure within an application, with well-defined API, that could potentially be swapped out for another implementation" (Humble & Farley 2010). This definition happens to coincide with how components are described in the literature about software architecture. Thus, components are much larger than units and require more sophisticated tests.

Integration Test

The term *integration test* is unfortunately both ambiguous and overloaded. The ambiguity comes from the fact that "integration" may refer to either two systems or components talking to each other via some kind of remote procedure call (RPC), a database, or message bus; or it may mean "an integration test is that which is not a unit test and not a system test."

Actually there's a point in maintaining this distinction. Testing whether two systems talk to each other correctly is a black box activity. Because the systems communicate through a (hopefully) well-defined interface, that communication is most likely to be verified using black box testing. Traditionally, this would fall into the tester's domain.

It's the second definition, encountered frequently enough, that gives rise to the overloading. The common reasoning goes something like the following, where Tracy Tester and David Developer argue about a test:

Tracy: Have you tested that the complex customer record is written correctly to the database?

David: Sure! I wrote a unit test where I stubbed out the database. Piece of cake!

Tracy: But the database contains both some triggers and constraints that could affect the persistence of the customer record. I don't think your unit test can account for that.

David: Then it's your job to test it! You're responsible for the system tests.

Tracy: I'm not sure whether the database is a "system." After all it's your way of implementing persistence. And besides, wouldn't you want to be certain that persisting the complex customer record won't be messed up by somebody else on the team? Sure, I can test this manually, but there are only so many times I can do it.

David: You're right, I guess. I need a test that runs in an automated manner, like a unit test, but more advanced. It must talk to the database. Hmm . . . Let's call this an integration test! After all, we're integrating the system with the database.

Tracy: . . .

Based on the preceding logic, a test that opens a file to write "Hello world" to it or just outputs the same string on the screen isn't a unit test. Because it's definitively not a system test, it must be an integration test by analogy. After all, something is integrated with the file system. Confused yet?

Integration tests, as per the second definition, are often intimately coupled to the source code. Given that the line where a test stops being a unit test and becomes something else is blurry and debated, many integration tests will feel like advanced or slower unit tests. Because of this, it shouldn't be controversial that integration testing really is a developer's job. The hard part is defining where that job starts and ends.

System Test

Systems are made up of finished and integrated building blocks. They may be components or other systems. *System testing* is the activity of verifying that the *entire* system works. System tests are often executed from a black box perspective and exercise integrations and processes that span large parts of the system. A word of caution about system testing: if the individual systems or components have been tested in isolation and have gone through integration testing, system testing will actually target the overall functionality of the system. However, if the underlying building blocks have remained untested, system tests will reveal defects that should have been caught by simpler and cheaper tests, like unit tests. In the worst cases, organizations with inferior and immature development processes, that is, where the developers just throw code over the wall for testing, have to compensate by running only system tests by dedicated QA people.[2]

Acceptance Test

In its traditional meaning *acceptance testing* refers to an activity performed by the end users to validate that the software they received conforms to the specifications and their expectations and is ready for use. Alas, the term has been kidnapped. Nowadays the aforementioned activity is called *user acceptance testing (UAT)* (Cimperman 2006), whereas acceptance testing tends to refer to automated black box testing performed by a framework to ensure that a story or part of a story has been correctly implemented. The major acceptance test frameworks gladly promote this definition.

Test Types

Test type refers to the purpose of the test and its specific objective. It may be to verify functionality at some level or to target a certain quality attribute. The most prevalent distinction between test types is that between functional and nonfunctional testing. The latter can be refined to target as many quality attributes as necessary. Regression

---

2. This is, by the way, the opposite of building quality in.

testing is also a kind of testing that can be performed at all test levels, so it makes sense to treat it as a test type.

Functional Testing

Functional testing constitutes the core of testing. In a striking majority of cases, saying that something will need testing will refer to functional testing. Functional testing is the act of executing the software and checking whether its behavior matches explicit expectations, feeding it different inputs and comparing the results with the specification,[3] and exploring it beyond the explicit specification to see if it violates any implicit expectations. Depending on the scope of the test, the specification may be an expected value, a table of values, a use case, a specification document, or even tacit knowledge. At its most fundamental, functional testing answers the questions:

- Does the software do what it was intended to do?

- Does it not do what it was not intended to do?

Developers will most often encounter functional tests at the unit test level, simply because they create many more of such tests in comparison to other types of tests. However, functional testing applies to all test levels: unit, integration, system, and acceptance.

Behavior

You will see the word *behavior* many times in this book. One reviewer, Frank Appel, pointed out that this term is used very often in the industry without really being defined. He suggested defining a component's behavior as the outcome produced by its functionality under certain preconditions.

I think this is a great definition that captures the meaning of this elusive term. Because this is a chapter on terminology, I feel obliged to warn about the use of the word *component*, though. Later in the book, I introduce the term *program element*, which I think is a better fit.

---

3. Here the word *specification* doesn't need to refer to a thick document. It could mean a user story or any other way of expressing what the software should do.

Nonfunctional Testing

Nonfunctional testing, which by the way is a very unfortunate name, targets a solution's quality attributes such as usability, reliability, performance, maintainability, and portability, to name a few. Some of them will be discussed further later on.

Quality attributes are sometimes expressed as nonfunctional requirements, hence the relation to nonfunctional testing.

Functional versus Nonfunctional Testing

A good way of memorizing the difference between functional and nonfunctional tests is remembering that functional tests target the *what*, whereas nonfunctional tests target the *how*. For example, a functional unit test of a sorting algorithm would verify that the input is indeed sorted. A nonfunctional unit test would time it to make sure that it runs within a specified time constraint.

Performance Testing

Performance testing focuses on a system's responsiveness, throughput, and reliability given different loads. How fast does a web page load? If a user clicks a button on the screen, are the contents immediately updated? How long does it take to process 10,000 payment transactions? All of these questions can be asked for different loads.

Under light or normal load, they may indeed be answered by a performance test. However, as the load on the system is increased—let's say by more and more users using the system at the same time, or more transactions being processed per second—we're talking about *load testing*. The purpose of load testing is to determine the system's behavior in response to increased load. When the load is increased beyond the maximum "normal load," load testing turns into *stress testing*. A special type of stress testing is *spike testing*, where the maximum normal load is exceeded very rapidly, as if there were a spike in the load. Running the aforementioned tests helps in determining the capacity, the scaling strategy, and the location of the bottlenecks.

Performance testing usually requires a specially tailored environment or software capable of generating the required load and a way of measuring it.

Security Testing

This type of testing may require a very mixed set of skills and is typically performed by trained security professionals. Security testing may be performed as an audit, the purpose of which is to validate policies, or it may be done more aggressively in the form of a penetration test, the purpose of which is to compromise the system using black hat techniques.

FIGURE 3.2   The CIA security triad.

There are various aspects of security. The security triad known as CIA is a common model that brings them all together (Stallings & Brown 2007). Figure 3.2 provides an illustration of the concepts in the triad. They include the following:

- **Confidentiality**
  - *Data confidentiality*—Private or confidential information stays that way.
  - *Privacy*—You have a degree of control over what information is stored about you, how, and by whom.

- **Integrity**
  - *Data integrity*—Information and programs are changed by trusted sources.
  - *System integrity*—The system performs the way it's supposed to without being compromised.

- **Availability**
  - Resources are available to authorized users and denied to others.

Each leg of the CIA triangle can be subject to an infinite number of attacks. Whereas some of them will assume the shape of social engineering or manipulation of the underlying operating system or network stack, many of them will make use of exploits that wouldn't be possible without defects in the software (developer work!). Therefore, it follows that knowing at least the basics of how to make an application resilient to the most common attacks is something that a developer should know by profession.

Security for Developers 101

Security is an incredibly broad field, and this book will not even attempt to address it. However, I couldn't resist including this short list.

- Most network protocols are not secure, and sending sensitive data over the network is usually a bad idea.
- Searching for Joe accounts, that is, accounts with easily guessed credentials, is a common practice among digital villains.
- Computers are fast; cracking a simple password may take minutes or even seconds.
- SQL injections wouldn't be possible without developer ignorance, or most likely laziness.[a]
- The same is true for various file system traversal vulnerabilities.
- If your program contains a fixed-size buffer for user input and that input isn't truncated, someone will send too much of it and either crash the program or escalate privileges.
- People can get very creative in attempts to put JavaScript code in HTML forms, which is known as cross-site scripting (XSS).

[a] Even in 2013, SQL injections were still the number-one threat according to the OWASP top 10 list (OWASP 2015).

The way security testing has been described so far really makes it sound like non-functional testing. However, there does exist a term like *functional security testing* (Bath & McKay 2008). It refers to testing security as performed by a "regular" tester. A functional security test may, for example, be about logging in as a nonprivileged user and attempting to do something in the system that only users with administrative privileges are allowed to do.

Normally, when we talk about security testing, we refer to the nonfunctional kind.

Regression Testing

How do we know that the system still behaves like it's supposed to once we've changed some functionality or fixed a bug? How do we know that we haven't broken anything? Enter *regression testing*.

The purpose of regression testing is to establish whether changes to the system have broken existing functionality or caused old defects to resurface. Traditionally, regression testing has been performed by rerunning a number of, or all, test cases on a system after changes have been made. In projects where tests are automated, regression testing isn't much of a challenge. The test suite is simply executed once more. In fact, as soon as a test is added to an automated suite of tests, it becomes a regression test.

The true challenge of regression testing faces organizations that neither have a traditional QA department or tester group, nor automate their tests. In such organizations, regression testing quickly turns into the Smack-a-Bug game.

Putting Test Levels and Types to Work

Maintaining a clear distinction between the various test levels and types may sound quite rigid and academic, but it can have its advantages.

The first advantage is that all cards are on the table. The team clearly sees what activities there are to consider and may plan accordingly. Some testing will make it to the Definition of Done for every story, some testing may be done on an iteration basis, and some may be deferred to particular releases or a final delivery.[4] Some might call this "agreeing on a testing strategy." If this isn't good enough and the team has decided on continuous deployment, having a chart of what to automate and in what order helps the team make informed decisions. Combinations of test levels and types map quite nicely to distinct steps in a continuous delivery pipeline.

A second positive effect is that the team gets to talk about its combined skill set, as the various kinds of tests require different levels of effort, time, resources, training, and experience. Relatively speaking, unit tests are simple. They take little time to write and maintain. On the other hand, some types of nonfunctional tests, like performance tests, may require specific expertise and tooling. Discussing how to address such a span of testing work and the kind of feedback that can be gained from it should help the team reach shared learning and improvement goals.

Third, we shouldn't neglect the usefulness of having a crystal-clear picture of what *not* to do. For example, a team may decide not to do any nonfunctional integration testing. This means that nobody will be blamed if an integration between two components is slow. The issue still needs to be resolved, but at least it was agreed that testing for such a problem wasn't a priority.

Finally, in larger projects where several teams are involved, being explicit about testing and quality assurance may help to avoid misunderstandings, omissions, blame, and potential conflicts. Again, a simple matrix of test levels and test types may serve as the basis for a discussion.

---

4. Ideally your team can perform all its testing always, constantly, and continually. In my experience, such cases are rare. Even great cross-functional teams may lack competence or resources to perform certain kinds of nonfunctional testing.

The Agile Testing Quadrants

A chapter on testing terminology wouldn't be complete without the *Agile Testing Quadrants*[5] shown in Figure 3.3.

Instead of focusing on levels and types, this model emphasizes the difference between *business-facing* and *technology-facing* tests. Business-facing tests are tests that make sense to a person responsible for business decisions. A typical example could be:

> *If a customer uses direct bank payments to pay for our product and pays too much, does he or she get a refund, or is the excess amount stored and used in the next transaction?*

Technology-facing tests are expressed using technical terms and implemented by the developers:

> *If validation of the credit card fails, the transaction enclosing the purchase is rolled back, nothing is stored in the database, and the event is logged.*

Another dimension of the testing quadrants is the distinction between tests that *guide development*, like tests written by developers to ensure that the produced code is correct, and tests that *critique the product*. The latter are directed toward the finished product and attempt to find deficiencies in it.

In my opinion, this is one of the most usable models in the domain of software testing. No, it's *the* most usable. It facilitates teamwork by turning testing into a cooperative activity, instead of an adversarial one, while at the same time reminding us of the duality of guiding/supporting testing and the critiquing kind. The model also tells us that in order for a team to deliver a product that functions correctly, delights the users, and solves the business problem, it must view its testing activities from several disparate perspectives.

When projected onto the Agile Testing Quadrants, developer tests cover the whole of the lower left quadrant, large parts of the upper left quadrant, and a fair share of the lower right quadrant.

---

5. The model was originally created by Brian Marick (2003) and has been popularized by Lisa Crispin and Janet Gregory (2008). It has been challenged, adapted, and revised, so there's plenty of material available online. Gojko Adzic's (2013) and Michael Bolton's (2014) work on the topic are good entry points to this material.

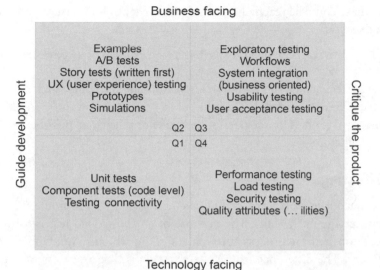

FIGURE 3.3 Agile Testing Quadrants as presented in the book *More Agile Testing* by Lisa Crispin and Janet Gregory (2014).

Some Other Types of Testing

The vocabulary of testing is indeed rich and plentiful. Next follow some terms that get thrown around frequently enough and that are related to developer testing in one way or another.

Smoke Testing

The term *smoke testing* originated from engineers testing pipes by blowing smoke into them. If there was a crack, the smoke would seep out through it. In software development, smoke testing refers to one or a few simple tests executed immediately after the system has been deployed. The "Hello World" of smoke testing is logging into the application.[6] Trivial as it may seem, such a test provides a great deal of information. For example, it will show that

- The application has been deployed successfully

- The network connection works (in case of network applications)

---

6. Because the "Hello World" of applications is an application that requires logging in.

- The database could be reached (because user credentials are usually stored in the database)

- The application starts, which means that it isn't critically flawed

Smoke tests are perfect candidates for automation and should be part of an automated build/deploy cycle. Earlier we touched on the subject of regression tests. Smoke tests are the tests that are run first in a regression test suite or as early as possible in a continuous delivery pipeline.

End-to-End Testing

Sometimes we encounter the term *end-to-end testing*. Most commonly, the term refers to system testing on steroids. The purpose of an end-to-end test is to include the entire execution path or process through a system, which may involve actions outside the system. The difference from system testing is that a process or use case may span not only one system, but several. This is certainly true in cases where the in-house systems are integrated with external systems that cannot be controlled. In such cases, the end-to-end test is supposed to make sure that all systems and subsystems perform correctly and produce the desired result.

What's problematic about this term is that its existence is inseparably linked to one's definition of a system and system boundary. In short, if we don't want to make a fuss about the fact that our e-commerce site uses a payment gateway operated by a third party, then we're perfectly fine without end-to-end tests.

Characterization Testing

Characterization testing is the kind of testing you're forced to engage in when changing old code that supposedly works but it's unclear what requirements it's based on, and there are no tests around to explain what it's supposed to be doing. Trying to figure out the intended functionality based on old documentation is usually a futile attempt, because the code has diverged from the scribblings on a wrinkled piece of paper covered with coffee stains long ago.[7] In such conditions, one has to assume that the code's behavior is correct and pin it down with tests (preferably unit tests), so that changing it becomes less scary. Thus, the existing behavior is "characterized."

---

7. My experience is that truly old specifications always come in paper form only! It's not that they predate text files, but the original document has been lost forever in a disk crash, reorganization of the shared network drive, or somebody's project directory cleanup frenzy.

Characterization tests differ from regression tests in that they aim at stabilizing *existing* behavior, and not necessarily the *correct* behavior.

Positive and Negative Testing

The purpose of *positive testing* is to verify that whatever is tested works as expected and behaves like it's supposed to. In order to do so, the test itself is friendly to the tested artifact. It supplies inputs that are within allowed ranges, in a timely fashion, and in the correct order. Tests that are run in such a manner and exercise a typical use case are also called *happy path* tests.

The purpose of *negative testing* is to verify that the system behaves correctly if supplied with invalid values and that it doesn't generate any unexpected results. What outcome to expect depends on the test level. At the system level, we generally want the system to "do the right thing": either reject the faulty input in a user-friendly manner, or recover somehow. At the unit level, throwing an exception may be the right thing to do. For example, if a function exercised with a unit test expects a positive number and throws an `IllegalArgumentException` or `ArgumentOutOfRange-Exception` in a negative test that may be fine. What's important is that the developer has anticipated the scenario.

Small, Medium, and Large Tests

When it comes to pruning terminology, Google may serve as a source of inspiration. To avoid the confusion between terms like end-to-end test, system test, functional test, Selenium[8] test, or UI test, the engineers at Google divided tests into only three categories—small, medium, and large (Stewart 2010).

- **Small tests**—Correspond closely to unit tests; they're small and fast. They're not allowed to access networks, databases, file systems, and external systems. Neither are they allowed to contain sleep statements or test multithreaded code. They must complete within 60 seconds.

- **Medium tests**—May check the interactions between different tiers of the application, which means that they can use databases, access the file system, and test multithreaded code. They should stay away from external systems and remote hosts, though, and should execute for no longer than 300 seconds.

- **Large tests**—Not restricted by any limitations.

---

8. Selenium is a browser automation framework.

Summary

Many of the terms in this chapter have multiple meanings and can be interpreted differently in different contexts. The purpose of this chapter is to bring to light several key terms that are used during discussions about software development and testing.

Human mistakes are called *errors* in testing speak. Errors frequently lead to software *defects*—bugs. Bugs may lead to software *failures*.

White box testing assumes having access to the source code and targets the internal structure of a system, whereas *black box* testing is done "from the outside" and targets the functionality.

Unit tests ensure that a small unit of code, like a function, a class, or a group of classes, works as expected. *Integration tests* verify that components/systems can talk to each other, but sometimes the term is used to describe tests that are somewhere between unit tests and system tests. *System tests* are run to verify an entire system. Finally, *acceptance tests* are performed by the customer to make sure that the expected system has been delivered, whereas *automated acceptance tests* are written by the team and executed by a testing framework to verify that a story or scenario has been implemented.

The *Agile Testing Quadrants* is a model that divides tests into dimensions of technology versus business oriented, as well as guiding the development versus critiquing the product.

Classifying tests can clarify discussions about responsibility and what to test, when, and how. The important thing is to use a classification that everybody in the organization agrees on (or at least is familiar with).

Chapter 4

TESTABILITY FROM A DEVELOPER'S PERSPECTIVE

Testability means different things to different people depending on the context. From a bird's eye view, testability is linked to our prior experience of the things we want to test and our tolerance for defects: the commercial web site that we've been running for the last five years will require less testing and will be easier to test than the insulin pump that we're building for the first time. If we run a project, testability would be about obtaining the necessary information, securing resources (such as tools and environments), and having the time to perform various kinds of testing. There's also a knowledge perspective: How well do we know the product and the technology used to build it? How good are our testing skills? What's our testing strategy? Yet another take on testability would be developing an understanding of what to build by having reliable specifications and ensuring user involvement. It's hard to test anything unless we know how it's supposed to behave.[1]

Before breaking down what testability means to developers, let's look at why achieving it for software is an end in itself.

Testable Software

Testable software encourages the existence of tests—be they manual or automatic. The more testable the software, the greater the chance that somebody will test it, that is, verify that it behaves correctly with respect to a specification or some other expectations, or explore its behavior with some specific objective in mind. Generally, people follow the path of least resistance in their work, and if testing isn't along that path, it's very likely not going to be performed (Figure 4.1).

That testable software will have a greater chance of undergoing some kind of testing may sound really obvious. Equally apparent is the fact that lack of testability, often combined with time pressure, can and does result in bug-ridden and broken software.

Whereas testable software stands on one side of the scale, The Big Ball of Mud (Foote & Yoder 1999) stands on the other. This is code that makes you suspect that

---

1. For an in-depth breakdown of testability, I recommend James Bach's work on the subject (2015).

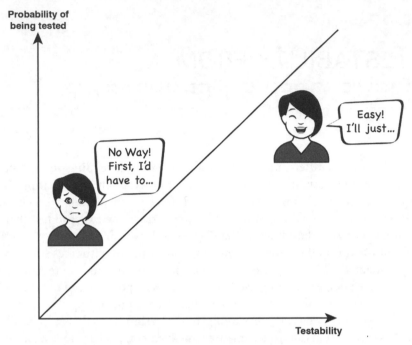

FIGURE 4.1   Is untestable software going to be tested?

the people who wrote it deliberately booby-trapped it with antitestability constructs to make your life miserable. A very real consequence of working with a system that's evolved into The Big Ball of Mud architecture is that it'll prevent you from verifying the effects of your coding efforts. For various reasons, such as convoluted configuration, unnecessary start-up time, or just the difficulty to produce a certain state or data, you may actually have a hard time executing the code you've just written, not to mention being able to write any kinds of tests for it!

For example, imagine a system that requires you to log in to a user interface (UI) and then performing a series of steps that require interacting with various graphical components and then navigating through multiple views before being able to reach the functionality you've just changed or added and want to verify. To make things more realistic (yes, this is a real-life example), further imagine that arriving at the login screen takes four minutes because of some poor design decisions that ended up having a severe impact on start-up time. As another example, imagine a batch program that has to run for 20 minutes before a certain condition is met and a specific path through the code is taken.

Honestly, how many times will you verify, or even just run, the new code if you have to enter values into a multitude of fields in a UI and click through several screens (to say nothing of waiting for the application to start up), or if you must take a coffee break every time you want to check if your batch program behaves correctly for that special almost-never-occurring edge case?

Testers approaching a system with The Big Ball of Mud architecture also face a daunting task. Their test cases will start with a long sequence of instructions about how to put the system in a state the test expects. This will be the script for how to fill in the values in the UI or how to set the system up for the 20-minute-long batch execution. Not only must the testers author that script and make it detailed enough, they must also follow it . . . many times, if they are unlucky. Brrr.

Benefits of Testability

Apart from shielding the developers and testers from immediate misery, testable software also has some other appealing qualities.

Its Functionality Can Be Verified

If the software is developed so that its behavior can be verified, it's easy to confirm that it supports a certain feature, behaves correctly given a certain input, adheres to a specific contract, or fulfills some nonfunctional constraint. Resolving a bug becomes a matter of locating it, changing the code, and running some tests. The opposite of this rather mechanical and predictable procedure is playing the guessing game:

> Charlie: Does business rule X apply in situation Y?
>
> Kate: Not a clue! Wasn't business rule X replaced by business rule Z in release 5.21 by the way?
>
> Charlie: Dunno, but wasn't release 5.2 scrapped altogether? I recall that it was too slow and buggy, and that we waited for 5.4 instead.
>
> Kate: Got me there. Not a clue.

Such discussions take place if the software's functionality isn't verifiable and is expressed as guesses instead. Lack of testability makes confirming these guesses hard and time consuming. Therefore, there's a strong probability that it won't be done.

And because it won't be done, some of the software's features will only be found in the lore and telltales of the organization. Features may "get lost" and, even worse, features may get imagined and people will start expecting them to be there, even though they never were. All this leads to "this is not a bug, it's a feature" type of arguments and blame games.

It Comes with Fewer Surprises

Irrespective of the methodology used to run a software project, at some point some-body will want to check on its progress. How much work has been done? How much remains? Such checks needn't be very formal and don't require a written report with milestones, toll gates, or Gantt charts. In agile teams, developers will be communicat-ing their progress at least on a daily basis in standup meetings or their equivalents.

However, estimating progress for software that has no tests (because of poor test-ability) ranges between best guesses and wishful thinking. A developer who believes he is "95 percent finished" with a feature has virtually no way of telling what fraction of seemingly unrelated functionality he has broken along the way and how much time it'll take to fix these regressions and the remaining "5 percent". A suite of tests makes this situation more manageable. Again, if the feature is supposedly "95 percent finished" and all tests for the new functionality pass, as well as those that exercise the rest of the system, the estimate is much more credible. Now the uncertainty is reduced to poten-tial surprises in the remaining work, not to random regressions that may pop up any-where in the system. Needless to say, this assumes that the codebase is indeed covered by tests that would actually break had any regression issues taken place.[2]

It Can Be Changed

Software can always be changed. The trick is to do it safely and at a reasonable cost. Assuming that testable software implies tests, their presence allows making changes without having to worry that something—probably unrelated—will break as a side effect of that change.

Changing software that has no tests makes the average developer uncomfort-able and afraid (and it should). Fear is easily observed in code. It manifests itself as duplication—the safe way to avoid breaking something that works. When doing code archaeology, we can sometimes find evidence of the following scenario:

At some point in time, the developer needed a certain feature. Alas, there wasn't anything quite like it in the codebase. Instead of adapting an existing concept, by gener-alizing or parameterizing it, he took the safe route and created a parallel implementa-tion, knowing that a bug in it would only affect the new functionality and leave the rest of the system unharmed.

---

2. A slight variation of this is nicely described in the book *Pragmatic Unit Testing* by Andrew Hunt and David Thomas (2003). They plot productivity versus time for software with and without tests. The productivity is lower for software supported by tests, but it's kept constant over time. For software without tests, the initial productivity is higher, but it plummets after a while and becomes negative. Have you been there? I have.

This is but one form of duplication. In fact, the topic is intricate enough to deserve a chapter of its own.

Why Care about Testability

Ultimately, testable software is about money and happiness. Its stakeholders can roll out new features quickly, obtain accurate estimates from the developers, and sleep well at night, because they're confident about the quality. As developers working with code every day, we, too, want to be able to feel productive, give good estimates, and be proud of the quality of our systems. We also want our job to feel fulfilling; we don't want to get stuck in eternal code-fix cycles, and, above all, we don't want our job to be repetitive and mind numbing. Unfortunately, unless our software is testable, we run that risk. Untestable software forces us to work *more* and *harder* instead of *smarter*.

Tests Are Wasteful

by Stephen Vance

This may sound heretical in a book on developer testing and from the author of another book on code-level testing, but bear with me. Agile methods attempt to improve the software we write, or more generally, the results of our knowledge work. I'm very careful to phrase this in a way that highlights that the results are more important than the methods. If some magical Intention Machine produced the software we want without programming, this entire book would be academic. If we could achieve the results without software altogether at the same levels of speed and convenience, our entire discipline would be irrelevant. In some sense, as advanced as we are compared to the course of human history, the labor-intensive-approach trade we ply is quite primitive. Before we wither at the futility of it all, we realize we can only achieve this magical future through improvement.

Most Agile methods have some basis in the thinking that revolutionized manufacturing at the end of the twentieth century. Lean, Total Quality Management, Just-in-time, Theory of Constraints, and the Toyota Production System from the likes of Juran, Deming, Ohno, and Goldratt completely changed the state of manufacturing. Agile methods take those insights and apply them to a domain of inherent invention and variability. Although the principles must be significantly adapted, most of them still apply.

A key principle is the elimination of waste. The Toyota Production System even has three words for waste, *muda*, *mura*, and *muri*, and *mura* has at

---

least seven subcategories captured in the acronym TIMWOOD. Much of our testing focuses on the waste of defects, but does so by incurring inventory and overprocessing.

We incur inventory waste when we invest capital (i.e., coding time) in product that has not yet derived value. Since tests are never delivered, they are eternal inventory. They are an investment with no direct return, only indirect through the reduction and possible prevention of defects.

We incur overprocessing waste by spending the extra attention required to write the tests as compared to the raw production code. The extra attention may pay off compared to the debugging time to get it right at first, the rework for the defects we don't catch, and the refamiliarization on each maintenance encounter. It is clearly additional to getting the code right naturally from the start.

The previous alternatives clearly show that tests are better than the problems they address. That just means they're the best thing we have, not the best we can do. Ultimately, we care about correctness, not tests. We need to keep looking for better ways to ensure the correctness of our software.

I haven't found the answer yet, but there are some interesting candidates.

Domain-Specific Languages

Domain-specific languages (DSLs) have promise. They simplify the work for their users and avoid the repetitive creation of similar code. They bring us closer to being able to say exactly what we mean in the language of the problem we are solving by encapsulating potentially complex logic in a higher-order vocabulary. If the author guarantees the correctness of the elements of the DSL, whole layers of code are correct before we try to use them.

However, good DSLs are notoriously hard to write. Arguably, almost every API we use should be a good DSL, but how many are? Creating a good DSL requires not only taking the time to understand the domain, but also playing with different models of the domain and its interactions to optimize its usability and utility. Additionally, there may be multiple characteristic usage patterns, differing levels of relevant abstractions, varying levels of user expertise, and impactful technological changes over time.

Take, for example, the Capybara acceptance test framework for Ruby, often cited as an example of a well-crafted DSL in the context of its host language. With a set of actions like `visit`, `fill_in`, `click_button` and matchers like `have_content`, it is well suited to static web pages. Under the covers, it has adapted to the rapid evolution of underlying tools like Selenium, but not without challenges at times. However, it still has difficulty dealing with the dynamic, time-dependent behaviors of single-page applications.

Formal Methods

Formal methods sound good. They provide formal proof of the correctness of the code. Unfortunately, we have had a hard time adapting them to larger problems, they are very labor intensive, and most programmers I've met prefer not to deal in that level of mathematical rigor. The research continues, but we're not there yet.

Types

Types bridge the gap between mainstream languages and formal methods in my opinion. By using a subset of formal specification, they help you ensure correctness by cleanly and compactly expressing your illegal "corner cases" in the context they can be most readily applied.

Others

Other approaches provide partial, complex, or laborious solutions. If you're so inclined, maybe you can find that great breakthrough. Until then, keep testing.

Testability Defined

Testability is a quality attribute among other "ilities" like reliability, maintainability, and usability. Just like the other quality attributes, it can be broken down into more fine-grained components (Figure 4.2). Observability and controllability are the two cornerstones of testability. Without them, it's hard to say anything about correctness. The remaining components described next made it to the model based on my practical experience, although I hope that their presence isn't surprising or controversial.

When a program element (see "Program Elements") is *testable*, it means that it can be put in a known state, acted on, and then observed. Further, it means that this can be done without affecting any other program elements and without them interfering. In other words, it's about making the black box of testing somewhat transparent and adding some control levers to it.

Program Elements

From time to time I'll be using the term *program element*. The meaning of the term depends on the context. Sometimes it's a function, sometimes a method, sometimes a class, sometimes a module, sometimes a component, or sometimes all of these things. I use the generic term to avoid clumsy sentences.

Using a catch-all term also solves the problem of emphasizing the difference between programming paradigms. Although the book favors object-oriented code, many techniques apply to procedural and functional constructs too. So instead of writing "class" and "method" everywhere, I can use "program element" and refer to "function" or "module" as well, like a C file with a bunch of related functions.

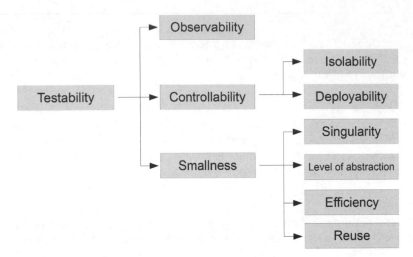

FIGURE 4.2   The testability quality attribute decomposed.

Observability

In order to verify that whatever action our tested program element has been subjected to has had an impact, we need to be able to observe it. The best test in the world isn't worth anything unless its effects can be seen. Software can be observed using a variety of methods. One way of classifying them is in order of increasing intrusiveness.

The obvious, but seldom sufficient, method of observation is to examine whatever output the tested program element produces. Sometimes that output is a sequence of characters, sometimes a window full of widgets, sometimes a web page, and sometimes a rising or falling signal on the pin of a chip.

Then there's output that isn't always meant for the end users. Logging statements, temporary files, lock files, and diagnostics information are all output. Such output is mostly meant for operations and other more "technical" stakeholders. Together with the user output, it provides a source of information for nonintrusive testing.

To increase observability beyond the application's obvious and less obvious output, we have to be willing to make some intrusions and modify it accordingly. Both testers and developers benefit from strategically placed observation points and various types of hooks/seams for attaching probes, changing implementations, or just peeking at the internal state of the application. Such modifications are sometimes frowned upon, as they result in injection of code with the sole purpose of increasing observability. At the last level, there's a kind of observability that's achievable only by developers. It's the ability to step through running code using a debugger. This certainly provides maximum observability at the cost of total intrusion. I don't consider this activity testing, but rather writing code. And you certainly don't want debugging to be your only means of verifying that your code works.

Too many observation points and working too far from production code may result in the appearance of *Heisenbugs*—bugs that tend to disappear when one tries to find and study them. This happens because the inspection process changes something in the program's execution. Excessive logging may, for example, hide a race condition because of the time it takes to construct and output the information to be logged.

Logging, by the way, is a double-edged sword. Although it's certainly the easiest way to increase observability, it may also destroy readability. After all, who hasn't seen methods like this:

```
void performRemoteReboot(String message) {
    if (log.isDebugEnabled()) {
        log.debug("In performRemoteReboot:" + message);
    }
    log.debug("Creating telnet client");
    TelnetClient client = new TelnetClient("192.168.1.34");
    log.debug("Logging in");
    client.login("rebooter", "secret42");
    log.debug("Rebooting");
    client.send("/sbin/shutdown -r now '" + message + "'");
    client.close();
    log.debug("done");
}
```

As developers, we need to take observability into account early. We need to think about what kind of additional output we and our testers may want and where to add more observation points.

Observability and information hiding are often at odds with each other. Many languages, most notably the object-oriented ones, have mechanisms that enable them to limit the visibility of code and data to separate the interface (function) from the implementation. In formal terms, this means that any proofs of correctness must rely solely on public properties and not on "secret" ones (Meyer 1997). On top of that, the general opinion among developers seems to be that the kind of testing that they do should be performed at the level of public interfaces. The argument is sound: if tests get coupled to internal representations and operations, they get brittle and become obsolete or won't even compile with the slightest refactoring. They no longer serve as the safety net needed to make refactoring a safe operation.

Although all of this is true, the root cause of the problem isn't really information hiding or encapsulation, but poor design and implementation, which, in turn, forces us to ask the question of the decade: *Should I test private methods?*[3]

Old systems were seldom designed with testability in mind, which means that their program elements often have multiple areas of responsibility, operate at different levels of abstraction at the same time, and exhibit high coupling and low cohesion. Because of the mess under the hood, testing specific functionality in such systems through whatever public interfaces they have (or even finding such interfaces) is a laborious and slow process. Tests, especially unit tests, become very complex because they need to set up entire "ecosystems" of seemingly unrelated dependencies to get something deep in the dragon's lair working.

In such cases we have two options. Option one is to open up the encapsulation by relaxing restrictions on accessibility to increase both observability and controllability. In Java, changing methods from private to package scoped makes them accessible to (test) code in the same package. In C++, there's the infamous `friend` keyword, which can be used to achieve roughly a similar result, and C# has its `Internals-VisibleTo` attribute.

The other option is to consider the fact that testing at a level where we need to worry about the observability of deeply buried monolithic spaghetti isn't the course of action that gives the best bang for the buck at the given moment. Higher-level tests, like system tests or integration tests, may be a better bet for old low-quality code that doesn't change that much (Vance 2013).

With well-designed *new* code, observability and information hiding shouldn't be an issue. If the code is designed with testability in mind from the start and each program element has a single area of responsibility, then it follows that all interesting abstractions and their functionality will be primary concepts in the code. In object-oriented languages this corresponds to public classes with well-defined functionality (in procedural languages, to modules or the like). Many such abstractions may be too specialized to be useful outside the system, but in context they're most meaningful and eligible for detailed developer testing. The tale in the sidebar contains some examples of this.

Testing Encapsulated Code

Don't put yourself in the position where testing encapsulated code becomes an issue. If you're already there and can't escape in the foreseeable future, test it!

---

3. Or functions, or modules, or any program element, the accessibility to which is restricted by the programming language to support encapsulation.

The Tale of the Math Package

Let's assume that we're setting out to build a math package with a user interface. Users will enter different expressions or equations somehow, and the software will compute the result or perform a mathematical operation like differentiation or integration.

If built iteratively in increments, possibly in a test-driven manner, the entire application may initially start in a single class or module, which will do everything: accept input, parse it, evaluate it, and eventually output the results. Such a program can easily be tested via its public interface, which would be somewhere around accepting unparsed input and returning the results of the computation. Maybe like so:

```
DisplayableResult evaluate(String userInput)
```

However, as the code grows, new program elements will be introduced behind this public interface. First a parser may appear, then something that evaluates the parsed input, then a bunch of specialized math functions, and finally a module that presents the output somehow—either graphically or using some clever notation. As all these building blocks come into existence, testing them through only the first public entry point becomes ceremonious, because they're standalone abstractions with well-defined behavior. Consequently, all of them operate on their own data types and domains, which have their own boundary values and equivalence partitions (see Chapter 8, "Specification-based Testing Techniques") and their own kind of error and exception handling. Ergo, they need their share of tests. Such tests will be much simpler than the ones starting at the boundary of the public interface, because they'll hit the targeted functionality using its own domains and abstractions. Thus, a parsing module will be tested using strings as input and verified against some tree-like structure that represents the expression, whereas an evaluation module may be tested using this tree-like representation and returning something similar. If the underlying math library contains a tailor-made implementation of prime number factorization, that, too, will need specific testing.

If built with some degree of upfront design (be it detailed or rough), that design will reveal some interesting actors, like the parser or the evaluation engine, and their interfaces from the start. At this stage it will be apparent that these actors need to work together correctly, but also exhibit individual correctness. Enter tests of nonpublic behavior . . .

So what happens if, let's say, the parsing code is replaced with a third-party implementation? Numerous tests will be worthless, because the new component happens to be both well renowned for its stability and correctness and well tested. This wouldn't have happened if all tests targeted the initial public interface. Well, this is the "soft" in software—it changes. The tests that are going to get thrown away once secured the functionality of the parser, given its capabilities and implementation. The new parsing component comes with new capabilities, and certainly a new implementation, so some tests will no longer be relevant.

Controllability

Controllability is the ability to put something in a specific state and is of paramount importance to any kind of testing because it leads to *reproducibility*. As developers, we like to deal with determinism. We like things to happen the same way every time, or at least in a way that we understand. When we get a bug report, we want to be able to reproduce the bug so that we may understand under what conditions it occurs. Given that understanding, we can fix it. The ability to reproduce a given condition in a system, component, or class depends on the ability to isolate it and manipulate its internal state.

Dealing with state is complex enough to mandate a section of its own. For now, we can safely assume that too much state turns reproducibility, and hence controllability, into a real pain. But what is *state*? In this context, state simply refers to whatever data we need to provide in order to set the system up for testing. In practice, state isn't only about data. To get a system into a certain state, we usually have to set up some data and execute some of the system's functions, which in turn will act on the data and lead to the desired state.

Different test types require different amounts of state. A unit test for a class that takes a string as a parameter in its constructor and prints it on the screen when a certain method is called has little state. On the other hand, if we need to set up thousands of fake transactions in a database to test aggregation of cumulative discounts, then that would qualify as a great deal of state.

Deployability

Before the advent of DevOps, deployability seldom made it to the top five quality attributes to consider when implementing a system. Think about the time you were in a large corporation that deployed its huge monolith to a commercial application server. Was the process easy? Deployability is a measure of the amount of work needed to deploy the system, most notably, into production. To get a rough feeling for it, ask:

"How long does it take to get a change that affects one line of code into production?" (Poppendieck & Poppendieck 2006).

Deployability affects the developers' ability to run their code in a production-like environment. Let's say that a chunk of code passes its unit tests and all other tests on the developer's machine. Now it's time to see if the code actually works as expected in an environment that has more data, more integrations, and more complexity (like a good production-like test environment should have). This is a critical point. If deploying a new version of the system is complicated and prone to error or takes too much time, it won't be done. A typical process that illustrates this problem is manual deployment based on a list of instructions. Common traits of deployment instructions are that they're old, they contain some nonobvious steps that may not be relevant at all, and despite their apparent level of detail, they still require a large amount of tacit knowledge. Furthermore, they describe a process that's complex enough to be quite error prone.

Manual Deployment Instructions

A list of instructions for manual deployment is a scary relic from the past, and it can break even the toughest of us. It's a sequence of steps written probably five or more years ago, detailing the procedure to manually deploy a system. It may look something like this:

1. Log in to prod.mycompany.com using ssh with user `root`, password `secret123`.
2. Navigate to the application server directory:

   `cd /data/opt/extras/appserver/jboss`
3. Stop the server by running the following:

   `./stop_server_v1_7.sh`
4. On your local machine, run the build script:

   `cd c:\projects\killerapp, ant package`
5. Use WinSCP version 1.32 to copy killerapp.ear to the deployment directory.
6. Remove the temporary files in `/tmp/killerapp`.
7. Clear the application cache:

   `rm -rf server/killerapp/cache*)`
8. More steps . . .

Being unable to deploy painlessly often punishes the developers in the end. If deployment is too complicated and too time consuming, or perceived as such, they may stop verifying that their code runs in environments that are different from their development machines. If this starts happening, they end up in the good-old "it works on my machine" argument, and it *never* makes them look good, like in this argument between Tracy the Tester and David the Developer:

> Tracy: I tried to run the routine for verifying postal codes in Norway. When I entered an invalid code, nothing happened.
>
> David: All my unit tests are green and I even ran the integration tests!
>
> Tracy: Great! But I expected an error message from the system, or at least some kind of reaction.
>
> David: But really, look at my screen! I get an error message when entering an invalid postal code. I have a Norwegian postal code in my database.
>
> Tracy: I notice that you're running build 273 while the test environment runs 269. What happened?
>
> David: Well . . . I didn't deploy! It would take me half a day to do it! I'd have to add a column to the database and then manually dump the data for Norway. Then I'd have to copy the six artifacts that make up the system to the application server, but before doing that I'd have to rebuild three of them. . . . I forgot to run the thing because I wanted to finish it!

The bottom line is that developers are not to consider themselves finished with their code until they've executed it in an environment that resembles the actual production environment.

Poor deployability has other adverse effects as well. For example, when preparing a demo at the end of an iteration, a team can get totally stressed out if getting the last-minute fixes to the demo environment is a lengthy process because of a manual procedure.

Last, but not least, struggling with unpredictable deployment also makes critical bug fixes difficult. I don't encourage making quick changes that have to be made in a very short time frame, but sometimes you encounter critical bugs in production and they have to be fixed immediately. In such situations, you don't want to think about how hard it's going to get the fix out—you just want to squash the bug.

What about Automated Deployment?

One way to ensure good deployability is to commit to continuous integration and then adapt the techniques described in the book *Continuous Delivery*. Its authors often repeat: "If it's painful, do it more often" (Humble & Farley 2010), and this certainly refers to the deployment process, which should be automated.

Isolability

Isolability, modularity, low coupling—in this context, they're all different sides of the same coin. There are many names for this property, but regardless of the name, it's about being able to isolate the program element under test—be it a function, class, web service, or an entire system.

Isolability is a desirable property from both a developer's and a tester's point of view. In modular systems, related concepts are grouped together, and changes don't ripple across the entire system. On the other hand, components with lots of dependencies are not only difficult to modify, but also difficult to test. Their tests will require much setup, often of seemingly unrelated dependencies, and their interactions with the outside world will be artificial and hard to make sense of.

Isolability applies at all levels of a system. On the class level, isolability can be described in terms of *fan-out*, that is, the number of outgoing dependencies on other classes. A useful design rule of thumb is trying to achieve a low fan-out. In fact, high fan-out is often considered bad design (Borysowich 2007). Unit testing classes with high fan-out is cumbersome because of the number of test doubles needed to isolate the class from all collaborators.

Poor isolability at the component level may manifest itself as difficulty setting up its surrounding environment. The component may be coupled to other components by various communication protocols such as SOAP or connected in more indirect ways such as queues or message buses. Putting such a component under test may require that parts of it be reimplemented to make the integration points interchangeable for stubs. In some unfortunate cases, this cannot be done, and testing such a component may require that an entire middleware package be set up just to make it testable.

Systems with poor isolability suffer from the sum of poorness of their individual components. So if a system is composed of one component that makes use of an enterprise-wide message bus, another component that requires a very specific directory layout on the production server (because it won't even run anywhere else), and a third that requires some web services at specific locations, you're in for a treat.

Smallness

The smaller the software, the better the testability, because there's less to test. Simply put, there are fewer moving parts that need to be controlled and observed, to stay consistent with this chapter's terminology. Smallness primarily translates into the quantity of tests needed to cover the software to achieve a sufficient degree of confidence. But what exactly about the software should be "small"? From a testability perspective, two properties matter the most: the number of features and the size of the codebase. They both drive different aspects of testing.

Feature-richness drives testing from both a black box and a white box perspective. Each feature somehow needs to be tested and verified from the perspective of the user. This typically requires a mix of manual testing and automated high-level tests like end-to-end tests or system tests. In addition, low-level tests are required to secure the building blocks that comprise all the features. Each new feature brings additional complexity to the table and increases the potential for unfortunate and unforeseen interactions with existing features. This implies that there are clear incentives to keep down the number of features in software, which includes removing unused ones.

A codebase's smallness is a bit trickier, because it depends on a number of factors. These factors aren't related to the number of features, which means that they're seldom observable from a black box perspective, but they may place a lot of burden on the shoulders of the developer. In short, white box testing is driven by the size of the codebase. The following sections describe properties that can make developer testing cumbersome without rewarding the effort from the feature point of view.

Singularity

If something is singular, there's only one instance of it. In systems with high singularity, every behavior and piece of data have a single source of truth. Whenever we want to make a change, we make it in one place. In the book *The Pragmatic Programmer*, this has been formulated as the DRY principle: Don't Repeat Yourself (Hunt & Thomas 1999).

Testing a system where singularity has been neglected is quite hard, especially from a black box perspective. Suppose, for example, that you were to test the copy/paste functionality of an editor. Such functionality is normally accessible in three ways: from a menu, by right-clicking, and by using a keyboard shortcut. If you approached this as a black box test while having a limited time constraint, you might have been satisfied with testing only one of these three ways. You'd assume that the others would work by analogy. Unfortunately, if this particular functionality had been implemented by two different developers on two different occasions, then you wouldn't be able to assume that both are working properly.

The tester sees . . .	The developer implemented . . .
📋 Copy	`EditorUtil.copy`
	`currentEditorPanel.performCopy`
	A third version?

This example is a bit simplistic, but this scenario is very common in systems that have been developed by different generations of developers (which is true of pretty much every system that's been in use for a while). Systems with poor singularity appear confusing and frustrating to their users, who report a bug and expect it to be fixed. However, when they perform an action similar to the one that triggered the bug by using a different command or accessing it from another part of the system, the problem is back! From their perspective, the system should behave consistently, and explaining why the bug has been fixed in two out of three places inspires confidence in neither the system nor the developers' ability.

To a developer, nonsingularity—duplication—presents itself as the activity of implementing or changing the same data or behavior multiple times to achieve a single result. With that comes maintaining multiple instances of test code and making sure that all contracts and behavior are consistent.

Level of Abstraction

The level of abstraction is determined by the choice of programming language and frameworks. If they do the majority of the heavy lifting, the code can get both smaller and simpler. At the extremes lie the alternatives of implementing a modern application in assembly language or a high-level language, possibly backed by a few frameworks. But there's no need to go to the extremes to find examples. Replacing thread primitives with thread libraries, making use of proper abstractions in object-oriented languages (rather than strings, integers, or lists), and working with web frameworks instead of implementing Front Controllers[4] and parsing URLs by hand are all examples of raising the level of abstraction. For certain types of problems and constructs, employing functional or logic programming greatly raises the level of abstraction, while reducing the size of the codebase.

The choice of the programming language has a huge impact on the level of abstraction and plays a crucial role already at the level of toy programs (and scales accordingly as the complexity of the program increases). Here's a trivial program that adds its two command-line arguments together. Whereas the C version needs to worry about string-to-integer conversion and integer overflow . . .

```c
#include <stdio.h>
#include <stdlib.h>

int main(int argc, char *argv[])
{
  int augend = atoi(argv[1]);
  int addend = atoi(argv[2]);

  // Let's hope that we don't overflow...
  printf("*drum roll* ... %d", augend + addend);
}
```

---

4. https://en.wikipedia.org/wiki/Front_Controller_pattern

. . . its Ruby counterpart will work just fine for large numbers while being a little more tolerant with the input as well.

```
puts "*drum roll* ... #{ARGV[0].to_i + ARGV[1].to_i}"
```

From a developer testing point of view, the former program would most likely give rise to more tests, because they'd need to take overflow into account. Generally, as the level of abstraction is raised, fewer tests that cover fundamental building blocks, or the "plumbing," are needed, because such things are handled by the language or framework. The user won't see the difference, but the developer who writes the tests will.

Efficiency

In this context, efficiency equals the ability to express intent in the programming language in an idiomatic way and making use of that language's functionality to keep the code expressive and concise. It's also about applying design patterns and best practices. Sometimes we see signs of struggle in codebases being left by developers who have fought valorously reinventing functionality already provided by the language or its libraries. You know inefficient code when you see it, right after which you delete 20 lines of it and replace them with a one-liner, which turns out idiomatic and simple.

Inefficient implementations increase the size of the codebase without providing any value. They require their tests, especially unit tests, because such tests need to cover many fundamental cases. Such cases wouldn't need testing if they were handled by functionality in the programming language or its core libraries.

Reuse

Reuse is a close cousin of efficiency. Here, it refers to making use of third-party components to avoid reinventing the wheel. A codebase that contains in-house implementations of a distributed cache or a framework for managing configuration data in text files with periodic reloading[5] will obviously be larger than one that uses tested and working third-party implementations.

This kind of reuse reduces the need for developer tests, because the functionality isn't owned by them and doesn't need to be tested. Their job is to make sure that it's plugged in correctly, and although this, too, requires tests, they will be fewer in number.

---

5. Now this is a highly personal experience, but pretty much all legacy systems that I've seen have contained home-grown caches and configuration frameworks.

Mind Maintainability!

All of the aforementioned properties may be abused in a way that mostly hurts maintainability. Singularity may be taken to the extreme and create too tightly coupled systems. Too high a level of abstraction may turn into some kind of "meta programming." Efficiency may turn into unmotivated compactness, which hurts readability. Finally, reuse may result in pet languages and frameworks being brought in, only to lead to fragmentation.

A Reminder about Testability

Have you ever worked on a project where you didn't know what to implement until the very last moment? Where there were no requirements or where iteration planning meetings failed to result in a shared understanding about what to implement in the upcoming two or three weeks? Where the end users weren't available?

Or maybe you weren't able to use the development environment you needed and had to make do with inferior options. Alternatively, there was this licensed tool that would have saved the day had but somebody paid for it.

Or try this: the requirements and end users were there and so was the tooling, but nobody on the team knew how to do cross-device mobile testing.

After having dissected the kind of testability the developer is exposed to the most, I'm just reminding that there are other facets of testability that we mustn't lose sight of.

Summary

If the software is designed with testability in mind, it will more than likely be tested. When software is testable, we can verify its functionality, measure progress while developing it, and change it safely. In the end, the result is fast and reliable delivery.

Testability can be broken down into the following components:

- *Observability*—Observe the tested program element in order to verify that it actually passes the test.

- *Controllability*—Set the tested program element in a state expected by the test.

- *Smallness*—The smaller the system or program element—with respect to the number of features and the size of the codebase—the less to test.

Chapter 5

PROGRAMMING BY CONTRACT

Structuring code so that it's testable, whereby increasing its probability of being tested isn't the only way to aim for correct software. Another approach would be to go down the road of *formal methods*, that is, mathematical proofs. In this chapter, we examine yet another alternative, which is modeling the software as transactions between a client and supplier, who agree on a contract that forces them to uphold certain obligations to each other (see Figure 5.1). In exchange, both get some benefits. If the contract is violated, the application stops. For such an approach to be effective, the contract must be constantly checked at runtime, as opposed to running a suite of tests now and then or proving a fact about the program on paper.

When software is written in this way, we're talking about *Programming by Contract*.[1] This technique is quite characteristic for Eiffel, where it's built right into the language.[2] However, even without full language support it's still quite usable.

Contracts Formalize Constraints

Contracts define constraints that apply throughout the execution of an application. The life span of a constraint depends on its type. Some must be satisfied upon entering or exiting a method; others must be upheld during the entire lifetime of the application.

If a constraint is violated, the application should abort execution with an exception or error that's not meant to be caught or handled; it should be unrecoverable, the reason being that a violation should happen as a result of exceptional conditions. In practice, this turns contracts into the last line of defense and a complement to the application's validation logic and test suite. Relying solely on contracts is neither feasible nor practical, and not even languages that have full support for them encourage that they replace validation and common sense in programming.

---

1. Actually, the more well-known term is "Design by Contract," but the term is trademarked and won't be used in this book.
2. According to Wikipedia, roughly 15 languages have built-in contract support (http://en.wikipedia.org/wiki/Design_by_contract).

Invocation contract

<Calling code>, henceforth known as "Client", and *<method/function>*, henceforth known as "Supplier", enter into this agreement of representation for the lifetime of the system.

The Supplier will provide service to the Client upon invocation.

Furthermore, the Supplier and Client agree to these <u>obligations</u>:

- The Client promises to send valid parameters to the Supplier
- The Supplier works according to specification

Whereupon they are entitled to the following <u>benefits</u>:

- The Client gets a valid result without surprises
- The Supplier gets valid parameters and doesn't need to verify them

Client name	Client signature
Supplier name	Supplier signature

FIGURE 5.1   In the nomenclature of contract programming, the caller of a method/function is its client and the callee is the supplier (because it supplies some chunk of work).

Contract Building Blocks

In the language of Programming by Contract a caller of a method/function is a *client*, and the callee is a *supplier*. The basic building blocks of contracts are preconditions, postconditions, and class invariants.

Preconditions are constraints that need to be met when calling the supplier. They are typically a function of the supplied arguments and any internal state of the supplier. If the constraint isn't met, the supplier terminates before executing. Preconditions are short lived. They are checked upon entering a method. Some possible examples include the following:

- When retrieving an element from an indexed collection, is the index positive or zero?

- When popping a stack, is the stack non-empty?

- When computing a checksum for a given input, is the input's format correct?

Postconditions are constraints on the supplier's internal state and often the return value. They need to be met prior to returning from a call to the supplier. If such a constraint isn't met, the supplier terminates before returning. Postconditions are also short lived. They apply only when returning to the calling client. All of the following would make reasonable postconditions:

- When transferring funds between accounts, the same amount is added to one account and subtracted from the other.

- When creating an object, its member variables have all been initialized to legal values.

- When adding an element to a linked list, the new element becomes the list's head and it points to the previous head of the list.

Invariants are the third building block of contracts. Two common types of invariants are class invariants and loop invariants. *Class invariants* are constraints that are always upheld for a class's internal state. For example, if we have a class that represents time and uses integers to store hours and minutes, a reasonable class invariant would require that they be in the ranges 0–23 and 0–59. Constraints upheld by class invariants can live as long as the executing program. For example, consider a class invariant on a collection of bank accounts stating that the sum of all transactions must equal the total balance.

Contracts in Eiffel

The following routine, written in Eiffel, uses preconditions to check that its parameters are valid and a postcondition to verify that the return value is reasonable. As we see, contract checking is clearly supported by the language.

```
Seconds_in_24h: INTEGER = 86400

to_seconds (hour, minute: INTEGER): INTEGER
require
    hour >= 0 and hour < 24
    minute >= 0 and minute < 60
do
    Result := hour * 3600 + minute * 60
ensure
    Result >= 0 and Result <= Seconds_in_24h
end
```

Implementing Programming by Contract

Full-fledged Programming by Contract is one strategy among several to achieve software correctness and constitutes a strong complement to testing at any level. That said, the most popular programming languages only partially, if at all, support it. On the other hand, the technique has much to offer, regardless of whether it's 100 percent supported by the programming language or if we have to make do with bits and pieces of it. In this section, we'll explore what to take away from contract programming and how.

Thinking in Contracts

Irrespective of your favorite language's support for contracts, the major shift when employing them comes from having to think about the produced code in terms of clients and suppliers and the consequences of formalizing responsibilities. In languages where contracts are supported natively, specifying the contract prior to writing any code is an established design practice.

Establishing preconditions, postconditions, and maybe even invariants for the program elements that we create slows us down—but in a good way. We need to think about where responsibilities lie and which part of the code should do what. Whether we strive to uphold the contract at runtime or not is secondary in my opinion. Specifying the contract is the critical aspect of this technique.

This may sound obvious, but think about this: How many times have you had to consider where to put the responsibility for ensuring that the arguments passed to a method/function/routine are valid? In the majority of systems that I've worked with, this question has been ignored or subject to heated debate, thereby producing the full spectrum of possibilities:

- **The caller ensures that the arguments are correct**—This stance is typically taken by libraries and reusable components, which are supposed to be clean and easy to understand, as opposed to sprinkled with various null and range checks. Routines in such libraries may crash badly if incorrect arguments are supplied. Thus, the contracts are clearly stated, but not enforced.

- **The callee checks the arguments**—It's perfectly logical for the callee to check the values of the input parameters (and, in fact, a must) in code exposed to public use. Publicly available remote procedure calls (RPCs) or web services make good examples. Because they don't know the intentions of the caller, whose objective may be to crash the callee for fun or privilege escalation, they must take their own protective measures. Routines that are to be called by unknown and potentially malicious clients should be crafted appropriately and apply additional checks to their input parameters. Common vulnerabilities like buffer overflows and SQL injections are often a result of missing or too lenient parameter checking.

  Legacy systems maintained by generations of developers, where nobody can trust anything, are another example. Such systems tend to have islands where defensive programming has been applied and where arguments are checked more thoroughly. The person who wrote the code probably thought: "Everything is so buggy. I can't trust anything, but at least I can make sure that *my* routine doesn't swallow the garbage without a fight." This is a brave attempt to enforce some kind of contract.

- **The responsibility isn't formalized**—Different generations of developers and programming styles, combined with lack of conventions, typically lead to a clear absence of argument checking, duplicated effort, or mishmash of the two preceding strategies.

Contracts, be they part of the language or just a mental model, blend naturally with object-oriented design. If it's clear what kind of contract each object honors, especially its construction logic, many tedious and verbose checks and validations may be omitted. Suppose that we implement the classic time difference function: given two dates, it returns the time difference between them. A naïve implementation using integers as arguments would have to start by checking that the arguments indeed are valid dates—for example, that they follow the format `yyyymmdd`. On the other hand, if the same function would accept two date objects, it could stop worrying about validating them and just perform the computation. In other words, the contract of the class representing the date would save the date difference function from performing extraneous checks. In fact, this example also illustrates how contracts can help us to follow the Single Responsibility Principle (Martin 2002) by taking validation and parameter checking off the table.

Enforcing Contracts

Once we decide to actually adopt contracts as a design technique, we have multiple options at our disposal for how to enforce them. Our choice will be affected by the availability of the technique in question in our current programming language and our intention to aim for runtime enforcement, in contrast to expressing the intention of contracts and more indirect means of enforcement.

Assertions

Assertions are by far the most common way to achieve contract verification. They're runtime checks that verify a boolean condition and make the program terminate with a diagnostic message if that condition isn't satisfied. A feature of assertions is that they can be turned off, which means that code executed in them mustn't be critical to the execution of the program.

Warning: Don't Try This at Home!

Assertions can be turned off, so executing code in them, like incrementing a counter, is a very bad idea.

```
assert(important++ < MAGIC_NUMBER);
```

The fact that failed assertions terminate in a way that aborts the execution of the application without further ado makes them totally inappropriate for verifying parameters to public functions or input supplied by the user. This is, by the way, in line with the philosophy of Programming by Contract, according to which contract checking should be preceded by normal validation logic. Imagine a typical constructor for a simple time class:

```
public Time(int hour, int minute) {
    assert hour >= 0 && hour < 24 :  "Hour out of range";
    assert minute >= 0 && minute < 60 : "Minute out of range";
```

```
    this.hour = hour;
    this.minute = minute;
}
```

Using assertions like this would be incorrect, because we don't want the program to crash just because invalid parameters have been passed to a public constructor. Also, we don't want the constructor to start accepting arbitrary values just because we decided to deactivate assertions.

In short, precondition verification and assertions apply to situations where we want to guard against programming errors and incorrect caller behavior, which isn't the case for public APIs. Such APIs should use normal error or exception handling to reject bad input.

```
public Time(int hour, int minute) {
    if (hour < 0 || hour > 23) {
        throw new IllegalArgumentException("Hour out of range: " + hour);
    }
    if (minute < 0 || minute > 59) {
        throw new IllegalArgumentException("Minute out of range: " + minute);
    }
    this.hour = hour;
    this.minute = minute;
}
```

Assertions have a slight impact on performance. The cost varies from language to language and platform to platform, but we can expect at least an additional conditional to be executed for every assertion.[3]

Libraries that Support Contracts

Many libraries are available that help in implementing contract programming in one form or another. Two are quite popular: Guava and Code Contracts.

Google's Guava libraries, available for Java developers, contain a collection of static utility methods for checking preconditions. Given that roughly a dozen methods are available and that they only support verifying preconditions, this might seem rather thin.[4] However, the design of these methods makes them interesting. The

---

3. Saving nanoseconds at the cost of turning off assertions may be a bad idea, but the point of this argument is that we don't want assertions that aren't used. They use up the few nanoseconds, but they also clutter the code if used incorrectly and in excess.
4. There are dedicated Programming by Contract libraries for Java, like Cofoja, but I haven't seen them used in practice.

methods go by names like `checkArgument`, `checkState`, or `checkNotNull` and expect booleans or the value to be checked for null as arguments. The interesting thing about their design is that they throw catchable runtime exceptions, which means that they can not only be used to verify contracts in the strictest sense, but also to perform validation.

Using Guava's utility methods, the constructor for a time class would look like the following:

```
public Time(int hour, int minute) {
    checkArgument(hour >= 0 && hour <= 23, "Valid hours are between 0 and 23");
    checkArgument(minute >= 0 && minute <= 59, "Valid minutes are between 0 and 59");
    this.hour = hour;
    this.minute = minute;
}
```

In my opinion, this better shows the intent and is more readable than `if` statements. In addition, it indicates the presence of a contract and its preconditions.

C# developers have a more versatile tool at their disposal in Code Contracts, which is a package that adds pretty much full-fledged contract support to C# (RiSE 2015). This highly configurable package allows verifying the different building blocks of contracts at both runtime and to some extent statically.

Discussing the full functionality of Code Contracts is beyond the scope of this book, but as a teaser, the following snippet shows that the library can be used to both validate arguments by throwing a developer-specified runtime exception and to truly enforce a precondition by throwing an unrecoverable `ContractException` (Microsoft 2013):

```
public Time(int hour, int minute)
{
    Contract.Requires<ArgumentException>(hour >= 0 && hour <= 23);
    Contract.Requires(minute >= 0 && minute <= 59);
    this.hour = hour;
    this.minute = minute;
}
```

Unit Tests

My personal experience is that neither assertions nor specialized libraries have had a major breakthrough or have reached the large masses. Hopefully, it's not because developers don't know or care about these techniques and building blocks, but because they specify and verify their contracts with unit tests. Using tests to express a contract is an indirect means of enforcement, but that doesn't make the technique less effective. After all, unit tests are perfectly capable of verifying preconditions, postconditions, and invariants once the hard work—specifying them—has been done. Obviously, the test-based approach takes away the runtime checking and, more important, the explicit documentation of the contract in the production code, but in spite of these drawbacks, it's the most popular choice.

Static Analysis

If runtime enforcement of contracts is at one side of a scale, static analysis is on the other. Still, static analysis together with type metadata can be used to express the intention of a contract. When using languages that allow annotating types somehow, we can make the IDE or a static analysis tool help us to uphold some rudimentary constraints for variables, method arguments, and return values (depending on which of these can be annotated). This can be considered a method of enforcing, or at least expressing, contracts in a way, but it's limited to the level of sophistication of the type metadata and compile-time checking.[5]

The flagship of this technique is some form of null check, like the `@Nonnull` or `@NotNull` annotations in Java (JCP 2006) and the `[NotNull]` attribute in C#.[6] While other annotations exist, this is the one that seems to have caught on the most at the time of writing.

Summary

Programming by Contract is a technique complementary to testing and is about run-time verification of constraints defined by contracts. Such constraints may be *pre-conditions*, *postconditions* and different types of *invariants*. The constraints ensure that calls are made using valid parameters and that the program is in a sound state. A constraint violation is an unrecoverable error.

Methods designed with a contract in mind (either explicitly enforced or just as a design aid) will have clearer responsibilities and will be easier to understand. This, in turn, simplifies testing.

The majority of languages don't support contracts directly; rather, they use asser-tions to achieve the effect of contract checking. Caution should be exercised in such cases, because assertions don't necessarily make it into production.

The big takeaway from this chapter is that designing program elements with con-tracts in mind helps give these elements clear responsibility and helps determine what kinds of tests, and how many, we need in order to verify that a contract is indeed sup-ported. Once a contract has been defined, we can verify it using secondary techniques like unit testing or static analysis.

---

5. Actually, one can use aspect-oriented programming to provide runtime checks, but I've never seen it done in practice.
6. This attribute comes from the JetBrains.Annotations package and is interpreted by ReSharper (JetBrains 2016).

Chapter 6

DRIVERS OF TESTABILITY

Some constructs and behaviors in code have great impact on its testability. This chapter is about exploring and harnessing them. Let's start by looking at two snippets of code. The first one—matrix multiplication—is a typical programming exercise for fresh computer science students.

```
static multiply(double[][] m1, double[][] m2) {
    if (m1[0].length != m2.length) {
        throw new IllegalArgumentException(
                "width of m1 must equal height of m2"
        )
    }

    final int rh = m1.length
    final int rw = m2[0].length

    double[][] result = new double[rh][rw]
    for (int y = 0; y < rh; y++) {
        for (int x = 0; x < rw; x++) {
            for (int xy = 0; xy < m2.length; xy++) {
                result[y][x] += m1[y][xy] * m2[xy][x]
            }
        }
    }
    return result
}
```

The second snippet could easily be found in any enterprise codebase.

```
public void dispatchInvoice(Invoice invoice) {
    TransactionId transactionId = transactionIdGenerator.generateId();
    invoice.setTransactionId(transactionId);
    invoiceRepository.save(invoice);
    invoiceQueue.enqueue(invoice);
    processedInvoices++;
}
```

If your brain is wired like mine, you'll find the second snippet more readable and easier to understand. However, from a testability point of view, the differences aren't in the variable names, nested loops, and opportunities for off-by-one errors. What truly makes these snippets different is the amount of direct and indirect input and output in each of them and how they handle state.

Direct Input and Output

When a program element's behavior is affected solely by values that have been passed in via its public interface, it's said to operate on *direct input*. In the case of a function like `multiply`, it means that whatever the function operates on is supplied as arguments. This notion can be taken further: other program elements, like entire classes or even components, may depend only on direct input, but for practical purposes, let's confine the discussion to methods/functions.

Reliance on only direct input is quite a desirable property.[1] From a testing perspective, it means that the largest concern is to find relevant inputs to pass in as arguments to the tested method, without caring about any other actors or circumstances that may affect its behavior.

Direct output is analogous to direct input. Output is said to be direct if it's observable through the program element's public interface. This, too, has a great impact on testability. It means that tests only need to query whatever the tested program element exposes. In the case of a method, it would be its return value.

In summation, `multiply` operates only on direct input and output, and testing it from a black box perspective would amount to finding good equivalence classes and boundary values.[2]

Indirect Input and Output

Conversely, let's have a look at the `dispatchInvoice` method. Unless you multiply matrices for a living, it's easier to grasp than `multiply`. On the other hand, testing it is harder. One of the differences is its reliance on indirect input and on the indirect output it produces. Input is considered *indirect* if it isn't supplied using the program element's public interface. An easy way to spot indirect input is to put the black box testing hat on and ask: "Would I be able to test this without having access to the source code?" If the answer is "no," then we're most likely dealing with indirect input.

---

1. It's one of those properties that comes with trade-offs, however. In some cases, relying on only direct input may conflict with object-oriented design and encapsulation.
2. Equivalence classes and boundary values are mentioned a few times in this chapter, but are properly introduced in Chapter 8, "Specification-based Testing Techniques."

The indirect input to `dispatchInvoice` is the result of `transactionId-Generator.generateId()`. The generated identifier is certainly not modifiable through the public interface, but constitutes input that's critical to the operation of the method. This makes testing harder, because the test must gain control of that input and make it predictable.

In the previous example, a collaborating object is the source of indirect input, but there are many other possible sources. Static variables/methods, system properties, files, databases, queues, and the system clock are all sources of indirect input. The notorious Singleton pattern is shunned for being the mother source of indirect input.

Finally, *indirect output* is any kind of output that isn't observable through the public interface. In the case of `dispatchInvoice` there are two such outputs[3]: first the saving of the updated invoice, then the enqueuing (what these actions actually result in isn't relevant here). In addition, `dispatchInvoice` doesn't return anything, so it clearly signals that *if* it produces any output, then it certainly is indirect.

Pure Functions and Side Effects

The two previous methods can be analyzed from a different perspective—in terms of pureness and side effects. A function is *pure* if

1. **It's consistent**—Given the same set of input data, it always returns the same output value, which doesn't depend on any hidden information, state, or external input.
2. **It has no side effects**—The function doesn't change any variables or data of any type outside of the function. This includes output to I/O devices.

Given this definition, functions that have no indirect input or output are pure. As for side effects, these typically involve

- Changing the value of a variable outside the scope of the function
- Modifying data referenced by a parameter (call by reference)
- Throwing an exception
- Doing some I/O

For testing purposes, there's no real difference between pure functions and functions that only operate on direct input and output. However, given the popularity of functional languages, it doesn't hurt to clarify the relation between these two terms.

---

3. Actually, we can count three. A counter is incremented too, but this will be treated later.

State

Let's return to the `dispatchInvoice` method once more. Its last line, where a counter is incremented, presents a challenge in itself when it comes to testing. The code is written so that we don't know whether `processedInvoices` is a class variable or a member variable, but we do know that some state is changed. The counter may have numerous uses, spanning from plain simple logging to triggering some critical business rule.

What if the last line of `dispatchInvoice` were changed to this instead:

```
if (++processedInvoices == BATCH_SIZE) {
    invoiceRepository.archiveOldInvoices();
    invoiceQueue.ensureEmptied();
}
```

Suddenly the state triggers something important, and any tests written against the method need to take that into account. A test that wants to trigger the condition needs to do one of the following:

- Access the `processedInvoices` variable directly and modify it; something that many people would argue would break encapsulation.

- Start by making `BATCH_SIZE - 1` calls to `dispatchInvoice` to arrive at the correct state (given that we know when `processedInvoices` is zero).

- Force some kind of refactoring that would enable modifying or ignoring the value of `processedInvoices` without making the code significantly worse.

None of these options are trivially obvious. You have to make the trade-off between violating encapsulation, writing a more complex test, or reworking the code. Do keep in mind that the example was about something as simple as a class or member variable and that there are many more elaborate and intricate ways to introduce state.

Databases, by nature, are piles of state. If you've ever had to debug an invoicing algorithm that applied a myriad of business rules to tens of thousands of customers, all of which had unique purchasing histories, you know the meaning of both state and pain. The same goes for reports, network-aware applications, page navigation, and so on.

The point is that all but the most trivial applications will have state, and we need to take that into account when designing testable code. The question we must ask ourselves is: "How do I set up a test so that I reach the correct state prior to verifying the expected behavior?" Or a better question may in fact be: "How do I keep the amount of state down and isolated so that I don't have to ask myself the former question too often?"

Temporal Coupling

Temporal coupling is a close cousin of state. "Temporal" means that something has to do with time. In this case, it's the time of invocation or, more specifically, the *order* of invocation. Given a program element with functions f_1 and f_2, there exists a temporal coupling between them if, when f_2 is called, it expects that f_1 has been called first—that is, it relies on state set up by f_1.

Imagine the `multiply` function from the example at the beginning of this chapter being moved to a class and the parameters being set using an old-fashioned initializer method.

```
class MatrixMultiplier {
    private double[][] m1
    private double[][] m2

    def initialize(double[][] m1, double[][] m2) {

        if (m1[0].length != m2.length) {
            throw new IllegalArgumentException(
                    "width of m1 must equal height of m2"
            )
        }

        this.m1 = m1
        this.m2 = m2
    }

    double[][] multiply() {
        // Same as before, but with member variables
    }
}
```

This change, deliberately crude to get your attention, introduces temporal coupling. A call to `multiply` now requires first calling `initialize`. Otherwise, it will reward you with a `NullPointerException`. Code in the wild will be just as ruthless. It will either crash if things are called out of order or perform some convoluted initialization spanning different layers of abstraction while violating a whole host of design practices and all forms of logic—all to make it impossible for you to even *dare* move a single line within a method.

In essence, temporal coupling arises as soon as one program element needs something to have happened in another program element in order to function correctly.

Usually, this isn't the end of the world. In many cases, it's quite apparent that there's some kind of life cycle or otherwise intuitive order of execution. Temporal coupling becomes dangerous if the succession of invocations isn't apparent and if calling a method out of order puts the application in an invalid state or results in some kind of error, like a `NullPointerException`.

Temporal coupling is quite common. Many libraries, especially those written in procedural languages, rely on it for initialization. Knowing what it looks like, there's no glory in creating more of it, especially in object-oriented languages that have constructors.

Data Types and Testability

Consider the simplest possible age check, the type you perform to make sure that people are of legal age and are allowed to engage in financial transactions.

```
public void signup(String firstName, String lastName, int age, ... ) {

    if (age < 18) {
        throw new UnderAgedException(age);
    }
    // Rest of the code that performs the signup
```

Integers in modern languages are usually 32-bit numbers ranging from roughly minus 2 billion to plus 2 billion. This means that the `age` parameter needs some more thorough checking to make sure that the value stored in the oversized data type is reasonable. How about this?

```
public void signup(String firstname, String lastname, int age, ... ) {

    if (age < 0 || age >= 120) {
        throw new IllegalArgumentException("Invalid age: " + age);
    } else if (age < 18) {
        throw new UnderAgedException(age);
    }
    // Rest of the code that performs the signup
```

Now the code ensures that the business rule is applied to a reasonable value. This needs to be done at every place in the code where age is used.[4] But what about validation? Sure, validating age someplace else would do the trick, provided that it is done

---

4. Actually it doesn't, but would you feel comfortable about people of age 432544 years passing the check?

everywhere that age is being checked, but this introduces temporal coupling between the validation and any logic that relies on age. Now, given that validation usually resides in another layer and may be written in a different language by—heaven forbid—another person, this type of coupling isn't something you want to rely on.

The age example may seem trivial, so let's list some other candidates for this type of behavior:

- Currency
- National identification numbers
- Date of birth
- Date/time

These are typical building blocks of standard business applications, and my experience is that they're passed around as numbers or strings more often than one would care to admit. As a consequence, the codebase gets sprinkled with random checks and conditionals, which, in turn, results in incomplete validation and trivial bugs. The problem is that the data type is either too large or just not appropriate for the value it stores. Reading code is also harder. If everything is just a number or a string, you need to keep track of what operations you can perform on each. For example, if a national identification number is stored as an integer, what happens if you multiply it by −1?

Object-oriented languages offer a natural solution to this problem. By creating a class that enforces all invariants and business rules for the type, we move the responsibility of upholding them to that one place. In the previous chapter we have seen that some languages have that mechanism built in.

```
public class Age {
    private int years;

    public Age(int years) {
        if (years < 0 || years >= 120) {
            throw new IllegalArgumentException("Invalid age: " + age);
        }
        this.years = years;
    }
}
```

This class can be extended to handle comparisons with other age objects or integers, and in some designs putting an `isOfLegalAge` method there would make real sense.

What about Languages that Aren't Object Oriented?

In languages that aren't object oriented but statically typed, we can at least choose the data type that matches the expected range of a variable's value as much as possible. In C, we would probably store age as an unsigned short or, even better, uint8_t. Actually, C allows defining new types, and supplementing the new type with a library of functions makes it almost look like a class (but without inheritance and polymorphism, of course).

When working with languages that are dynamically typed and offer no functionality for upholding contracts, all we can do is write a lot of unit tests to ensure that they do what we want them to.

How Can Types Take the Place of Tests?

by Alex Moore-Niemi

Consider this proscription from a page of Eiffel's Design by Contract documentation[a]

A routine body should *never* test for the precondition.

It's incredibly common, however, to see several patterns violating that assertion in code: switch statements, a guard clause, inspection on the object to ensure it receives a method, etc. Even in Eiffel, I always felt a bit like it was cheating on this goal. Here's a snippet:

```
class CHECK
feature -- Divy up.
split_by (num_of_people: INTEGER) -- Split a check by diners.
    require
        non_negative: num_of_people >= 1
    do
        ... split it up here ...
    ensure
        split_checks: check_count = old check_count + 1
end
```

Isn't require inside the routine body? Technically no, because the routine body starts with do. It still seemed weird to me, though, semantically, to have the precondition anywhere but immediately before the feature name.

Better yet, I wondered: Can I get this precondition entirely out of my function definition?

Looking again at our precondition num_of_people >= 1, it's nothing magical, just a predicate. How else can we encode a predicate instead of as a precondition inside a function? In Eiffel, the answer would be to encode in

---

another class. In other words, `num_of_people` wouldn't be an integer; it would become a new, more constrained class that wraps integers. So `num_of_people: INTEGER` would become `num_of_people: DINERS`, and the `DINERS` class would constrain its possible values to nonzero ones in its constructor.

This is an effective strategy for encoding guarantees into programs, but how can it be improved? I think statically typed functional programming offers some worthwhile enhancements. In functional programming we operate with basically two entities, functions and data, and they have one thing in common: types.[b] At a minimum, types define sets of values; depending on language, types may also define a set of operations that can be performed in common on a set of values. Classes, then, are just a type coupled with its constructor function (and commonly some kind of inheritance, too). In functional programming, we gain composability and genericism by keeping functions separate from the data they will operate on. But then on what basis do we know a function is applicable to some data? By its type.

An operation on a value can transform its type,[c] and that's where the power and the danger come in. In the useful case, we may transform values from something like `type FormData` to `type Customer`. But in the dangerous case, the operation "breaks" its value outside of its original type, or any useful type, into an error type. Dividing by zero is an example of this: what starts as an operation on two integers results in an undefined value. If we have a type representing positive integers and restrict the function of division to that type, then we know we'll never hit the undefined value.

Types are a powerful machinery for validating your program by shaping data. Used well, types can constrain what's possible to "say" in your program from the get-go so that we never "say" invalid things. Or, as Yaron Minsky put it in an article[d] on ML:

Make illegal states unrepresentable.

Via types, we construct which states are "legal" for our program. Just like with our classes that constrain values by their constructors, a value becoming "well typed" means it has also been verified to meet the precondition of its definition. These can be checked at compile time, which gives us a different and faster feedback mechanism than usual unit testing. (Unit testing, after all, requires a runtime.) In a robust type system, we'll also get a way to implicitly define first-order logical predicates in our type system. That sounds a bit academic, but we can see it in practical action.

Let's found a start-up for processing I9 forms. To verify that an employee is eligible to work in the United States, you need a document from List A or two documents from Lists B **and** C on the form. How do we encode that restriction via types? Let's try it in F#:

```
type FederalId = FederalId of string
type StateId = StateId of string
type ListA =
  | PassportOnly of FederalId
type ListB =
  | DriversLicenseOnly of StateId
type ListC =
  | SocialSecurityCardOnly of FederalId
type Identification =
  | PrimaryId of ListA A>
  | TwoValidForms of ListB * ListC
type Employee =
  {
  identification: Identification;
  }
let fedIdNumber = FederalId "C00001549"
let passport = PassportOnly fedIdNumber
let primaryId = PrimaryId passport
let employee = { identification = primaryId }
```

Now we don't need to test for each case because it's literally impossible in our system to be an employee and not have the necessary ID.[e] Instead, we incrementally build valid data, always guaranteed to have a "legal" state. Essentially we have implicit preconditions living in our types. How? It's hiding right in plain sight: we actually have logical operators operating on our types! In F#, sum types are represented with | and product types are represented with *. These correspond to the logical operators ∨ (or) and ∧ (and), respectively.

The more you work in this way, the easier it becomes to see how to encode valuable business logic out of preconditions in functions, or out of functions entirely, and into our data types. Does this remove the need for unit tests entirely? In my experience, no. But the more logic you move into your type system, the less you will need to test.

---

[a] https://docs.eiffel.com/book/method/et-design-contract-tmassertions-and-exceptions.

[b] Even functions have types because in a functional language you have higher order functions that operate on other functions!

[c] Formally, not all operations are "closed under" a type.

[d] https://blogs.janestreet.com/effective-ml-revisited/.

[e] You may ask: What if we need to represent people who aren't yet employees? (And thus don't have ID.) You'd create a new type!

Domain-to-Range Ratio

Speaking of data types and their ranges naturally takes us to this chapter's last piece of theory. How would we test a function, *f*, that supposedly says whether a number is odd or even and returns 0 if it's odd and 1 if it's even?

Given that we accept that 0 is an even number, the first test that comes to mind is calling the function with 0 and comparing the result to 0. Next, we'd probably call it with a 1, and expect 1 in return. Then what? Is *f(10) = 0* a good test? Or maybe *f(9999) = 1*? That depends.

Let's leave the world of software and go for a more mathematical definition. *f* maps the set of natural numbers to [0, 1]. This means that we no longer have to concern ourselves with things like *f("hello world")*. The *range* of *f* is the set consisting of 0 and 1, whereas its *domain* is the set of natural numbers. Given these definitions, the *domain-to-range ratio* (DRR) can be introduced. It's the quotient of the number of possible inputs over the number of different outputs. In a more mathematical language, we can state this as the cardinality of the function's domain over the cardinality of its range (Woodward & Al-Khanjari 2000):

$$DRR = \frac{|D|}{|R|}$$

Why is that interesting? Let's reduce the size of our problem and replace the infinite set of natural numbers with the set of numbers from 1 to 6. Thus, the size of the domain is 6, which makes the Domain-to-Range Ratio equal to 6/2. The measure tells us something about the information loss that occurs when multiple values in the input map to the same output. In the example, three input values map to the same output value, three to another. It would be tempting to create only two test cases for this scenario; after all, there are two reasonable equivalence classes here—odd and even numbers.

Now, suppose that *f* looks like this:

$$f(1) = 1$$
$$f(2) = 0$$
$$f(3) = 1$$
$$\mathbf{f(4) = 1}$$
$$f(5) = 1$$
$$f(6) = 0$$

It's almost a function that determines whether a number is even or odd, but it has an exception built in. If there's no test for f(4), we're in for a surprise. This is an example of how bugs can creep into areas that suffer from information loss. The problem is amplified if the input domain (and consequently the DRR) grows. Without getting too formal, we can say that the DRR is a measure of risk; the higher it is, the more unsafe it'll be to have very few tests.

The previous example illustrates how a trivial function with obvious equivalence partitions can include surprises that may remain unfound, unless the DRR isn't considered. Naturally this doesn't mean that we should throw equivalence partitioning out the window. Rather, it means that we should be careful both in situations involving discontinuous large input domains that cannot be easily partitioned and in situations where there's information loss (as indicated by the DRR). It's also yet another reason for keeping data type sizes close to the range of the variable that they hold and to introduce abstractions that uphold invariants and keep the size of the domain down.

Summary

Several constructs and behaviors in code affect testability. *Direct input/output* is observable through a program element's public interface. This makes testing easier, because the tests need only be concerned about passing in interesting arguments and checking the results, as opposed to looking at state changes and interactions with other program elements.

Conversely, *indirect input/output* cannot be observed through the public interface of a program element and requires tests to somehow intercept the values coming in to and going out from the tested object. This usually moves tests away from state-based testing to interaction-based testing.

The more complex state a program element allows, the more complex the tests need to become. Therefore, keeping state both minimal and isolated leads to simpler tests and less error-prone code.

Temporal coupling arises if one method requires another method to be invoked first. Typical examples are initializer methods. Temporal coupling is actually state in disguise and should therefore be avoided if possible.

The *Domain-to-Range Ratio* is a measure of information loss in functions that map large input domains to small output domains, which may hide bugs. It's yet another tool when determining what abstractions to use and how many tests there should be.

Chapter 7
UNIT TESTING

Unit testing is the professional developers' most efficient strategy for ensuring that they indeed complete their programming tasks, that the code they write works in accordance with their assumptions,[1] and that it can be changed by them and their peers.

A hobby hack written and used by one person doesn't need to have unit tests. One person suffers the consequences of bugs, and if any refactorings take more time than necessary or totally break the project, that's probably fine too. If the project is more about coding for fun than producing something that an actual customer is willing to pay money for and that can be developed and maintained by more than one person for a longer period of time, having no unit tests is a viable strategy.

Why Do It?

Why should you invest time in writing unit tests when working with software professionally? Here are a couple of reasons. Some of them echo arguments made previously in the book, but it doesn't make them less true. Unit tests

- **Enable scaling**—Software development simply doesn't scale without the code being supported by various types of tests, of which unit tests are the base. It's hard to have collective code ownership without unit tests. Having several people or teams working on a codebase that's not covered by tests leads to accidental overwriting of code, regression defects, and us-and-them type of conflicts between teams, at worst, and long release cycles prolonged by days of manual testing, at best.

- **Lead to better design**—Code written so that it can undergo unit testing can't get totally rotten. When developers exercise a unit of work with a test, they'll tend to make it small and to the point, and they'll be mindful of its dependencies. The mere existence of unit tests, or even just the awareness of what it takes to achieve testability at the unit level, will save the code from some of the following:

---

1. It's tempting to write "works correctly" instead of "works in accordance with their assumptions," but proving that a program is correct is impossible, except for simplistic snippets used in a university course on formal methods.

- Methods with too many parameters
- Monster methods
- Global state (in static classes and singletons)
- Excessive dependencies
- Side effects

Such constructs tend to make developers' lives miserable in the world of untestable legacy code.

- **Enable change**—Adding and removing features to software requires redesign and refactoring, as do smaller changes. Whoever makes the changes to one part of a system has to know what other parts need to be re-executed to verify that it hasn't been broken. This effectively stops developers that are new on the team from making changes to critical areas of the system, because they can't possibly know what to retest or rerun. Not only that, but even more seasoned developers will refrain from changing and refactoring code if they risk breaking it in some unforeseen manner. Automated tests, and among them unit tests, provide the safety net needed to make changes without fear of unexpected breakdowns.

- **Prevent regressions**—In the absence of tests, the only practical way to verify that the software seems to be working is by running it. There are some downsides to this approach. First, running the software over and over again to verify that a certain part of it seems to work (the part that's just been written or modified) is monotonous and boring. Second, as pointed out previously, it's not always obvious what to rerun. Third, time is not unlimited. As the system grows, manual testing will be able to cover a smaller and smaller fraction of its functionality, and doing exhaustive regression testing will be impossible. A suite of unit tests executed by the developer while changing the code, along with a build server running the tests on a continuous basis, will catch regressions in areas covered by tests almost as soon as defects are introduced.

- **Provide a steady pace of work**—Writing unit tests is a way to achieve and maintain a steady pace of work. Code written in tandem with tests tends to lead to fewer surprises or last-minute problems. If everything implemented up to a point is passing unit tests, it most likely works on a functional level at least. Furthermore, if a bug is found in code with unit tests, fixing it is a matter of adding yet another unit test and adjusting the code without the drama and potential delays of last-minute manual regression testing.

- **Free up time for testing**—Unit tests are the simplest, fastest, and cheapest way to perform fundamental checking like verification of boundary values, input validation, or invocation of the happy path. This allows testing performed manually to uncover things that are far more interesting than, let's say, off-by-one errors. Conversely, teams and organizations that lack unit tests will have to compensate by manual means, which translates into manual checking.

- **Specify behavior and document the code**—Ideally, a unit test is a description of some behavior of the tested code; that is, an example of how the code should work or implement a specific business rule. It's documentation. And what documentation tends to actually get read—a dryly written, autogenerated method description or working code?

Making People Responsible for Code

One strategy for trying to control change and regression is making a person or a team truly responsible for an area of the system. This strategy suffers from some obvious drawbacks, like people going on vacation, quitting their jobs, or just becoming bottlenecks. It will also encourage some individuals to keep information to themselves as a means of work protection.

If you really want to walk down this path, I suggest seeking inspiration in open-source projects, which have many contributors, who supply changes and patches, and few committers, who review these and commit them to the trunk. Because the contributors deliver complete change sets, the committers only have to review them, in contrast to implementing the changes themselves. This makes them less of a bottleneck.

Just a reminder, though: this way of working also comes with unit tests. They simplify the committer's job and prevent regressions.

What Is a Unit Test?

As we've seen in Chapter 3, "The Testing Vocabulary," nailing testing terminology down is hard. Defining the exact meaning of *unit test* is no different. Many details and technicalities can easily be debated. In this book, I've chosen to combine several sources[2] to provide a definition of unit test that, although probably not unchallenged in some circles, should be quite acceptable to the developer community.

A unit test is a piece of code that tests a unit of work—a method, class, or cluster of classes that implement a single logical operation, which is accessible through a public interface.[3] Unit tests have the following properties:

---

2. The following definition is inspired by Osherove (2009); Langr, Hunt, and Thomas (2015); and Feathers (2004).
3. This is one of these rules that has exceptions, but stop and think before testing encapsulated, nonpublic behavior.

- **They're fully automated**—Unit tests can be executed with minimal effort whether through an IDE, a build script, or by using a specialized tool. Driver programs that are executed manually aren't unit tests.

- **They're self-verifying**—A unit test doesn't just execute code; it verifies that the code behaves as expected (by the test) and communicates that result.

- **They're repeatable and consistent**—They provide the same inputs and expect the same results for every run and can be executed as many times as necessary.

- **They test a single logical concept**—One unit test should verify one thing only about the tested code.

- **They run in isolation**—A test *is not* a unit test if

  - It talks to the database
  - It communicates across the network
  - It touches the file system
  - It can't run at the same time as any of your other unit tests
  - You have to do special things to your environment (such as editing configuration files) to run it.

- **They're fast**—One unit test takes a few milliseconds to run; an entire suite of thousands of such tests takes *at most* a few minutes. Together with the requirement of isolation, this disqualifies tests that require accessing slow resources, such as networks and databases, and algorithmically complex tests.

The last two points are sometimes subject to debate, but in this book they're part of the definition.

Fundamental Truth of Tests

Tests that take a long time to run or are somehow cumbersome to execute won't be executed!

When writing a test that adheres to the preceding definition, it's quite hard to make it complex. Another good reason for following the aforementioned constraints is environment independence (portability). Unit tests have to be portable across all developers' environments. They also have to be runnable in environments used for continuous integration. Such environments will most likely be quite different from the average developer machine. They may run another operating system, establish network connections to other hosts, use a different directory layout, and so on. For these reasons it's vital that unit tests don't involve external resources.

All Tests Executed by a Unit Testing Framework Aren't Unit Tests

Don't fall into the trap of believing that a test is automatically a unit test because it's being executed by a framework like JUnit or MSTest.

A unit testing framework is a very good vehicle for launching arbitrarily complex tests. This means that integration tests that may do everything a unit test isn't allowed to and possibly automated acceptance tests will also make use of such a framework. That doesn't make them unit tests!

The Life Cycle of a Unit Testing Framework

Figure 7.1 illustrates the life cycle of an xUnit-based testing framework. All such frameworks follow the same model of execution. They execute methods marked as tests and treat them as successful if no assertions (see later) are violated and no run-time errors occur. Thus, an empty test method will count as a passed test if executed.

Test Methods

Different frameworks use different mechanisms for test discovery. If the programming language in which the tests are written supports metadata (such as annotations or attributes), this mechanism tends to be the first choice. Such is the case for JUnit 4.x, NUnit, and MSTest, to mention just a few. In other cases, the framework relies on naming conventions. Methods prefixed with `"test"` are considered tests in JUnit 3.x, Ruby's Test::Unit, PHPUnit,[4] and XCTest for Objective-C and Swift. Finally, in some frameworks everything must be done "by hand," like in CUnit, where the test methods are added to the test suite programmatically. In general, the frameworks make no guarantees about the order of execution of the individual test methods, and some even randomize the execution order on purpose. This is a good thing, because it makes it virtually impossible to create tests that are coupled to each other.

Test Initializers and Cleanups

In order to become repeatable and consistent, unit tests must be executed from a known state. A fixed state of program elements that the test depends on is called a *test fixture,* and it's the purpose of a test initializer method to set it up. The need for initializers becomes apparent once the test class/module contains three or more tests

---

4. Actually PHPUnit uses a hybrid approach. It relies on naming conventions, but also supports annotations.

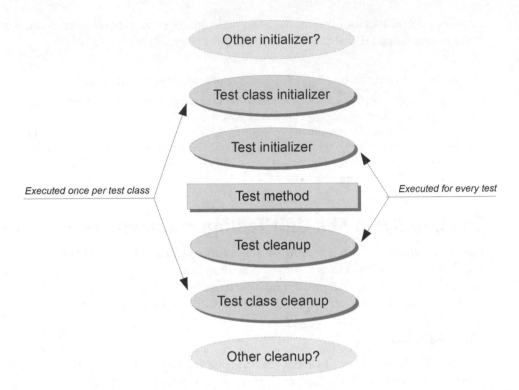

FIGURE 7.1 The life cycle of a unit testing framework. Most frameworks don't provide the outermost initializers/cleanup methods.

that run the same or very similar setup code. Moving such code to a common initializer eliminates duplication and enhances readability. Think of this initializer as the tests' constructor.

There's one downside to test initializers: they spread out a test's code across different locations. When reading a test, you must also take the code in the initializer into account, and if it doesn't fit on the screen together with the test's code, you'll need to scroll back and forth. For many tests this won't matter, whereas some will really suffer. I can't give a general pointer, but consider extracting common setup code to well-named methods and call them at the beginning of the test if you feel that it makes the test more readable and easier to understand.

After each test a cleanup method, commonly called *teardown*, is called (again analogous to a destructor). A good rule of thumb is to avoid using cleanup methods when writing unit tests. Since unit tests are supposed to run in isolation, the mere presence of a cleanup method should raise suspicion, especially when working with a language that has automatic garbage collection.

Initializer methods are called once per test, although many unit testing frameworks support initializers that are called once per class or even less frequently.[5] Such initializers are rarely needed by unit tests and are meant for tests that require lengthy setup, like connecting to a database or setting up some lightweight server. Such tests are, by this book's definition, not unit tests.

Test Classes without Common Setup Code

Sometimes test classes just don't contain common setup code that should be run before every test method. Half of the tests wouldn't use it, and it would just create confusion. This is often a sign to split the test class in two (or more) new classes. There's no golden rule that says you must have only one test class. Maybe half of the tests focus on interactions and require setting up test doubles, whereas the other half exercises an algorithmic aspect that requires setting up a data structure.

Then again, this might be a sign of the tested code violating the Single Responsibility Principle (Martin 2002) and a reason to do some redesign.

Constructors and Destructors

If the language running the test framework is object oriented, the test class's constructor will obviously be invoked sometime. This often happens before the test initializer method is called. Most frameworks don't speak of the test class's constructor, and therefore no assumptions whatsoever should be made about when and how many times it's invoked (Fowler 2004). The same goes for destructors. Just don't use them! Put any common setup code in the designated initializer or directly in the test.

There are exceptions to every rule! The xUnit.net framework lacks initializers/ cleanup methods and relies on the constructor of the test class and an implementation of `IDisposable.Dispose` for cleanup, so the previous advice obviously doesn't apply. However, frameworks that operate like this are in the minority at the time of writing.

Naming Tests

Naming tests is difficult. Coming up with a name that conveys both what's **specific** about the test and an **expected outcome** may often be quite a challenge. Furthermore, the name of a test should make it distinguishable from other tests in the same suite or category.

---

5. For example, MSTest supports the `AssemblyInitialize` attribute, which enables calling an initializer method once for an entire assembly.

Most test names you'll encounter will be influenced by one of the following naming conventions, or a variation thereof (see Kumar [2014] for more naming schemes).

Mandated by the Framework

Test frameworks that don't or can't make use of language features like annotations or attributes to discover tests have to rely on naming conventions. In practice this means that test method names have to start with a prefix like "`test`" or "`t_`."

Using a special prefix isn't that bad. It's just mandatory white noise. What *is* bad, though, is adopting the following style: `test`*MethodName*. A name like that doesn't say anything about what to expect from the test and creates some other problems as well.

- **It steers the developer toward thinking in terms of methods instead of behavior**—Imagine the simplest possible case: a `testAdd` method. Whoever sees that method gets biased toward thinking about what to do with the `add` method and not about the outcome of an addition.

- **It leads to silly names**—To test even something as simple as addition, more than one test is required. If the name `testAdd` has been used, what's the next test going to be called? Should it be `testAdd2`?

Therefore, just pretend that the prefix isn't there and use one of two remaining naming conventions after the prefix.

Behavior-driven Development Style

This convention is based on the sentence template: "the class **should** do something" (North 2006). It's supposed to keep the developer focused on the fact that a specific class is being tested, like "a calculator should add numbers together." If you can't express the behavior you're about to test so that it fits this template, it most likely means that the behavior belongs in another class. Starting the test name with "should" also encourages you to think about the test's premises and assumptions, and it helps you make a claim about what you think the system should be doing in a given situation, like

```
ShouldAlertUserIfAccountBalanceIsExceeded
```

or

```
ShouldFailForNegativeAmount
```

Unit of Work, State under Test, Expected Behavior

This naming style acknowledges that a unit test may exercise more than a single method. The first part, the *unit of work*, may indeed correspond to a method, but it may also start in a public method and span several other methods, or even classes. It may end with a value being returned, a state change, or a call to a collaborating object (Osherove 2005).

The second part of the name should describe the action performed—what's being done, what's passed in, what's interesting in this test? This is the *state under test*. Finally, the last part of the name should convey an *expectation*—what's supposed to happen? What result is expected: a value or an error? For example, `Atm_NegativeWithdrawal_FailsWithMessage` or `Divide_DenominatorIsZero_ExceptionThrown`.

Picking a Naming Standard

If you've worked on several projects and maybe in different organizations, then no doubt you have seen traces of all the preceding styles. Still, I'd like to offer some tips and pointers:

- Don't get trapped by mandatory prefixes! If your framework mandates that test method names start with a prefix like "test" (and you can't swap it for another or upgrade), then don't turn this into an excuse for writing bad test names. The prefix has to be there, but the rest of the name should be as good as they come.

- If you're quite new to unit testing and just need a "do like this" pointer, then use the third naming style. It forces you to think about both what makes the test interesting (state under test) and the expected outcome.

- Combine! After having written some tests you'll realize that the rigid form of the third naming style may not actually be the best for the type of test you're about to write, and you may start questioning the rationale behind the "should" ("what if it doesn't?"). I often find that the best test names are definitive statements about the conditions of the test and the outcome. See the next code snippet—the one about the magic hat—for an example.

- Let the context decide. Often, the type of code that you're writing tests for and their design will push you toward a preferred naming standard for these particular tests. Don't be surprised if other code and tests in the same codebase will make you want to choose another naming convention.

Experiment!

Don't be afraid of experimenting with test names. I certainly wasn't when writing the sample code for this book. I ended up using different naming conventions and variations on purpose throughout the book to illustrate how they play out.

Structuring Tests

A common way of organizing code in a test method is following the "triple A" structure: *Arrange. Act. Assert.* It helps in dividing a test into three distinct phases, where the first is dedicated to setting things up, the second to executing the code to be tested, and the third to verifying the outcome.

```
[TestMethod]
public void MagicHatConvertsRedScarfIntoWhiteRabbit()
{
    // Arrange
    var magicHat = new MagicHat();
    magicHat.PutInto(new Scarf(Color.Red));

    // Act
    magicHat.TapWithMagicWand();
    var itemFromHat = magicHat.PullOut();

    // Assert
    var expectedItem = new Rabbit(Color.White);
    Assert.AreEqual(expectedItem, itemFromHat);
}
```

The previous example raises a question. Does `magicHat.TapWithMagic-Wand` really belong in the "Act" section, or is it really about arranging? In this case, it's not really important. The Arrange-Act-Assert structure is about protecting the test from doing a little setup first, then doing some asserting, then executing something, then asserting again, then changing some value and executing something again . . . You get the picture.

More Names for the Three Phases

Arrange-Act-Assert is one name for the idea of organizing tests into three phases. There are others. You may come across names like Build-Operate-Check, Given-When-Then, or Setup-Execute-Verify-Teardown. The last name includes cleanup, which the others don't.

You might want to agree on the terminology in your team or organization, but the important thing is the structure, not the name, especially because the words seldom make it to the tests.

Assertion Methods

Because unit tests are self-verifying, they must somehow communicate success or failure. *Assertion methods* provide a standardized way to express the outcome of the test so that the checking can be automated by the test framework, while the test remains readable to the developer (Meszaros 2007). An assertion method that fails will make the framework fail the test—and produce the dreaded red bar in the majority of frameworks. For a test to pass, none of its assertions[6] may fail.

Types of Assertions

Assertions come in different flavors. The types and number of assertions vary from framework to framework. Table 7.1 presents a lowest common denominator of one C# and one Java-based framework.

Functionality starts to differ beyond this minimal subset, so it's always worthwhile to read the framework's documentation. For example, some frameworks have

TABLE 7.1   Comparison of assertions from MSTest and JUnit.

Assertion type	MSTest	JUnit
Object equality	AreEqual AreNotEqual	assertEquals
Object identity	AreSame AreNotSame	assertSame assertNotSame
Boolean	IsFalse IsTrue	assertTrue assertFalse
Null check	IsNull IsNotNull	assertNull assertNotNull
Fail test	Fail	fail

---

6. From now on the term *assertion* will be used instead of *assertion method*. Although it clashes with how the word was used in Chapter 5, "Programming by Contract," it does make the text more fluent.

more "core" assertions, whereas others make use of helper classes, like MSTest's `CollectionAssert` and `StringAssert` classes. What's important is that you should use the assertions from your framework that best communicate your intent.

Finally, although assertion methods have been around from the dawn of time and are the foundations of an absolute majority of unit testing frameworks, you *can* get away without using them. Groovy's Spock Framework (or just "Spock") is designed around *blocks*, such as `given:`, `when:`, `then:`, or `expect:`. This structure allows it to treat everything in the `then:` and `expect:` blocks as assertions, which means that Spock tests use normal comparisons (or any kind of predicates) where an xUnit framework would employ an assertion method. The subsequent chapters contain some tests written using Spock, but here's a sneak peek:

```
def "Magic hat converts red scarf into white rabbit"() {
    given: "A magic hat with a red scarf in it"
    def magicHat = new MagicHat()
    magicHat.putInto(new Scarf(Color.RED))

    when: "The hat is tapped with the magic wand"
    magicHat.tapWithMagicWand()

    then: "A white rabbit is pulled out"
    magicHat.pullOut() == new Rabbit(Color.WHITE)
}
```

How Many Assertions per Test?

A unit test should verify one specific piece of functionality, and it should fail for one specific reason. The easiest way to achieve this is to have it end with a single assertion. Such tests will only fail if the assertion fails or if there's an error. Thus, ending tests with a single assertion helps in error localization.

As with many rules of thumb and guidelines, there are some exceptions. The first is *guard assertions* (Meszaros 2007). These are safety checks used to avoid conditional logic that protects a test from runtime errors. The simplest one is the null check.

```
var orderDetails = new OrderRepository().FindOrderById(1234567);
Assert.IsNotNull(orderDetails);
Assert.AreEqual(customerAddress.StreetName,
    orderDetails.ShippingAddress.StreetName);
```

Another common guard assertion is checking the size of a collection before examining its contents. For example, before examining some property of the second element of a tested collection, a guard assertion is used to ensure that the collection indeed contains two elements.

Failures and Errors

Some frameworks like to keep separate counters for failures and errors. A test is considered failed if an assertion fails. If a test crashes because the tested code threw an exception or failed unexpectedly, then this is counted as an error. This difference is slightly academic. After all, the test doesn't pass!

The second exception is more of a clarification. As stated in the previous paragraph, the reason for having a single assertion is to have the test fail for a single reason. However, that single reason may not be captured by merely one assertion. In such cases we need to make a distinction between *syntax* and *semantics*. Let's say that we want to test something like the classic split function. Semantically, splitting strings is one concept. Syntactically, it may require several assertions:

```
String[] parts = "Adam,Anderson,21".Split(',');
Assert.AreEqual("Adam", parts[0]);
Assert.AreEqual("Anderson", parts[1]);
Assert.AreEqual("21", parts[2]);
```

Then again, it may not:

```
String[] parts = "Adam,Anderson,21".Split(',');
CollectionAssert.AreEqual(new String[] {"Adam", "Anderson", "21"}, parts);
```

This example illustrates how one semantic concept may or may not require several assertions depending on the syntax. In just a few paragraphs, I'll describe the `AssertThat` mechanism, which allows lumping together arbitrarily complex logic into a single assertion. This is yet another reason for not striving for ending a test with a single assertion slavishly.

A pragmatic developer may identify a third category of exceptions to the "one assertion per test" guideline—the tedious tests, those that don't exercise an intricate piece of logic or a clever algorithm. Such tests are necessary, because they protect from copy and paste mistakes, off-by-one errors, and other bugs easily introduced when working with repetitive patterns. They're usually not software engineering masterpieces and may contain multiple assertions without suffering too much. Often these tests verify one thing semantically, but the syntactic implementation may be quite offending.

```
[TestMethod]
public void CreatePersonEntityFromTransferObject()
{
    var dto = new PersonDTO { FirstName = "Brian", LastName = "Brown", Age = 25 };
    var newEntity = PersonCreator.CreateEntity(dto);
    Assert.IsNotNull(newEntity.Id);
```

```
Assert.AreEqual("Brian", newEntity.FirstName);
Assert.AreEqual("Brown", newEntity.LastName);
Assert.AreEqual(25, newEntity.Age);
Assert.AreEqual(DateTime.Now.ToShortDateString(),
    newEntity.Created.ToShortDateString());
}
```

Verbosity of Assertions

Did you notice how the values of the names and the age were repeated in the previous example? Due to their very nature, tests tend to contain some duplicated code. Consider the following test of a method that loops through a list of people and puts their first names in a comma-separated list:

```
[TestMethod]
public void CollectFirstNames_ThreePersons_ResultContainsThreeNames()
{
  var adam = new Person { FirstName = "Adam", LastName = "Anderson" };
  var brian = new Person { FirstName = "Brian", LastName = "Brown" };
  var cecil = new Person { FirstName = "Cecil", LastName = "Clark" };

  var actual = NameUtils.CollectFirstNames(new
      List<Person>() { adam, brian, cecil });
  var expected = "Adam,Brian,Cecil";
  Assert.AreEqual(expected, actual);
}
```

Notice that the first names appear in both the setup code and the verification. Is this duplication annoying? Sometimes we might feel tempted to rewrite the test to eliminate such duplication. In the preceding example, the line containing the expected value could be rewritten to:

```
var expected = adam.FirstName + "," + brian.FirstName + "," +
    cecil.FirstName;
```

Surely this would eliminate the duplication, but it would introduce another problem. It so happens that the tested method looks like this:

```
public static string CollectFirstNames(List<Person> persons)
{
    return String.Join(",",  persons.Select(p => p.FirstName));
}
```

Now, suppose that some time passes and in a few weeks another developer decides to modify the method so that it also capitalizes the first names. Ignorant of

Command/Query Separation principle (Meyer 1997), lazy, or just human, that developer adds a line of seemingly clever code—and introduces a bug by modifying the incoming names!

```
public static string CollectFirstNames(List<Person> persons)
{
    persons.ForEach(p => p.FirstName = p.FirstName.ToUpper());
    return String.Join(",", persons.Select(p => p.FirstName));
}
```

This modification doesn't break the test, because the value of the `expected` variable is a result of concatenating all first names *after* they have been accidentally modified. With this behavior, the test is dubious at best, or simply utterly wrong. In this particular case, putting the assignment of `expected` prior to the call would repair the situation. This, however, would introduce temporal coupling in the test. Instead, by allowing a small amount of duplication, we can protect the test from code that introduces side effects that may fool the verification.

Is allowing a degree of duplication a rule then? No! At the end of the day, it boils down to communicating intent. In some tests, it's better to use constants in both input and expected values to highlight correlated values, whereas others may be made more readable and understandable by some duplication.

Asserting Equality

The most commonly used assertion is by far that which checks for object equality. In many cases this is very unproblematic. For example:

```
Assert.AreEqual("Hello World", String.Join(" ", new[] { "Hello", "World" }));
Assert.AreEqual(3, 1 + 2);
Assert.AreEqual(3.5, 1.5 + 1.99, 0.01);
```

But what would happen if we had to assert that two `Person` objects from one of the previous examples were equal?

```
[TestMethod]
public void TwoPersonsWithIdenticalAttributesAreIdentical()
{
    var aPerson = new Person { FirstName = "Adam",
        LastName = "Anderson", Age = 21};
    var anotherPerson = new Person { FirstName = "Adam",
        LastName = "Anderson", Age = 21};
    Assert.AreEqual(aPerson, anotherPerson);
}
```

Does the previous test succeed or fail? Whether it succeeds depends entirely on whether the `Person` class has an `Equals` method with a reasonable implementation; one that tells whether two persons are equal in the context of the domain. Forgetting to provide the `Equals` method or its equivalent is an extremely common source of errors in unit tests.

In some rare cases[7] we can't implement the equality method in a way that makes it usable for testing. In other cases, initializing an object just to make a comparison, as in the preceding example, seems to defeat the very purpose of the test. If the `Person` class contained 10 more fields, like gender, address, and some flags that somehow always make it to such classes, it would do more harm than good to set up such an object and then rely on one assertion. In such cases, having multiple assertions per test is quite acceptable. Or it could be an opportunity to make use of more sophisticated assertions.

Constraints and Matchers

At this point, it's time to introduce the most powerful of the assertion methods: `AssertThat`. Compared to the very narrow methods presented so far, like `AreEqual` or `IsTrue`, it offers next to endless possibilities. Instead of asserting something very specific, it lets us provide *our own* predicate that will determine the outcome of the assertion. In NUnit, such predicates are called *constraints*; in JUnit they're called *matchers*. Providing custom predicates opens up new interesting verification opportunities.

Specialized Assertions

Remember the `Person` class from the previous examples? It contained an `Age` attribute. What if you wanted to test whether a person is an adult, that is, not underage or retired? As a first test, an example with a reasonable adult age would do fine[8]:

```
[Test]
public void PersonAged45_IsAnAdult()
{
    var person = new Person { Age = 45 };
    Assert.IsTrue(person.Age >= 18 && person.Age < 65);
}
```

---

7. I'm mostly thinking of objects that are persisted in a database and where the database generates a surrogate key. In such cases "equality" may become the subject of debate: Are the objects equal if all their fields are equal, or are they equal if their "primary keys" are the same?

8. At the time of writing, Microsoft's unit testing framework didn't support custom constraint assertions, so the tests in this section are written with NUnit.

But what if you wanted to make your test even more explicit? How about changing the test to this?

```
[Test]
public void PersonAged45_IsAnAdult()
{
    var person = new Person { Age = 45 };
    Assert.That(person, Aged.Adult);
}
```

When this test fails, it's going to fail with a message like:

```
Expected: a person of age 18 to 65
But was:  a person aged 12
```

To get this rather detailed output, some work is required. First, we need a constraint based on the Constraint class.

```
public class IsAdultConstraint : Constraint
{
    public override void WriteDescriptionTo(MessageWriter writer)
    {
        writer.Write("a person of age 18 to 65");
    }

    public override void WriteActualValueTo(MessageWriter writer)
    {
        if (actual is Person)
        {
            writer.Write("a person aged " + ((Person)actual).Age);
        }
        else
        {
            base.WriteActualValueTo(writer);
        }
    }

    public override bool Matches(object actual)
    {
        base.actual = actual;
        if (actual is Person)
        {
            var person = (Person) actual;
            return person.Age >= 18 && person.Age < 65;
```

```
        }
        return false;
    }
}
```

At this point, we can write an assertion like this:

```
Assert.That(person, new IsAdultConstraint());
```

Second, to get to `Aged.Adult` a small helper is required.

```
public static class Aged
{
    public static IsAdultConstraint Adult
    {
        get { return new IsAdultConstraint(); }
    }
}
```

In Java and JUnit 4, constructs with `assertThat` and matchers come out even nicer. Because of static imports, the assertion would look like the following, given that there was a `Person` object at hand:

```
assertThat(person, isAdult());
```

To get to this form, a simple factory class would be required.

```
public class MatcherFactory {
    public static IsAdult isAdult() {
        return new IsAdult();
    }
}
```

The implementation of `IsAdult` is very similar to the previous C# version but would be based on the `org.hamcrest.BaseMatcher` class.

Syntactic sugar or not, *specialized* assertions is one area of use for custom constraints/matchers.

Fluent Assertions

Specialized assertions aren't the most popular use of custom constraints. Most of us actually start out by using *fluent assertions*. The fluency is achieved by switching the order of arguments[9] in the call to `Assert.That` style of assertions and the kind of syntactic sugar we've seen so far. So

```
Assert.AreEqual(10, quantity);
```

becomes

```
Assert.That(quantity, Is.EqualTo(10));
```

Apart from increasing readability, which becomes evident when combining several constraints, the fluent syntax produces better messages.

```
Assert.IsTrue("Hello World!".Contains("Worlds"));
```

fails with

```
Expected: True
But was:  False
```

whereas

```
Assert.That("Hello World!", Is.StringContaining("Worlds"));
```

fails with

```
Expected: String containing "Worlds"
But was:  "Hello World!"
```

Different unit testing frameworks come with different fluent assertions. As the preceding example shows, they may contain some quite convenient features.

Tip

There are specialized fluent assertions libraries! In C#, extension methods provide a very elegant way of implementing fluent assertions, which are utilized by the Fluent Assertions library. In Java, AssertJ provides a set of custom `assertThat` methods that return assertion objects with methods that can be chained to form fluent assertions.

---

9. To be precise, not all unit testing frameworks want the expected value as the first parameter and the actual value as the second parameter to the assertion. In some, the order is the opposite, and some don't document any preference.

"Partial" Verification

A third area of use for custom constraints could be described as "partial" verification. In an earlier example, a `Person` object was constructed by copying values from a data transfer object (DTO). Then a GUID and a date were added. The test that verified the object had been constructed correctly coped with these two fields by using rather loose assertions. The code is repeated here for convenience:

```
Assert.IsNotNull(newEntity.Id);
Assert.AreEqual("Adam", newEntity.FirstName);
Assert.AreEqual("Anderson", newEntity.LastName);
Assert.AreEqual(21, newEntity.Age);
Assert.AreEqual(DateTime.Now.ToShortDateString(),
    newEntity.Created.ToShortDateString());
```

This code looks the way it does because there's virtually no way to construct a `Person` object that would be equal to the object created by the factory.[10] The GUID is "random" and there's a time instance. On the other hand, these values may not be very interesting from the perspective of the test. At least that's what the test indicates by just checking for a non-null GUID and performing coarse matching of the creation time.

In such cases, a custom constraint might come in handy. Because we can't make persons equal (not in the sense of an equality method), we can at least try to make them "similar." The following test shows how to achieve that by ignoring the `Id` and `Created` attributes in the comparison.

```
[Test]
public void AllValuesAreCopiedFromPersonDtoToNewEntity()
{
  var personDto = new PersonDTO { FirstName = "Adam",
      LastName = "Anderson", Age = 21};

  var expectedPerson = new Person { FirstName = "Adam",
      LastName = "Anderson", Age = 21};

  Assert.That(PersonCreator.CreateEntity(personDto),
      new IsSamePersonConstraint(expectedPerson));
}
```

The `Matches` method of the constraint is implemented the way one would expect:

---

10. Of course, `PersonCreator`, the factory, could be "opened up" and its GUID and timestamp functions controlled by the unit test in one way or another, but that's not the point here.

```
public override bool Matches(object actual)
{
    base.actual = actual;
    if (actual is Person)
    {
        var person = (Person)actual;
        return expected.FirstName == person.FirstName
                && expected.LastName == person.LastName
                && expected.Age == person.Age;
    }
    return false;
}
```

This technique and variations of it can be applied in many situations. Candidates for partial verification are

- Objects with tricky attributes that are irrelevant to the test

- Objects that are created in a way that we cannot control

- Large/compound objects where only a few fields out of the object graph are interesting

Testing Exceptions

Error conditions change the execution flow and must therefore be tested. Most languages used these days use exceptions to communicate that an error has occurred. Not only has this the benefit of actually altering the flow of control so that there's no question whether the operation has succeeded or not, it also saves the developer from clunky checks of return values, calling things like `GetLastError`, inspecting the value of `errno`,[11] or the like.

The generic way to test for an exception is:

```
[TestMethod]
public void OperationBlowsUpWithADramaticException()
{
    try
    {
        DoSomethingThatBlowsUp();
```

---

11. `GetLastError` is a function in the Win32 API that returns the last-error code value on the calling thread, whereas `errno` is a global variable or function used in UNIX C programs for the same purpose.

```
          Assert.Fail("Expected an exception");
    }
    catch (CrashBoomBangException e) { }
}
```

This is the oldest way of verifying that an exception has been thrown, and this technique still has two benefits:

- It'll always work. Because nothing in the test uses any fancy features of the unit testing framework, this technique can be applied in Java, C#, C++, JavaScript, PHP, and Ruby (with slightly different keywords), to mention some widely used languages.

- It's still the most flexible and intuitive way if you need to scrutinize the caught exception, if you need to verify the exception message in a sophisticated way, if you need to inspect a chain of nested exceptions, or if the exception carries some payload, like the offending object.

That said, this *is* the oldest way, and there are better options for most cases. Nowadays, frameworks come with annotations like `@Test(expected=)`, `[Expected-Exception(...)]`, or `@expectedExeption`, which enable condensing tests of exception code to something like this:

```
[TestMethod]
[ExpectedException(typeof(CrashBoomBangException))]
public void OperationBlowsUpWithADramaticException()
{
    DoSomethingThatBlowsUp();
}
```

Because this book contains a lot of Java code, I feel obliged to mention that JUnit has taken things in the right direction by introducing the `ExpectedException` rule,[12] which brings back the flexibility to do more advanced processing of the caught exception (the second benefit of the generic approach). For example:

```
@Rule
public ExpectedException thrownException
        = ExpectedException.none();

@Test
```

---

12. http://junit.org/apidocs/org/junit/rules/ExpectedException.html

```
public void operationBlowsUpWithADramaticException() {
    thrownException.expect(CrashBoomBangException.class);
    thrownException.expectCause(isA(IllegalStateException.class));
    thrownException.expectMessage(startsWith("Ooops!"));

    doSomethingThatBlowsUp();
}
```

This test not only verifies that the `CrashBoomBangException` has been thrown, but also that the exception causing it is `IllegalStateException` and that the exception message starts with a specific string. Because Hamcrest matchers are used, arbitrarily sophisticated analysis of the exception is possible—something that's lost or limited when using an annotation.

Finally, languages that support higher-order functions offer yet another option. In such languages you can pass a block of code that's expected to fail with an exception to a function that will execute that block in a surrounding try-catch. This is what the technique would look like if implemented by hand.

```
[TestMethod]
public void OperationBlowsUpWithADramaticException()
{
    ExpectCrashBoomBang(() => DoSomethingThatBlowsUp());
}

public static void ExpectCrashBoomBang(Action action)
{
    try
    {
        action();
        Assert.Fail("Expected an exception");
    }
    catch (CrashBoomBangException) { }
}
```

We don't need to sweat, though. Many testing frameworks contain assertions that work like this out of the box. NUnit's `Assert.Throws`, Groovy's `GroovyAssert.shouldFail`, and JUnit's `Assertions.assertThrows` all make use of mechanics similar to that of the preceding example (but allow specifying the expected exception, of course). So, the preceding test would look like this in JUnit[13]:

---

13. At the time of writing, this assertion was in the alpha version of JUnit 5, so the final version may differ somehow.

```
@Test
public void operationBlowsUpWithADramaticException() {
    assertThrows(CrashBoomBangException.class, () ->
            doSomethingThatBlowsUp());
}
```

Behavior-driven Development–Style Frameworks

Most of the material in this chapter applies to all unit testing frameworks. However, there's a family of frameworks that I'll refer to as *BDD-style frameworks* that differs from the popular xUnit frameworks in certain ways and therefore needs some additional treatment. In some languages, like Ruby or JavaScript, such frameworks are often used for unit testing, regardless of whether the actual development style is behavior-driven design or not.

Test Structure

BDD-style frameworks use a test structure that reminds the developer about focusing on the behavior, rather than the details of the tested implementation. RSpec for Ruby and Jasmine and Mocha for JavaScript do this by enclosing tests in a function called it.

```
it("specifies a test", function() {
    expect(["Hello", "world!"].join(" ")).toEqual("Hello world!");
});
```

Tests are grouped together by wrapping them in a describe function. The frameworks discussed in this book allow nesting calls to describe to provide nested contexts. In RSpec there's even a method called context, which is syntactically equivalent to describe. Nested contexts can be used to create a separation between various states or variants when testing the same functionality.

```
describe "pay order" do
  let(:order_to_pay) { create(:order, :standard_order) }

  context "credit card" do
    # Credit card tests go here
  end

  context "direct bank transfer" do
    # Bank transfers are tested here
  end
```

```
context "Bitcoin" do
  # And digital currency here
end
end
```

Each context provides its own scope, and thus variables declared in different contexts get different lifetimes relative to the tests. The `order_to_pay` variable is created once and outlives the three payment method contexts and any tests that would execute within them. Powerful as this may seem, I urge you to count to 12 before constructing a complex hierarchy of nested contexts with tests that depend on different variable scopes. Not only is it easy to introduce temporal coupling in this way, but such tests are hard to read and understand.

Test initializers also exist in BDD-style frameworks. They work quite similarly to those of xUnit frameworks (per test method and per test class initialization). In addition, there are two caveats to keep in mind:

- How does initialization/fixture setup interact with nested contexts?

- Some frameworks provide more options for fixture initialization.[14]

Naming Tests

Using the `it` function encourages naming the tests in a certain way. Look at the test name and the output of the framework to decide whether the name makes sense. Because the name is just a string, it can contain whitespace and punctuation characters. This isn't the place to get too creative though. The test name should succinctly communicate the expected behavior, given the conditions that are specific to the test. If the name becomes too long, we can consider using contexts to make them more concise.

Matchers

To make tests pass or fail, BDD-style frameworks use functions that are more verbose and often read in a more natural way than assertion methods. To illustrate, I'll revisit the test of a simple utility function that just picks out the first names of the supplied persons.

---

14. RSpec, for example, provides two methods called `subject` and `let`, both of which in essence evaluate a block and store the result between tests. `subject` is used to initialize the tested object. This functionality is most useful when used implicitly, like in the coming magic wand example, in which the magic wand becomes the subject. `let` may be used to change the context of each test. This is a very superficial treatment of two quite powerful concepts, but the point is that they can both compete with and complement initialization methods. This has the potential to make the fixture setup very advanced and very complicated.

```
describe("NameUtils", function() {
    describe("collectFirstNames()", function() {
        it("creates a comma-separated list of first names", function()
        {
            var adam = new Person("Adam", "Anderson");
            var brian = new Person("Brian", "Brown");
            var cecil = new Person("Cecil", "Clark");
            expect(NameUtils.collectFirstNames([adam, brian,
                cecil])).toEqual("Adam,Brian,Cecil");
        });
    });
});
```

Just as xUnit testing frameworks come with a library of assertion methods, so do BDD-style frameworks; but they come with *matchers*—functions/methods that compare an expected value with the actual value. In Table 7.2, I present a handful of matchers that are similar between two widely used BDD-style frameworks. The purpose of Table 7.2 is to show how matchers differ from assertion methods syntactically.

Notice how a fluent syntax is achieved by combining `expect` with the matcher.

TABLE 7.2   Some matchers in Jasmine and RSpec.

Matcher type	Jasmine	RSpec
Expected value	expect(actual). (a matcher)	expect(actual).to (a matcher)
Negation	expect(actual).not. (a matcher)	expect(actual).not_to (a matcher)
Object equality	toEqual(expected)	eq(expected)
Object identity	toBe(expected) (*)	be(expected)
Boolean	toBeTrue() toBeFalse()	be true be false
Null check	toBeNull()	be_nil

(*) Object equality without type conversion.

> ### More Fluent Syntax
>
> BDD-style frameworks are typically found in the land of dynamic languages, which gives them some cool features. The RSpec test that follows not only creates a matcher on the fly, but also a very descriptive failure message.
>
> ```
> class MagicWand
>   def doing_magic?
>       false
>   end
> end
>
> describe MagicWand do
>     it { is_expected.to be_doing_magic }
> end
> ```
>
> It fails with the following message:
>
> ```
> 1) MagicWand should be doing magic
>    Failure/Error: it { is_expected.to be_doing_magic }
>      expected #<MagicWand:0x000000027d1200>.doing_magic? to return true, got false
> ```

BDD-style frameworks aren't that different from xUnit family frameworks, especially when it comes to unit test design and implementation. They're built around a different terminology and encourage thinking about behavior rather than implementation, but at the end of the day, they execute a comparison between an actual value and an expected value.

Summary

Unit tests are created to

- Allow scaling

- Lead to better design

- Enable change

- Prevent regressions

- Provide a steady pace of work

- Free up time for testing

- Specify behavior and document the code

If code can be unit tested, it can't be too poor. Some bad constructs will simply not make it into the codebase if unit tests are in place. Ultimately, if a feature isn't testable, it won't be tested.

Defining unit tests isn't uncontroversial. In this book, unit tests are fully automated, self-verifying, repeatable, consistent, and fast. They test a single logical concept and run in isolation.

There are three common naming standards for test methods:

- Mandated by the framework—Test names must start with a mandatory prefix. Don't let it ruin them.

- BDD style—Test names should read like spoken sentences in the domain language, and the program elements *should* do something.

- Unit of work, state under test, expected behavior—A solid template that contains everything needed to accurately describe a test.

Using Arrange-Act-Assert protects from arbitrarily complex test methods and gives all tests a similar structure.

Assertion methods provide a standardized way to express the outcome of a test. In addition, the majority of the unit testing frameworks provide some kind of "assert that," which enables custom constraints and fluent assertions.

Forgetting to implement an equality method is a very common error, which produces confusing messages from `assertEquals`, `Assert.AreEqual`, or the like.

BDD-style frameworks are used for unit testing in some languages. They use matchers instead of assertion methods and use a slightly different test structure in comparison to xUnit frameworks.

Chapter 8

SPECIFICATION-BASED TESTING TECHNIQUES

Every profession has its fundamental techniques. Software testing is by no means an exception. A tester will check for certain things and fall back on a range of well-established techniques when designing and executing tests. Obvious to the tester, and seemingly intuitive once familiar, these techniques somehow don't always make it into developer literature or tests written by developers. In my experience, one of the first questions developers who are new to unit testing (or to any kind of testing, for that matter) ask is:

Okay, I know how to write a unit test, but what should I test?

My hope is that this chapter will serve as a source of inspiration when the time comes for you to decide what to verify with your next test. The techniques covered here usually go by the name *specification-based techniques*, because the specification is their foundation. Variations of them can be applied at all test levels, but I've found them especially useful when writing unit tests and integration tests. They are basic techniques, and by keeping them in mind while developing code and tests, you will increase the quality of your code and save your testing colleagues from tedious and boring work. Ain't that a win-win?

Another reason for keeping these techniques in mind is that if developers and testers have different opinions on how certain features of the application should work, then discussions involving specification-based techniques will typically shed some light on the differences.

Equivalence Partitioning

Let's say that you're facing the daunting task of implementing an integer-based calculator—the kind of program one would write in an introductory programming class. When it comes to checking that it works, is it meaningful to test whether it can compute the sum of 5 + 5 if it computes the sums of 3 + 3 and 4 + 4 correctly? Or 10,000 + 20,000? Probably not, but why?

There's a similarity between 3, 4, 5, 10,000, and 20,000 in the context of a calculator that operates solely on integers.[1] All these numbers are in the same *equivalence partition*. Equivalence partitions, sometimes called equivalence classes, are subsets of data in which all values are equivalent to each other. The equivalence relation depends on the context. In this case, they are equivalent to each other from the perspective of integer addition, so adding two numbers together is sufficient to inspire confidence that addition will work within the equivalence class of integers of reasonable size.

For an integer calculator, reasonable partitions would be one for positive integers and one for negative integers, and two partitions just outside the positive and negative ranges of the data type to catch overflow errors.

Another partitioning could treat both negative and positive integers as one partition. Would such a partitioning be more correct? Now, here's the difference between how testers and developers would approach partitioning in the absence of a shared specification. A developer would know the range of the data type and base the partitioning on that, whereas the tester would probably think more about the domain and partition from that viewpoint. This could lead to different partitioning (see Figure 8.1).

Nothing says that equivalence partitions must consist of consecutive values. Mathematical functions or arbitrary predicates may be used to define equivalence, as well as sets of values that are considered equivalent in some context. Does this sound too abstract? Think of an average enterprise system that stores customer information. Depending on the context, some equivalence classes could be

- Males/females

- Those aged 0 to 17, 18 to 28, 29 to 44, 45 to 69, and 70 to 110

- Those whose national identification number is known

- Those registered in the system before the year 2000 and those after

- Prospects, regular, or premium customers

- Those who pay with Visa, MasterCard, or PayPal

- Those who have returned some merchandise and those who haven't

There are pretty much endless possibilities, and it's the specification and test scenario that should guide the choice of relevant equivalence partitions.

Equivalence partitioning is a very helpful tool for the developer. Suppose we want to ensure that a function that computes the risk premium for insured drivers works

---

1. Let's not get academic and dig out some ancient 8-bit integer type. Let's think 32-bit.

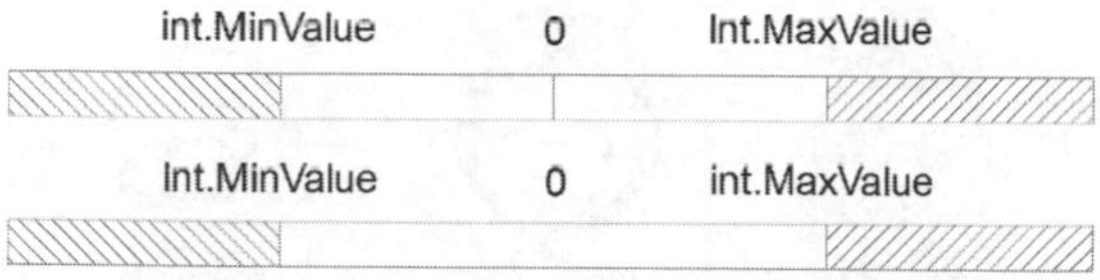

FIGURE 8.1 Two ways of partitioning input to an integer calculator. Is there a way to reach the partitions outside the range of the integer type? There could be, if the calculator accepted its input as strings that would be converted to integers.

correctly. According to this function, young drivers run a higher risk of accidents, the middle-aged have mastered driving, and older drivers tend to start getting involved in accidents again. A simple version of this function could look like the following:

```
public double getPremiumFactor(int age) {
    if (age >= 18 && age < 24) {
        return 1.75;
    } else if (age >= 24 && age < 60) {
        return 1;
    } else if (age >= 60) {
        return 1.35;
    }
}
```

Armed with a new tool, we immediately see three valid partitions, hence three tests. We also spot two partitions with illegal input. Ages below 18 and above, say, 100, don't make any sense. Thus this particular function needs at least five tests.

Another benefit of this technique is that it allows us to think about input visually, which hopefully lets us discover partitions that haven't been covered by tests yet. Sometimes drawing the input and partitions on paper or a whiteboard really helps (see Figure 8.2).

Parentheses and Brackets

When expressing intervals, square brackets next to values mean "in the interval" and parentheses mean "outside the interval." So the interval of integers [0, 11) includes numbers 0 to 10, but not 11.

Dividing data into equivalence partitions will only get us so far. In order to achieve reliable test coverage, tests at the *boundaries* of the partitions are required.

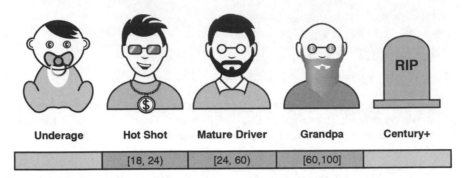

FIGURE 8.2 Dividing input into equivalence partitions can sometimes be quite a visual technique. Here, each partition has been illustrated with an avatar that could evolve into a persona in other test cases.

Boundary Value Analysis

Boundary values are values that occur at the boundary of an equivalence partition. If no equivalence partitions have been identified, think of boundary values as occurring at the edges of the domain of allowed input. Such values may also be called *edge cases*. Many software bugs lurk at the boundaries, which is why fortifying them with tests is crucial.

Let's look at the car driver premium example again. One of its equivalence partitions contained ages for mature drivers, 24 to 59 years. A boundary value analysis would suggest checking the values 23, 24, 59, and 60—two values at the very edge and two values outside the equivalence partition. Some authors suggest that checking 25 and 58 is also a good idea, even though they're in the partition (Bath & McKay 2008).

Just like equivalence partitions, boundary values can be derived from the specification, the size of a data type, or common sense. Checking boundary values is something testers do in their sleep, but unfortunately still manually to some extent. If the program contains an input field that the specification says accepts numbers from 1 to 10, one of the obvious first tests would be to type in the 0 and 11 to verify that values just around the edges of allowed input aren't accepted. The next step would most likely be to verify the accepted range by typing in 1 and 10.

Keeping boundary values in mind is crucial for developers, because having other people finding bugs around boundaries, be they testers, or, even worse, users, is simply embarrassing. When writing code, developers have both access to a specification and knowledge about the ranges of the data types they're using. There are simply no excuses for not checking something as obvious as edge cases.

Edge Cases and Gotchas for Some Data Types

We don't always need to resort to strict boundary value analysis and equivalence partitioning. These techniques do help us find values that are interesting to check, as well as edge cases, but for scenarios involving the most common data types, applying a set of heuristics may be sufficient.

Numbers

Finding boundary values for numbers is rather easy. If your input is valid for the range *m-n*, check what happens at *m − 1, m, n,* and *n + 1*. In some cases, try *m + 1,* and *n − 1*. Using 0 might or might not be a boundary value, but it's usually a good idea to investigate what happens around it.

For primitive integer types, it usually pays to look at what happens near the maximum represented by the data type, such as $2^{31} − 1$ or $2^{63} − 1$, and the minimum, like $−2^{31}$ or $−2^{63}$, while remembering that the sign bit causes an asymmetry between them. For certain types of programs, nasty bugs can be introduced because of integer overflow.

Many languages have constants that represent minimum and maximum values for their data types, for example, `Integer.MAX_VALUE` in Java and `int.Max-Value` in C#. Use them or introduce your own with care if the language doesn't have them. Don't put yourself in a position where you have to remember whether the maximum value of a signed 32-bit integer is $2^{31} − 1$ or $2^{32} − 1$.

In the case of floats, verify that a reasonable precision is used. A partition may change as the precision of the floating point number is adjusted.

Strings

The empty string is an obvious edge case. It can usually be traced back to blank user input or fixed-record file formats. It has a cousin called `null`[2] that may be returned from many standard libraries or functions in your legacy application. Irrespective of your personal feeling about nulls, you have to be prepared for them. Whereas one half of the code you're working with may go to great lengths to avoid nulls by using Null Objects and exceptions in creative ways, the other half, written by that other guy, won't exhibit this property and will throw nulls right in your face. Hence, add `null` to your list of edge cases.

In languages where strings are allocated directly on the stack or stored in fixed-size buffers on the heap, developers have to worry about memory corruption and buffer overflow. In newer languages the developer doesn't need to worry about strings

---

2. Or `nil` or `undef`.

overwriting part of the heap that belongs to another process, but checking around maximum input length is still a good idea.

Strings, especially in Unicode, may contain all sorts of characters. But in an average system, the partition of allowed characters is rather small in comparison to the entire Unicode character set. The challenge usually lies in the encoding. UTF-8, the most widely used encoding on the Web,[3] uses one byte to encode standard ASCII, but may use up to four bytes when encoding less common Unicode characters. Make sure that your parsing and string routines take this into account.

Dates and Time

Dates are difficult. If you don't agree, think back to the year 2000 bug. By their very nature they require careful boundary checking. Depending on the type of application, you may have different ambitions regarding your date boundaries. Regardless of ambition, if the dates can be either entered manually by a user or read from a file (in fact, any place where their format isn't enforced), be sure to hand the date over to a data type or date library to avoid boundary-related errors.

Remember that an unexpected locale can mess up date parsing and presentation and that the system's time zone can affect date arithmetic. The classic gotcha here are time zones without and with daylight saving time (DST), in which some days may have 23 and 25 hours. Cross–time zone tests may be necessary to understand the behavior of a client and a server on different continents.

Also, be explicit about the time of day component of the date—is it used or not? Should hours, minutes, and seconds be reset when working with *just* dates, or should they simply be ignored? Date precision also affects boundary values.

Choosing Date Pickers

When you decide on a date picker component, see what it does when you first select January 31 and then change the month to February.

Collections

The empty collection is a common edge case worth checking (because you *do* use empty collections and not nulls, right?). Too often, we encounter code that really relies on a collection actually having one element, like this archetypal piece of older code using Hibernate.

---

3. According to Wikipedia, 85 percent of all web pages were encoded using UTF-8 in 2015 (https://en.wikipedia.org/wiki/UTF-8).

```
Query query = session.createQuery("from Customer where id = :id ");
query.setParameter("id", "12345678");
Customer customer = (Customer) query.list().get(0);
```

This code will fail miserably when there's no customer with an id equal to 12345678. Also, there be dragons where developers balance on the edge between fetching and iterating over a collection. A close cousin to the preceding code, the iteration over a multivalued collection may at least have a fighting chance.

```
Query query = session.createQuery("from Customer where dob > :dob ");
query.setParameter("dob", 19750101);
for (Customer customer :
        Collections.checkedCollection(query.list(), Customer.class)) {

        // Do something interesting with the customer...
```

Constructs like the above aren't really a problem if you check the sizes of your collections or just iterate over them (while being prepared for the fact that they may actually be empty), but even if *you* do this, then *somebody else* won't have done it in the legacy code that you're maintaining. Ergo, paying extra attention to empty collections and those with one element usually pays off. Iterations over collections may also suffer from off-by-one errors if they rely on indexes and the collection's size. All of this is best summarized as *0-1-many*.

For some more ideas, see Hendrickson, Lyndsay, and Emery (2006).

State Transition Testing

Some applications or parts of a system are nicely modeled as state machines. Typical examples are various flows like "wizards" and navigation between pages. Other examples are control systems that depend on a sequence of known inputs. Many embedded systems run in devices that have a number of buttons that can be pressed in different order to achieve different things. The most trivial example is a digital clock that can be set with two buttons. A more mission-critical application would be software for controlling things in planes and cars.

Once we've decided that our problem is indeed best modeled as states and transitions, the next step is to draw a state diagram (see Figure 8.3) to get an overview of how the application should behave. The diagram is most helpful in identifying missing or invalid states and transitions.

Apart from *states* and *transitions*, a state transition model also includes *events* and *actions*. Events cause transitions. In the previous example, most events represent clicks on a button in the user interface, such as Next, or Accept license, with the

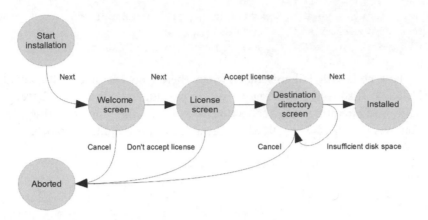

FIGURE 8.3   A simple installation wizard modeled as a state machine. In reality, there would be more states before *Installed*.

exception of a disk space check performed by the installer. Actions are the result of transitions. Again, in the example, most actions consist of showing a certain screen to the user, except for the final action, in which files are copied and some configuration is stored in the system.

Sometimes it may be helpful to rewrite the state transition diagram into a table. Personally, I've always found the diagram more understandable, but for exhaustive testing, a table might help.

State diagrams can be drawn at different levels of abstraction. That's probably the greatest strength of this technique. On one end, there's the detailed diagram depicting transitions between states in a regular expression matcher, where each encounter with a letter is a state transition. On the other end is the huge business application modeled with three states: logged in, working, and logged out. This flexibility translates directly to developer testing. Detailed, low-level state transitions fit nicely in unit tests. A diagram will help determine what tests to write. Sometimes the number of states and transitions will require using parameterized tests or theory tests (described in Chapter 10, "Data-driven and Combinatorial Testing") to avoid repetition. Coarse-grained state diagrams help when developing high-level tests, like browser-based UI tests, or just doing manual testing.

When working with state transition testing, we encounter the term *switch coverage*. 0-switch coverage refers to testing the individual transitions, 1-switch coverage means that pairs of transitions are tested, and so on. Exercising various switch coverages exhaustively may be very helpful in weeding out race conditions.

Decision Tables

Let's revisit the car insurance premium example one last time. This time the premium is also affected by the driver's gender. After all, statistics show women to be safer drivers. In addition, certain combinations of age and gender trigger a fraud investigation in the event of a claim.

To get an overview of these business rules, we can use *decision tables*, which capture all combinations of variables and possible outcomes.

Age	18–23	18–23	24–59	24–59	60+	60+
Gender	Male	Female	Male	Female	Male	Female
Premium factor 1	N	N	N	Y	N	N
Premium factor 1.05	N	N	Y	N	N	N
Premium factor 1.25	N	N	N	N	N	Y
Premium factor 1.35	N	N	N	N	Y	N
Premium factor 1.65	N	Y	N	N	N	N
Premium factor 1.75	Y	N	N	N	N	N
Fraud investigation	N	N	Y	Y	Y	N

Formally, a decision table is made up of *conditions, condition alternatives, actions,* and *action entries*. In the preceding table, the variables Age and Gender are conditions, whereas the different premium factors and Fraud investigation are actions. The values of Age and Gender are the condition alternatives. Finally, the Ys and Ns are the action entries.

The example already seems complicated enough due to the repetitive actions corresponding to the different premium factors. Personally, I don't think that experimenting with the notation is very dangerous, especially if it results in increased readability:

Age	18–23	18–23	24–59	24–59	60+	60+
Gender	Male	Female	Male	Female	Male	Female
Premium factor	1.75	1.65	1.05	1	1.35	1.25
Fraud investigation	N	N	Y	Y	Y	N

Why should developers care about decision tables? Obviously they can show gaps or inconsistencies in business rules, but there's another reason. Remember that the different flavors of behavior-driven development emphasize shared understanding and concrete examples. Tables, and among them decision tables, are a good format for capturing such concrete examples. Hence, a good decision table, or parts thereof, can be fed right into a tool like FitNesse, Concordion, or Cucumber as a first building block of an automated acceptance test.

At the unit test level,[4] turning the contents of a decision table into arguments to a parameterized test is a good foundation for achieving exhaustive coverage of a business rule.

Summary

Specification-based techniques are a great source of inspiration for developer tests. By being aware that such techniques will constitute the first wave of testing, developers can build software that is prepared to handle these tests. This increase in quality lets testers engage in more high-value testing.

The key specification-based techniques to consider when developing software are

- Equivalence partitioning—Divide the input into partitions where each partition contains data that's equivalent from the perspective of the test.

- Boundary value testing—Check the values at the edges of the partitions, as well as common edge cases.

- State transition testing—Model the target of the test with a state diagram to discover test scenarios.

---

4. I recommend running parameterized tests at the unit level only, because of their execution time. We don't want a slow test running off a huge table of values.

- Testing based on decision tables—Capture all combinations of relevant variables to uncover missing and interesting test cases and to achieve full coverage if need be.

Just as the name implies, specification-based techniques provide the fuel for discussions about concrete examples when doing specification by example (pun intended) or behavior-driven development.

Chapter 9
DEPENDENCIES

Developers who are new to unit testing and have just grasped its mere basics soon hit a barrier. From their perspective, the systems they encounter bear no resemblance to the examples in an introductory text or online tutorial on unit testing or test-driven development. In my experience, this can be very demoralizing and lead to conclusions like: "*Our* system can't be tested" or "Unit testing/test-driven development only works in green field projects." There are numerous reasons for such beliefs, some being a complex or botched architecture, inconsistent design, or simply code written with everything but testability in mind. However, in the majority of cases, the problem is much simpler and is spelled *dependencies*. Different parts of a system depend on each other in different ways, and the exact nature of these dependencies affects testability.

A white box developer test—most often a unit test—exercises a very small part of the system. It does this by creating the object it wants to exercise and calling methods on it. In object-oriented systems, the tested object will make use of other objects, from now on called *collaborators*, to provide its services.[1] Some collaborators are heavyweight and deeply entrenched in the system; others are simple and provide very narrow functionality. When dealing with either kind, we turn to test doubles, the topic of Chapter 12, "Test Doubles," but before skipping ahead, let's look at different kinds of dependencies and what challenges they present.

Relations between Objects

The dependency that first comes to mind is the relation between two objects. Such relations are fundamental to object-oriented programs. Modern systems are usually composed of thousands of classes, and their instances form intricate webs of relations between collaborating objects. Not much is needed for things to get interesting from the unit testing point of view; just let one object create another, like in this `Raffle` class.

---

1. If the language isn't object oriented, there will obviously be no objects and no collaborating objects. However, a tested function will still call code from other modules or libraries. Such dependencies will have to be dealt with within the constraints and functionality of the language in question. Michael Feathers touches on this topic in *Working Effectively with Legacy Code* (Feathers 2004).

```
public class Raffle
{
    private ISet<int> tickets;

    public int TicketCount
    {
        get { return tickets.Count; }
    }

    public Raffle()
    {
        tickets = new HashSet<int> { 3, 10, 6 };
    }
}
```

Okay, I confess. This isn't much of a raffle, but it's my way of trying to make a three-element set wrapped by another class appear exciting. An actual abstraction of a raffle would most likely shuffle its tickets, assign prizes to them somehow, and do the drawing. Here, I simplify all of this to just creating a fixed set of tickets and counting them. The point here is to make the constructor create another object, and thus rely on indirect input, to produce a class that's small and yet hard to test. By "hard to test," I mean that there's no way to write a unit test that would be able to establish a relation between the object created in the constructor and the class's public interface—in this case the `TicketCount` property. So, although it's plain to see that three tickets are created, writing a test that would expect three tickets would be a bad idea due to the nonexistent controllability.

In this example, there's no obvious way to control the indirect input; the code lacks a *seam*—a place in which the behavior of the code can be altered without editing it (Feathers 2004). The bulk of making code testable is dealing with such constructs in the most appropriate manner by adding seams at which dependencies can be broken. There are some generic ways of doing this, all of which can be applied to this particular piece of code with varying degrees of success and complications. To gain control of this dependency we need to make it explicit, which would involve one of the following:

- Pass in the collaborating object
- Create a factory method[2] that can be overridden
- Provide an external factory or builder[3]

---

2. See the Factory Method pattern in Gamma et al. (1994).
3. See the Builder pattern in Gamma et al. (1994).

Let's explore all three and learn what costs, benefits, and trade-offs each approach brings to the table.

Passing in Collaborators

Making collaborators explicit by passing them around is the simplest and most obvious way to increase testability. The downside is the increase in complexity and sometimes decrease in intuitiveness, especially in trivial cases. In the current example, instead of creating the set of tickets in the constructor, we can pass it as an argument. Alternatively, it can be provided using a *setter*[4] (property or method).

```
public class Raffle
{
    private ISet<int> tickets;

    public int TicketCount
    {
        get { return tickets.Count; }
    }

    public Raffle(ISet<int> tickets)
    {
        this.tickets = new HashSet<int>(tickets);
    }
}
```

Now the test becomes trivial.

```
[TestMethod]
public void RaffleHasFiveTickets()
{
    var testedRaffle = new Raffle
        (new HashSet<int> { 1, 2, 3, 4, 5 });
    Assert.AreEqual(5, testedRaffle.TicketCount);
}
```

Passing in collaborators using constructors or setters is usually appropriate when the dependent object isn't short lived and is at the same level of abstraction as the object that uses it.

---

4. One of my reviewers pointed out that this creates temporal coupling. This is usually not a problem, unless you're working with legacy spaghetti code, where it may be hard to find a good spot for calling that setter.

Using Factory Methods

Instead of having the constructor create the tickets, it could be made to call a factory method that would do the creating.

```
public class Raffle
{
    private ISet<int> tickets;

    public int TicketCount
    {
        get { return tickets.Count; }
    }

    public Raffle()
    {
        tickets = CreateTickets();
    }

    protected virtual ISet<int> CreateTickets()
    {
        return new HashSet<int> { 1, 2, 3 };
    }
}
```

The factory method would be made overridable so that any test code would be able to provide its own implementation.

```
[TestClass]
public class RaffleWithFactoryMethodTest
{
    [TestMethod]
    public void RaffleHasFiveTickets()
    {
        var testedRaffle = new FiveTicketRaffle();
        Assert.AreEqual(5, testedRaffle.TicketCount);
    }
}

class FiveTicketRaffle : Raffle
{
    protected override ISet<int> CreateTickets()
    {
        return new HashSet<int> { 1, 2, 3, 4, 5 };
    }
}
```

This approach often saves the day in legacy code, as it turns out to be a reasonable trade-off between complexity and readability. In this case, though, it may become catastrophic. Calling overridable methods from a constructor is bad practice because such methods can easily reference uninitialized member variables and crash the application by doing so. A static analysis tool would warn about this. That said, it's a fantastic example of constraints to think about when dealing with dependencies. In classes with more functionality, this wouldn't usually be a problem; the factory method would be called after the object has been created.

Controversy Warning

Some people feel very strongly about any changes to code that are made solely to simplify testing, such as changing the accessibility of some methods. In some cases, especially in legacy code, this sometimes *has* to be done. Whenever I do this, I remind myself that the code has *two* clients: the system that runs in production and the test code.

However, like everything else, this approach may be misused and lead to code where everything is public or protected, which virtually makes access modifiers meaningless.

Providing an External Factory or Builder

This approach is in a way a combination of the two aforementioned approaches. Instead of passing in the collaborating object directly to the constructor (or via a setter), pass in a factory or a builder. This may seem like overkill, and in many cases it will be. However, some designs will improve considerably when employing this technique. As a matter of fact, it wouldn't be unreasonable for a more sophisticated Raffle class to externalize the creation of its tickets if its other responsibilities included assigning prizes and drawing tickets. Here's what a factory-based solution would look like (just showing the constructor for brevity):

```
public Raffle(TicketsFactory ticketsFactory)
{
    this.tickets = ticketsFactory.CreateTickets();
}
```

The accompanying factory and the test:

```
public class TicketsFactory
{
    private int numberOfTickets;

    public TicketsFactory(int numberOfTickets)
    {
        this.numberOfTickets = numberOfTickets;
    }
```

```
    public ISet<int> CreateTickets() {
        return new HashSet<int>(Enumerable.Range(1, numberOfTickets));
    }
}


[TestMethod]
public void RaffleHasFiveTickets()
{
    var testedRaffle = new Raffle(new TicketsFactory(5));
    Assert.AreEqual(5, testedRaffle.TicketCount);
}
```

Finally, for our tiny set of integers representing ticket numbers, employing the Builder pattern would be way off target, but here's what it would look like.[5]

```
public class TicketsBuilder
{
    private int start = 100;
    private int end = 199;

    public TicketsBuilder StartingAt(int start)
    {
        this.start = start;
        return this;
    }

    public TicketsBuilder EndingWith(int end)
    {
        this.end = end;
        return this;
    }

    public ISet<int> Build()
    {
        return new HashSet<int>(Enumerable.Range(1, end - start + 1));
    }
}
```

In the test, we set up the builder to give us five tickets.

---

5. This builder is slightly more elaborate than it needs to be. A minimal builder could have its defaults set to starting at 1 and stopping at 5, but what's the fun in using a builder if we're just going with the defaults?

```
[TestMethod]
public void RaffleHasFiveTickets()
{
    var builder = new TicketsBuilder().StartingAt(1).EndingWith(5);
    Raffle testedRaffle = new Raffle(builder);
    Assert.AreEqual(5, testedRaffle.TicketCount);
}
```

Obviously, the small class with a three-element set didn't improve from throwing an external builder at it, so what designs do? Factories and builders are both creational patterns (Gamma et al. 1994). We normally turn to them when we need to construct complex objects.

The previous examples have illustrated that the basic relation between two objects can be handled in a number of ways. The solution will depend on the type and complexity of the objects and their exact relation. In addition, this kind of dependency will most likely be managed differently in new code, written with seams and testability in mind, and legacy code.

System Resource Dependencies

System resources tend to make a mess out of tests. In this context, the term *system resource* refers to an abstraction of an operating system artifact, most notably a file, the system clock, a network socket, or something similar. Although such resources are abstracted away in classes or other appropriate language constructs, they still have an impact on unit tests. Even though the test sees a seemingly simple abstraction, its use could trigger behavior and side effects way outside the test harness, like writes to disk or blocking reads. Let's look at a couple of examples.

Files

Nowadays not too many programs actually require direct access to files. Being Web applications, mobile apps, or cloud friendly, they tend to fetch their data or configuration in a different way. However, there are still lots of batch applications out there that read and write raw files.

Consider the first lines of a method that parses a file containing some payment transactions. Being written without testability in mind, it presents a tricky kind of file dependency—a filename.

```
public List<Payment> readPaymentFile(String filename) throws IOException {
    File paymentFile = new File(filename);
    BufferedReader reader
```

```
        = new BufferedReader(new FileReader(paymentFile));

String line;
while ((line = reader.readLine()) != null) {
    // Logic for parsing the file goes here...
```

Passing in a filename to a method is providing input to indirect input (read this sentence again). The `paymentFile` variable is indirect input, whereas the `filename` parameter is its input. This doesn't help when writing unit tests. A small improvement here would be to pass in a `File` object instead, but the problem would remain.

Two generic solutions work in the majority of programming languages for the problem of file dependencies.

Provide Your Own Abstraction

This solution is almost too generic, but will always do the trick. We can always just introduce another layer of indirection around the thing that's hard to test (in this case, the file I/O). When doing this, we have infinite freedom at the cost of having to test the new abstraction.

Imagine that we introduced a simple abstraction called `PaymentFile` that wrapped an instance of `File` to improve readability and testability of the `read-PaymentFile` method:

```
public List<Payment> readPaymentFile(PaymentFile file) throws IOException
{
    while (file.hasMoreLines()) {
        String line = file.readLine();
        // Logic for parsing the file goes here...
```

This new abstraction may even hide the fact that there's a file involved at all. Although *line* is used as the abstraction (as in lines in a file) it could just as well be changed to *unparsed payment*.

Test the Data Handled by the I/O Operation

As soon as a file has been opened, our programming language provides us with a convenient abstraction of its contents. In many cases it's a stream object, and if not, it's some kind of array or list of the file's contents. All these can easily be controlled by a unit test. In fact, splitting the pure file I/O from whatever's done with the contents of the file is a good refactoring that not only benefits testability, but also promotes separation of concerns. Here's an example:

```
public List<Payment> readPaymentFile(String filename) throws
```

```
IOException {
    return readFileContents(new FileInputStream(filename));
}

List<Payment> readFileContents(InputStream inputStream) throws IOException {
    List<Payment> parsedPayments = new ArrayList<>();
    BufferedReader reader = new BufferedReader(
            new InputStreamReader(inputStream));

    String line;
    while ((line = reader.readLine()) != null) {
        String[] values = line.split(";");
        parsedPayments.add(new Payment(parseReference(values[0]),
                parseAmount(values[1]),
                parseDate(values[2])));
    }
    return parsedPayments;
}
```

The corresponding test would set up the file contents as a string and create a stream from it:

```
@Test
public void parseLineIntoPayment() throws Exception {
    String line = "912438784;1000.00;20151115\n";

    List<Payment> payments = new PaymentFileReader().readFileContents(
            new ByteArrayInputStream(line.getBytes()));

    Payment expectedPayment = new Payment("912438784",
            new BigDecimal(1000.00,
                    new MathContext(2, RoundingMode.CEILING)),
            LocalDate.of(2015, Month.NOVEMBER, 15));
    assertEquals(expectedPayment, payments.get(0));
}
```

A Newer Version

This solution looks roughly the same in any language that has an I/O stream library, which is why I presented it here. Had this been a Java book, I'd have the readFileContents method take a Stream<String> instead, and the test would start with the following:

```
    String line = "912438784;1000.00;20151115";
    List payments = new PaymentFileReader()
        .readFileContents(Arrays.stream(new String[]{line}));
```

The System Clock

I said earlier that pretty much every dependency can be solved by introducing an abstraction around it. Code that depends on the system clock is no different. The routine that follows could easily be a part of the batch payment handling program listed previously. In its present form, it's hard to verify that the payment will indeed be treated as if arriving on time, because the system time is sampled directly, that is, it constitutes uncontrolled indirect input.

```
public void DispatchPayment(Payment payment)
{
    var now = DateTime.Now;
    if (now.Date.Equals(payment.DueDate))
    {
        ReceiveOnTimePayment(payment);
    }
    else
    {
        // Handle late and possibly incorrect payments
```

The standard way of dealing with this kind of dependency is introducing a simple "time source" that wraps the class that provides the time.

```
public interface ITimeSource
{
    DateTime Now {
        get;
    }
}

public ITimeSource TimeSource { get; set; }

public void DispatchPayment(Payment payment)
{
    var now = TimeSource.Now;
    if (now.Date.Equals(payment.DueDate))
    {
        ReceiveOnTimePayment(payment);
    }
    else
    {
        // Handle late and possibly incorrect payments
```

A test making use of such a time source would just set its date to match the date of the payment. As always, there's the price of complexity. Adding an interface and a trivial implementation just to make code testable may increase the overall complexity of the program. Depending on the implementation language and platform, there may be other options. Ruby, for example, has several gems[6] for controlling its primary time abstraction, the `Time` class. In Java, testing of time-dependent code has finally been simplified as of JDK 1.8 with the appearance of the abstract `Clock` class. The purpose of this class is to make providing different clock implementations easy, and it has been introduced with testing in mind. In the absence of such alternatives, introducing an abstraction for the time source is a simple technique, which will nearly always work.

Watch for Options . . .

. . . and their cost. Although generic methods work well, there might be some alternatives. Testing the `DateTime` class is actually the "Hello World" program for Microsoft's *Fakes* framework. This framework can replace calls to system components "under the hood" in runtime (Microsoft 2016a), which is ideal for a class like a time source. In older versions of Java, *PowerMock* could be used to achieve a similar outcome.

I'm rather cautious when it comes to using such frameworks, because they may help in postponing the pain of taking on untestable legacy code, instead of helping you to get rid of it. However, being aware of options is always a good thing.

Other System Resource Dependencies

With file and system clock dependencies out of the way, few other system resources should give us trouble. Code that uses raw sockets can usually be refactored in the same way as code that works on files. A stream or a byte array can be used instead. The same goes for different abstractions of memory.

Where more specific strategies fail, the more generic ones described earlier will work. Often the secret to handling system resource dependencies in any form is separating the pure I/O stuff from the processing of data resulting from the I/O operation.

Dependencies between Layers

An application doesn't have to grow large to get divided into layers. In fact, it's harder these days to find an application *without* layers than with layers.

---

6. The most widely used being Timecop.

Layers present a twofold challenge to developer testing. The first problem is intertwining. For various reasons, often best summarized as *technical debt*, layers never stack nicely on top of each other, as they would do in a design document.

Although a truly layered architecture enforces strict separation between the layers and dependencies in *one* direction, I'd say that in the majority of cases, such architectures tend to be more "flexible" and contain some bypasses (see Figure 9.1). Typical examples are the circumvented business layer or the data access layer that knows the workings of the presentation layer to the last bit.

For instance, consider the following data access method. Like pretty much every single example in this book, this one is also "based on a true story." In fact, it's typical legacy code, a decade old, and with more problems than just layer violations. What kind of dependency is this?

```java
public List<String> getCustomers() throws SQLException {
    Connection conn = null;
    PreparedStatement ps = null;
    ResultSet rs = null;
    List<String> customers = new ArrayList<String>();
    try {
        conn = getConnection();
        ps = conn.prepareStatement("SELECT name FROM customers");
        rs = ps.executeQuery();
        while (rs.next()) {
            customers.add("<li class=\"clist\"><b>"
                    + fixHtml(rs.getString("name"))
                    + "</b></li>");
        }
        return customers;
    } finally {
```

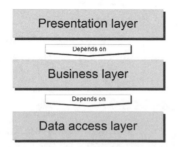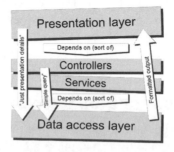

FIGURE 9.1   The layers of a typical Web application: To the left, a textbook version. To the right, something that resembles reality.

```
        DbUtils.closeQuietly(rs);
        DbUtils.closeQuietly(ps);
        DbUtils.closeQuietly(conn);
    }
}
```

Nasty, isn't it? This old DAO knows that the customers will be presented in an HTML list.

The second problem is that the quality of how layers are connected to each other may vary greatly. Sometimes decoupling layers from each other will be a walk in the park, and sometimes it'll require extensive refactoring.

A way that I wholeheartedly recommend to save convoluted and fragile layered designs is to start applying the *Dependency Inversion Principle* in conjunction with conservative use of *dependency injection*. This is where dependency injection frameworks come in handy. Such frameworks are put to best use when wiring together components from different layers or even tiers (if the technology permits it). Although dependency injection is a great pattern and the frameworks that support it are good tools, they can be overused.

Don't Overuse Dependency Injection

Wiring together classes for the sake of doing so or "because it's done in other places in the application" may lead to overcomplicated code that's hard to read and understand.

Dependency Inversion—A Short Introduction

Traditional layered architectures rely on one-way dependencies. Upper layers consume services from lower layers. If truly adhered to, such architectures present no special problems to testing, as long as the lower layers expose interfaces. The weakness of such architectures is that changes to interfaces in lower layers break the upper layers.

Dependency Inversion is a solution to this. When following this principle, higher-level layers only depend on interfaces that *they* own. These interfaces describe operations that are expected of lower-level services, which own and provide the implementation of these operations. Thus, the direction of the dependency is "inverted."

In the example in Figure 9.2, `Upper` wants a message from `Lower`. This will work as long as the `getMessage` method's signature remains untouched. If dependency inversion is applied, `Upper` will depend only on an interface, and `Lower` will provide the implementation that returns the message.

FIGURE 9.2 A layered version of "Hello World" implemented without and with dependency inversion.

Dependencies across Tiers

When an application is split across several physical machines, where each machine provides a different service, it's said to be *multitiered*. The archetypes for multitiered applications are the old client-server architecture and architectures where there's a presentation tier (Web servers), some kind of processing tier (application servers), and a data tier (database).

Because of the physical separation, the communication between tiers is performed using various network protocols (although many technologies try to hide this fact by using local proxies for abstracting remote endpoints). Typical ingredients in multitiered applications are databases, web services, message buses and queues, and various kinds of RPC technologies.

Micro-services, which can run in different tiers, are a more recent example of an architecture that introduces dependencies between components that communicate over a network. Micro-services are also typically distributed over different hosts for better scalability and availability, which increases the complexity of the dependencies and introduces the need for load and fail-over testing.

Dependencies across tiers may suffer from the same problems as dependencies across layers: they may be convoluted and intertwined, or secretly hidden in code where they don't belong. However, they differ from layer dependencies in the way that they almost exclusively either require initialization that may be very hard to do in a unit test (and it shouldn't be done), or they introduce a side effect that causes the test to crash. In the eyes of the inexperienced, such side effects tend be interpreted as "untestable code." Often they are easily fixed by refactoring and introducing proper abstractions and separations, and they can be avoided in the long run by some architecture work.

Summary

Various kinds of dependencies may make systems seem untestable. The trick is to recognize them and handle them in the right manner. This chapter speaks of four kinds of dependencies:

- **Between collaborating objects**—These are the fundamental relations between objects in an object-oriented program. This is where indirect input and output become a challenge. The key to handling these dependencies is to make them explicit. This can be done by injecting the collaborators directly (using constructors or setters), using factory methods, or passing in builders or factories.

- **On system resources**—These are simple dependencies on program elements that abstract a system resource that produces some kind of side effect or uncontrollable behavior. The canonical examples are files and the system clock. When testing on a unit level, files are best handled by separating code that performs the file I/O from code that works with the resulting data. Classes that represent the system clock can be wrapped in another abstraction that can be controlled. Please note that this is a generic method for handling dependencies.

- **Between layers**—Most applications are layered. Each layer has responsibility for some specific functionality, like presentation or business logic. Dependencies between layers are just dependencies between program elements and can be handled in the same way. Layers become challenging when they are violated and bypassed. A good way of wiring layers together that often ensures testability is using dependency inversion and a dependency injection framework.

- **Across tiers**—Applications that are physically split across tiers live on different machines. Dependencies between tiers tend to be more indirect and come in the form of various network-related protocols and technologies. From the programming point of view, the drivers and proxies are just abstractions. However, such abstractions may have quirky interfaces and produce side effects that aren't desirable from a unit testing point of view and that can be difficult even for some integration tests.

Working with dependencies can be emotional. Sometimes code has to be changed to facilitate testability at the cost of increased complexity or a slight accessibility violation. This is seldom required in code written with testability in mind, but may be the fastest, or only, way when working with older code.

Chapter 10

DATA-DRIVEN AND COMBINATORIAL TESTING

Occasionally we end up writing a lot of tests that look strikingly similar. It almost feels like we've turned a table containing inputs and expected outputs into identical test cases. In Chapter 8, "Specification-based Testing Techniques," in the "Boundary Value Analysis" section, there was an example of logic for computing a factor that would determine the cost of car insurance premiums. It was a discontinuous function, which means that thorough testing of it would involve several equivalence classes and strict boundary values. Here's the function again:

Age interval	Premium factor
18–23	1.75
24–59	1.0
60+	1.35

Given the importance age has on the final premium factor and the fact that the devil is in the details, it would seem rather prudent to focus some tests on the boundaries of the age intervals. However, doing it with normal unit tests would just produce a bunch of similar-looking examples and would quickly become repetitive and prone to error.

To illustrate how this would play out, let's revisit a slightly less trivial version of the car insurance premium calculation engine. This time, it's been extended to take gender into account, but it still remains very simple:

```
public double getPremiumFactor(int age, Gender gender) {
    double genderMultiplier = gender == Gender.FEMALE ? 0.9 : 1;
    if (age >= 18 && age < 24) {
        return 1.75 * genderMultiplier;
    } else if (age >= 24 && age < 60) {
        return 1 * genderMultiplier;
    } else if (age >= 60) {
        return 1.35 * genderMultiplier;
    }
```

```
        throw new IllegalArgumentException("Age out of range");
}
```

In this form, careful reading could provide enough confidence in the code. On the other hand, most rule engines don't come as 10-line methods, and their rules and parameters tend to change. Assuming that the computed factor has a significant impact on the final premium a customer would pay, off-by-one errors and simple arithmetic miscalculations aren't tolerated. Therefore, we would duly start by writing a test:

```
@Test
public void maleDriversAged18()   {
    assertEquals(1.75, new PremiumRuleEngine()
            .getPremiumFactor(18, Gender.MALE), 0.0);
}
```

It wouldn't be completely unreasonable to verify that male drivers aged 23 also get the same premium factor. After all, 23 is a boundary value.

```
@Test
public void maleDriversAged23()   {
    assertEquals(1.75, new PremiumRuleEngine()
            .getPremiumFactor(23, Gender.MALE), 0.0);
}
```

At this point, an observant reader may have noticed that the test names don't follow any of the naming conventions presented previously. Figuring that the tested function only returns a floating point number with no special significance, I felt that adding some expectation to the test name would feel contrived.

Actually, things got interesting already. When writing the second test, I stopped for a second, thinking about whether it shouldn't be something like this:

```
@Test
public void maleDriversAged23HaveTheSameFactorAsMaleDriversAged18() {
    PremiumRuleEngine prl = new PremiumRuleEngine();
    assertEquals(prl.getPremiumFactor(18, Gender.MALE),
            prl.getPremiumFactor(23, Gender.MALE), 0.0);
}
```

This approach would have the superficial advantage of explicitly tying the two factors together. Conversely, it could also lead to a cascade of bugs if the boundaries were to change. In addition, it would hide the fact that the essence of the function is to provide a numerical value.

Now, what about female drivers? They have a lower premium factor, which could be expressed as yet another test, but would start to feel awkward because of the duplication and similar structure of the tests. Here, it could be tempting to dodge the "one assert per test guideline" by grouping similar assertions into one test:

```
@Test
public void driversAged18()  {
    PremiumRuleEngine prl = new PremiumRuleEngine();
    assertEquals(1.75, prl.getPremiumFactor(18,  Gender.MALE), 0.0);
    assertEquals(1.575, prl.getPremiumFactor(18, Gender.FEMALE), 0.0);
}
```

A better way of doing this—and this was done in times when unit testing frameworks didn't support parameterized tests—is to extract the code that's common to all test cases and let the tests contain only the different arguments and expectations:

```
@Test
public void maleDriversAged18()  {
    verifyPremiumFactor(1.75, 18, Gender.MALE);
}

@Test
public void maleDriversAged23()  {
    verifyPremiumFactor(1.75, 23, Gender.MALE);
}
@Test
public void femaleDriversAged18()  {
    verifyPremiumFactor(1.575, 18, Gender.FEMALE);
}

private void verifyPremiumFactor(double expected, int age,
        Gender gender) {
    assertEquals(expected, new PremiumRuleEngine()
            .getPremiumFactor(age, gender), 0.0);
}
```

The invocation of the tested method is a one-liner, which makes this approach overkill. However, the example illustrates the technique and applies equally to cases where a bigger chunk of code is extracted into a parameterized method. This technique can be used in practically any testing framework to achieve a degree of parameterization.

Parameterized Tests

Nowadays many unit testing frameworks come with support for *parameterized tests* out of the box. Using Spock, a test that would cover 10 different premium factors would look like this:

```
@Unroll("""A #gender driver of #age has a premium factor
       of #expectedPremiumFactor""")

def "Verify premium factor"() {
    expect:
    new PremiumRuleEngine().getPremiumFactor(age, gender) ==
            expectedPremiumFactor

    where:
    age | gender        || expectedPremiumFactor
    18  | Gender.MALE   || 1.75
    23  | Gender.MALE   || 1.75
    24  | Gender.MALE   || 1.0
    59  | Gender.MALE   || 1.0
    60  | Gender.MALE   || 1.35
    18  | Gender.FEMALE || 1.575
    23  | Gender.FEMALE || 1.575
    24  | Gender.FEMALE || 0.9
    59  | Gender.FEMALE || 0.9
    60  | Gender.FEMALE || 1.215
}
```

This test works by expanding the table into 10 separate test instances (which is made explicit through the `@Unroll` annotation). As illustrated, the values fed to the test may be both primitive types and objects, and may be generated by arbitrary Groovy constructs. The JUnit equivalent is much more verbose and clunky, which is why I put it in the appendix.

NUnit's implementation is also quite elegant. The unnamed parameters of the `TestCase` attribute are fed directly to the method it annotates, and that method's return value is compared with the `ExpectedResult` parameter.

```
[TestCase(18, Gender.MALE, ExpectedResult = 1.75)]
[TestCase(23, Gender.MALE, ExpectedResult = 1.75)]
[TestCase(24, Gender.MALE, ExpectedResult = 1.0)]
// ...
public double VerifyPremiumFactor(int age, Gender gender)
{
```

```
    return new PremiumRuleEngine().GetPremiumFactor(age, gender);
}
```

Theories

Parameterized tests are ideal when a bunch of inputs can be compared to a bunch of known expected results. For example: 1 + 1 = 2, 2 + 3 = 5, 4 + 8 = 12, and so on. The same was true for the premium factor computation, where it was quite easy to determine the expected value. Thus, parameterized tests help in expressing tabular examples in a compact way, but are constrained by the number of available examples (rows in the parameter table).

Theories, on the other hand, offer a different approach. Instead of focusing on parameters and expected results, they provide a way of verifying a *statement* about the tested code (Saff & Boshernitsan 2006). This is extremely useful when the expected result is unknown, hard to compute, or just irrelevant. In such cases, verifying a statement, as opposed to an exact value, may be the most effective thing to do. Whereas normal tests and parameterized tests rely on singular examples, theories express "for all instances of . . ." type of reasoning.

So, how is the input determined? In reality, proving a theory on the entire input domain can be time consuming and unnecessary. Doing exhaustive testing also defeats the purpose of using equivalence classes. In practice, a theory test is executed on a number of *data points* that represent interesting values for which proving the theory is particularly important. It should be no surprise that boundary values make good data points.

Running an unconstrained theory test on parameters from different input domains is equivalent to verifying a statement on their Cartesian product.

Children from Europe, the United States, and Asia, blue-eyed, green-eyed, and brown-eyed, both boys and girls, like candy.

This example talks about three inputs: countries (three of them), eye colors (three as well) and genders (two). This theory would result in $3 \times 3 \times 2 = 18$ verifications. It's unconstrained, because all combinations are tried. Conversely, expressing this seemingly trivial test as a parameterized test would end up in a long and repetitive parameter table.

How would a theory test be applicable in the case of the premium factors? Let's assume that we want to verify that the premium factor always remains between 0.5 and 2.0 for a number of ages between 18 and 100 and for both genders. This would be done by choosing some data points and running a theory test that matches all ages with both genders and checks that the premium factor remains valid.

For example, if we sampled age at 18, 24, and 99 years, running a theory test would result in the following combinations being checked:

Gender	Age
FEMALE	18
FEMALE	24
FEMALE	99
MALE	18
MALE	24
MALE	99

Both JUnit and NUnit support theory tests and both use the same nomenclature. *Theories* rely on *data points* and use *assumptions* to establish conditions under which the theory is relevant (i.e., to constrain input).

```
public class PremiumFactorsWithinRangeTest
{
    [Datapoints]
    public Gender[] genders
        = new Gender[]{Gender.FEMALE,Gender.MALE, Gender.UNKNOWN};

    [Datapoints]
    public int[] ages
        = new int[]{17, 18, 19, 23, 24, 25,59, 60, 61, 100, 101};

    [Theory]
    public void PremiumFactorsAreBetween0_5and2_0(Gender gender, int age)
    {
        Assume.That(age, Is.GreaterThanOrEqualTo(18));
        Assume.That(age, Is.LessThanOrEqualTo(100));
        Assume.That(gender == Gender.Female || gender == Gender.Male);
        var premiumFactor = new PremiumRuleEngine()
            .GetPremiumFactor(age, gender);
        Assert.That(premiumFactor,  Is.InRange(0.5, 2.0));
    }
}
```

This example illustrates a theory that will be applied 18 times; there are nine valid values for age and two genders.[1] Sometimes not all combinations of data points make sense, or we want to filter out input that's irrelevant to the tested theory or handled in a way that would break the test (i.e., the tested code throws an exception). This would correspond to the case of the tested premium rule engine throwing exceptions if too low or too high ages were supplied. By the same token, we don't want to pass in null or unknown genders to the tested algorithm.

Assumptions are used to achieve this kind of filtering. Syntactically they look like assertions, but instead of failing a test, they just prevent it from running. Notice that the data points in the example contain values that will immediately be filtered out by the assumptions. This doesn't make sense if there's only one theory test that runs against one set of data points, although it's quite useful if different tests make use of the same data. We could, for instance, write a negative theory test that would "assume out" all valid ages and just run on the invalid ones and expect exceptions to be thrown. Alternatively, assumptions also protect from combinations of parameters that make no sense. Finally, one could also argue that stating the tested theory's pre-conditions as assumptions documents the test.

Assumptions are not unique to theory tests. They can be used whenever there's need to state a nonfailing precondition in a test.

Test Result Reporting

From a test execution perspective, parameterized tests and theory tests produce multiple instances of a test. For the sake of reporting, each instance is treated as a single test, so if a parameterized test with 10 different parameters fails once, most frameworks and IDEs will report nine successful tests and one failure. For theory tests, this worked slightly worse in Java than in C# at the time of writing, but it was still easy to find the offending combination of data points for a failing test.

Generative Testing

Theory tests are quite powerful. Still, they're limited by the number of data points and the way they're selected. If bad data points are chosen, a theory test will do little

---

1. The code would translate directly to Java/JUnit if [Datapoints] were swapped for @DataPoints, [Theory] for @Theory, and the class was annotated with @RunWith(Theories.class). Adjusting Assume and Assert should be easy for the keen reader. If we're willing to implement our own annotations, we can get rid of @DataPoints altogether. An example of this can be found in the appendix.

good. Suppose that we want to verify that an encryption algorithm works correctly. If it's a symmetric algorithm,[2] it can be verified by checking that decrypting encrypted plaintext produces the plaintext again. Testing an algorithm like this by using a parameterized test would require putting together a table of examples of interesting inputs.

Plaintext	decrypt(encrypt(plaintext))
an empty string	an empty string
a very long string	a very long string
A	A
BB	BB
CCC CCC CCC	CCC CCC CCC
Hello world!	Hello world!
/()=^.-@%<	/()=^.-@%<

Using a theory test would look more compact and mathematical, but would still suffer from the limitations imposed by selecting a few samples.

- **Data points:** *empty string, a very long string*, A, BB, CCC CCC CCC, Hello World!, /()=^.-@%<

- **Theory:** Given the data points, *plaintext = decrypt(encrypt(plaintext)*

In any case, when would we feel that we've provided enough samples to achieve confidence in the algorithm? What are the equivalence classes and boundary values? Does the mathematical nature of the algorithm require testing some inputs extra carefully?

Besides parameterized tests and theory tests, there's a third option: keep the theory, but let the computer generate the data points. Tell it how many, using what constraints, and whether they should be generated deterministically (so that the test can be repeated) or randomly (to cover different inputs for each test run).

```
@Test
public void encryptionRoundTrip() {
    Generator<String> plainTextGenerator
        = strings(integers(1, 128), characters());
```

---

2. Symmetric encryption algorithms use the same key to turn plaintext into ciphertext and vice versa.

```
    for (int i = 0; i < 100; i++) {
        String plainText = plainTextGenerator.next();
        assertEquals(plainText, MyFancyCipher
                .decrypt(MyFancyCipher.encrypt(plainText)));
    }
}
```

In this example, a Java version[3] of QuickCheck (Claessen & Hughes 2016) has been used. In essence, this implementation of QuickCheck provides a simple way to generate values, often randomized, in a convenient and controlled way. The test uses a *generator* in conjunction with a loop to generate 100 random strings that will be encrypted and decrypted.

A generator provides values in accordance with some rules, like minimum/maximum length or size, range, or statistical distribution. The preceding test combines three generators to produce randomized strings. The strings generator will generate strings of the specified length using the supplied character generator. An integers generator is used to produce a random value between 1 and 128, which will determine each string's length. The character generator will produce random characters from the latin1 character set, unless configured differently. There are many other generators in the library. There's also another library called *junit-quick-check* that extends JUnit theory tests with generator annotations.

Trying a similar approach on the premium rule engine example would make little sense. After all, there are only roughly 80 interesting ages and two genders. Still, this is what it would look like in NUnit, which has rudimentary support for data generation out of the box and can manage without extra libraries.

```
[Test]
public void PremiumFactorsAreBetween0_5and2_0(
    [Values(Gender.Female, Gender.Male)] Gender gender,
    [Random(18, 100, 100)] int age)
{
    double premiumFactor = new PremiumRuleEngine()
        .GetPremiumFactor(age, gender);
    Assert.That(premiumFactor, Is.InRange(0.5, 2.0));
}
```

Verifying the Results

Alluring as this kind of testing might seem, it should be used with caution. In many cases, relying on examples will be more than enough—as long as they're selected with care. Adding randomness to tests makes them nondeterministic. This is usually

---

3. https://bitbucket.org/blob79/quickcheck

something we *don't* want, because we want to be able to rerun a test if it fails. On the other hand, generative testing is a powerful technique, provided that we know how to verify the results of tests that are based on generated values. Here are some strategies:

- **Using inverse functions**—An inverse function is a function that produces the "reverse" of another function.[4] Symmetric key encryption, mentioned previously, is an archetypal example. If you know the inverse function of the function you want to test, verifying the results is usually very easy: just apply the inverse function on the value produced by the tested function and compare the result to the input (the generated value).

- **Verifying general properties**—Sometimes we can get away with less accuracy by just verifying a general property of the result of the computation. The test in the section on theories is an example of this. In that test, the exact result wasn't as important as the fact that it was within a certain range, that is, the premium factor remained between 0.5 and 2.0, regardless of the input age. Checks like this may be good enough in many cases. Here are some examples:

  - Is the result always positive?
  - Is the result within a certain range?
  - Is all input handled gracefully without errors and exceptions?
  - Is the result always non-null?

- **Using oracles**—This is the most demanding way of verifying results produced by generative testing. Without being too formal about the actual definition, we can say that an oracle is a black box that knows the answer to a problem. In this particular case, the oracle knows the correct result of the computation verified by the generative test. How does it know? You program it to!

  Yes, an oracle is an alternative implementation of the tested algorithm. For it to be useful, it has to be separated from the tested code somehow so that bugs and biases aren't repeated in both versions. One way is to have a different person or team implement the oracle. Another way could be to implement it in a different programming language—one that's fundamentally different from the language used to implement the tested algorithm. Naturally, these approaches can be mixed to achieve a higher degree of independence.

---

4. In mathematical jargon this is written as $f^{-1}(f(x))=x$, for all x.

Combinatorial Testing

Until now, the assumption has been that executing tests in large numbers—in the form of parameterized tests, theory tests, or with generated values—would be useful and feasible. This would certainly be true for unit tests and a reasonable number of test runs. Not all tests are unit tests, though! Some tests will remain manual, whereas some tests written by developers may involve a slow resource, like a database, a file system, or a network connection. In such cases the kind of close-to-exhaustive testing presented so far in this chapter won't work, which is why choosing *which* and *how many* tests to run becomes the real issue.

To illustrate the point, let's continue building on the premium rule engine example and make it more realistic by having it take yearly mileage, car model, safety features, and driving record into account. At this point the actual implementation isn't relevant. What's relevant is the fact that bringing in more parameters increases the complexity of the rule engine. To deal with this increased complexity, the new variables are divided into equivalence classes, just as the age was.

- **Yearly mileage**
  - Only owner: 0 km
  - Sunday driver: 1–1000 km
  - Casual driver: 1001–3000 km
  - Car enthusiast: 3001–6000 km
  - Professional driver: 6001+ km

- **Safety features**
  For the sake of the example, they're constrained to five classes:
  - No safety features
  - Airbag
  - Antilock Brake System (ABS)
  - Head Injury Protection (HIP)
  - Two or more safety features from the previous list

- **Car models**
  In a real application there would be hundreds; in this example only six:
  - Nissan
  - Volvo
  - Ferrari
  - Toyota

- Ford
- Volkswagen
- **Driving record**
  Analyzing a driving record can be arbitrarily complex. Here, just a few simple equivalence partitions are considered:
  - Model Driver (MD): no parking fines, no accidents, no other violations
  - Average Joe (AJ): 1–5 parking fines, no other violations, no accidents
  - Unlucky Ursula (UU): 1–2 parking fines, 1–2 accidents, no other violations
  - Bad Judgment Jed (BJJ): 1–2 parking fines, no accidents, drunk driving
  - Dangerous Dan (DD): >5 parking fines or >2 accidents or several cases of drunk driving or any other car-related violation.

This slightly more realistic rule engine would produce quite a few test cases if we went for total coverage:

Variable	# values
Gender	2
Age interval	3
Yearly mileage	5
Safety features	5
Car model	6
Driving record	5

In total, there are $2 \times 3 \times 5 \times 5 \times 6 \times 5 = 4{,}500$ variations. At this point exhaustive testing usually isn't an option, so we need a way to reduce the number of tests, while remaining confident in the results. Fortunately, some facts and techniques may help.

Single-mode Faults

A *single-mode fault* is a fancy name for a bug that occurs if a single variable's state isn't handled correctly. In this context, it could mean that the rule engine froze whenever Volvos were fed to it, or it returned a negative value for drivers aged 75. To guard against such faults, we need to ensure that every possible value is tried at least once. This can be done by just listing all parameters and their values in a table. It's usually easier to put the ones with the largest number of possible values to the left.

Car model	Driving record	Mileage	Safety features	Age	Gender
Nissan	MD	0	No features	18–23	Male
Volvo	AJ	1–1000	Airbag	24–59	Female
Ferrari	UU	1001–3000	ABS	60+	–
Toyota	BJJ	3001–6000	HIP	–	–
Ford	DD	6000+	Two or more	–	–
Volkswagen	–	–	–	–	–

The table shows what combinations of parameters are needed to test for single-mode faults (which is also called "achieving all singles"), and it says that six tests are required to do it. Had there been no Volkswagens in the example, only five tests would be required (because the last row only contains a value for the car model variable—Volkswagen). This technique may seem painfully obvious, but tends to be forgotten in the heat of battle.

Double-mode Faults

Often enough a combination of two parameters triggers a bug. Not surprisingly, this is called *double-mode faults*. Testing for double-mode faults is equivalent to testing *all pairs* of values; hence the name of the technique is *pairwise testing* (Bolton 2007).

Finding all pairs is cumbersome in all but the simplest cases, and even a relatively straightforward scenario, like the premium rule engine, would necessitate the help of a computer. For instance, if we started out with Nissans as car models, we would need to ensure that they were paired with all driving record types, mileage intervals, safety features, and so on.

For a few variables with few values, finding all pairs can be done by hand. Let's look at this table made up of three binary variables, V1, V2, and V3:

row	V1	V2	V3
1	A	X	Q
2	A	X	R
3	A	Y	Q
4	A	Y	R
5	B	X	Q
6	B	X	R
7	B	Y	Q
8	B	Y	R

To find all pairs, let's start from the top of the table and see how many rows can be removed. The pairs in the first row, (A, X), (A, Q), and (X, Q), can be found in rows 2, 3, and 5, so row 1 can be deleted. Row 2 must remain, because there's no other row that contains the pair (A, X) once row 1 has been deleted. The pair (A, Y) is in both rows 3 and 4, and (Y, Q) can be found in rows 3 and 7. However, (A, Q) only remains in row 3 after row 1 has been dropped, so row 3 has to stay. Row 4 can be dropped. (A, Y) has been kept in row 3, (A, R) in row 2, and (Y, R) can be found in row 8. Row 5 has to stay; after removing row 1, there's no other row with (X, Q). Following this procedure, rows 6 and 7 can be dropped. The final table looks like this:

row	V1	V2	V3
2	A	X	R
3	A	Y	Q
5	B	X	Q
8	B	Y	R

This isn't the only solution. If the same algorithm were applied from the bottom of the table going up, different rows would remain (1, 4, 6, 7). Doing this exercise by hand for a small table, like this one, quickly convinces us that performing this for bigger tables (like the one for the extended premium rule engine) is a task for the computer.

Writing a program to compute all pairs for larger tables is a fun exercise, but if that isn't what you want to spend your time doing, there's both commercial and free software that will do it for you. Two freely available programs are James Bach's `pairwise.pl` and ACTS from the National Institute of Standards and Technology. Running these two tools on the updated premium rule engine reveals that somewhere between 30 and 40 tests are needed to capture all pairs of variables. Compared to the initial 4,500 tests, it makes quite a difference! Armed with yet another tool, we see how valuable it is to be able to give parameterized tests a reasonably sized parameter table or a theory test a manageable number of data points. In this light, finding all singles and all pairs isn't only a technique for keeping down the number of manual tests, but also a technique for data selection in developer tests.

Beyond Double-mode Faults and All Pairs

Double-mode faults and pairs of variables aren't the end of the road. Obviously, triple-mode faults also occur, so finding all triplets and turning the solution into test cases wouldn't be wrong. This could go on and on. On the other hand, let's be practical. What's important in the context of this book is that pairwise testing is a well-documented technique, and it can be applied to both manual testing and when choosing parameters for developer tests. Going beyond all pairs *does* provide additional confidence, but is computationally more expensive and starts touching on an overly academic subject. In many applications, testing for single-mode and double-mode faults gives high enough confidence at a reasonable price (Kuhn, Kacker, & Lei 2010).

Summary

This chapter is about scenarios that require executing many tests. The first, more tool-oriented part, talks about some features of the more mature unit testing frameworks.

Parameterized tests help when the tests are mainly about matching input values with predefined expected values.

A *theory* is a statement about a property of the program. Theories answer the question: "Given a function *f(x)*, is property *p* true for some different values of *x*?" *Data points* are used to provide the different values. Specialized libraries exist to supply *generators* that produce values for either theory tests or just normal unit tests. The values can be randomized or deterministic.

The second part of the chapter describes what to do when not everything can be tested. *Single-mode* faults occur when the handling of a single variable's state fails. *Double-mode faults* occur when a combination of two variables is handled incorrectly.

Pairwise testing is a technique for dealing with combinatorial explosions in scenarios where all combinations of several unrelated variables must be tested. In such cases, testing only the unique pairs of variables tends to give a rather high payoff.

Chapter 11

ALMOST UNIT TESTS

Developers must do more than just write unit tests to ensure that their code indeed works. In the first chapter, I mentioned several other activities, two of which were to write integration tests and to automate tests in general. Such tests, which I'll refer to as "higher-level tests," are discussed later in the book. In the meantime, it's time to visit a family of tests that shares some characteristics with unit tests and some with higher-level tests, which tends to cause confusion and discussions among developers. A common trait of such tests is that they're *not* unit tests—at least not according to the definition advocated by this book, but they execute just fast enough—in the range of 1 to 2 seconds—to make it into the unit test suite. If it were up to me, I'd call them "bastard tests," the reason being that they look deceivingly simple and are fast, but they're often integration tests, or even system tests. In Google's nomenclature,[1] they'd be typical "Medium" tests, although they'd execute far below the upper time boundary, which is recommended to be 300 seconds for such tests. Therefore, I believe that it's only fair to call them *fast medium tests*. How do they make it into the unit test suite? Here are some plausible reasons:

- **Tests are not classified**—Unfortunately, not every developer cares about whether a test is a unit test, an integration test, or an end-to-end test (or simply doesn't know). If no attention is paid to how and when different tests are executed, some will end up in unexpected places.

- **The test suite is small**—If the test suite consists of a 100 unit tests in total, does it matter if 30 of them take a few extra seconds to run?

- **Laziness**—When this book was being written, it still took a certain amount of effort to make a build tool distinguish between different types of tests. This effort translated into reading up a little on the build tool and tweaking the build script accordingly. On the other hand, running all tests as unit tests requires practically no effort.

- **Hurry**—Sometimes you want to go really fast, especially at the beginning of a project. Maybe you just want to create a spike[2] or prove that the product has

---

1. Google's nomenclature has been covered in Chapter 3, "The Testing Vocabulary."
2. http://www.extremeprogramming.org/rules/spike.html

the potential to be commercially viable. In such cases, growing into a more advanced build as you go along isn't a bad idea. In this stage, fast medium tests may live in the unit test suite.

Examples

The easiest way to get a feeling for what the tests I speak of look and feel like is to look at some concrete examples. There are plenty to be found out there, and these are the ones that have been popping up rather consistently in my projects over the years.

Tests Using In-memory Databases

Several SQL-compliant in-memory database implementations exist that are very fast. Not only do they perform reads/writes much faster than databases that make use of disk storage, they're also easier to set up, because they require virtually no installation and provide programmatic APIs for configuration (including executing DML and DDL). Such databases are quite usable for tests that require a data source that doesn't make use of vendor-specific functionality, which is why you may encounter something like this in your test suite:

```
@Shared
private Connection conn

def setupSpec() {
    Class.forName("org.hsqldb.jdbc.JDBCDriver")
    conn = DriverManager.getConnection("jdbc:hsqldb:mem:db", "SA", "")
    Sql.newInstance(conn).execute(
            "CREATE TABLE users(id BIGINT IDENTITY, " +
                    "name VARCHAR(255), "+
                    "password_hash VARCHAR(255))")
}

def "Authenticate user"() {
    given:
    Sql.newInstance(conn).execute("INSERT INTO users " +
        "(id, name, password_hash) VALUES (NULL, 'joe', '%Gjk!4/P')")

    expect:
    new AuthenticationManager(conn).authenticate("joe", "secret")
}
```

This test assumes that whatever database is being used can be swapped out for HSQLDB, a database that can run in memory only and is implemented in Java. This is quite convenient if your code just relies on standard SQL statements without making use of vendor-specific features and extensions.

Given that the authentication is complicated, this is quite a good test. It shows that the `AuthenticationManager` class uses the database correctly and that password hashing seems to work as expected. However, it's not a unit test. It loads classes, starts a database, and establishes a connection to it. At the time of writing, it ran in less than a second.

Test-specific Mail Servers

The next test starts a simple mail server, which actually binds to the SMTP port. What's really convenient about setting up an entire server is that it doesn't require any seams in the code; only the server address needs to be specified. A test like this takes a mere second. Although definitely not the only way to test delivery of e-mails, a test like the following would be common enough (and look quite similar in both C# and Java[3]).

```
private SimpleSmtpServer smtpServer;

[TestInitialize]
public void Setup()
{
    smtpServer = SimpleSmtpServer.Start(25);
}

[TestCleanup]
public void TearDown()
{
    smtpServer.Stop();
}

[TestMethod]
public void CompanyInformationIsPresentInEmail()
{
    MailService testedService = new MailService("localhost");
    testedService.SendMail(new MailAddress("user@test.local"),
        "Dear customer", "We care!");
```

---

3. This example uses the Dumbster library, which is available in both Java and C#. See Appendix A, "Tools and Libraries."

```
    Assert.AreEqual(1, smtpServer.ReceivedEmailCount);

    SmtpMessage sentMail = (SmtpMessage)smtpServer.ReceivedEmail[0];
    Assert.AreEqual("support@company.local",
        sentMail.FromAddress.ToString());
    StringAssert.Contains(sentMail.Data, "Company Support");
}
```

Tests Using Lightweight Containers

Why settle for stripped-down test servers when you can run a full-blown implementation? Jetty is a very popular web server and servlet container. One of its features is that it can run embedded. This means that an entire web application can be launched using just a few lines of code. Powerful and relatively fast, the next test should definitely not live among unit tests.

```
private static Server server;

@BeforeClass
public static void setUpOnce() throws Exception {
    server = new Server(8080);
    final String pathToWarFile = "/tmp/myapp.war";
    server.setHandler(new WebAppContext(pathToWarFile,  "/webapp"));
    server.start();
}

@Test
public void applicationIsUp() throws Exception {
    HtmlPage mainPage = new WebClient()
            .getPage("http://localhost:8080/webapp");

    assertEquals("Fancy application", mainPage.getTitleText());
}

@AfterClass
public static void tearDownOnce() throws Exception {
    server.stop();
}
```

This test is even "worse" than the previous two. Here an entire server is started, a web application of arbitrary complexity contained in myapp.war is deployed, and an HTTP request is made using HtmlUnit. On the other hand, these few lines of code are sufficient to verify the deployment of an entire web application. In fact, it's a great test, but it's just not a unit test. At the time of writing, this test took no more than two seconds to execute.

The New-School Approach to Embedded Containers

The preceding implementation is an old-school approach that you may encounter in older test suites. A more recent way of starting embedded containers in Java is to use Spring Boot (http://projects.spring.io/spring-boot/).

Tests of Web Services

Arguably, the previous examples may feel kind of specific, so I'm ending with a scenario that few developers who write business applications these days have been able to dodge—invoking a RESTful web service, and an interaction test thereof. In this example, we want to test a class that monitors the stock market and sends a notification if a fictitious stock's price drops below a certain threshold. This would be useful in cases where you don't want your untested code to make actual financial transactions for you using some broker's API.

This particular test focuses on how the tested class interacts with two web services to ensure that the APIs are used correctly.

```
@Rule
public WireMockRule wireMockRule = new WireMockRule()

def "Notify by email when a monitored stock reaches threshold"() {

    final double askPriceThreshold = 20.6
    final String monitoredStock = "XYZ"

    given:
    def notificationReceiver = new ContactInformation(
            phoneNumber: '+1 202-555-0165', email: 'stockfan@test.local')

    stubFor(post(urlMatching("/.*"))
            .willReturn(aResponse().withStatus(200)));

    stubFor(get(urlPathEqualTo("/quotes"))
            .withHeader("Accept", equalTo("application/json"))
            .withQueryParam("s", equalTo(monitoredStock))
            .willReturn(aResponse()
            .withStatus(200)
            .withHeader("Content-Type", "application/json")
```

```
                .withBody("{\"symbol\": \"XYZ\", \"bid\": 20.2, "
                + "\"ask\": 20.6}")))
    and:
    def testedStockMonitor = new StockMonitor("localhost:8080")
    testedStockMonitor.add(notificationReceiver, monitoredStock,
            askPriceThreshold)

    when:
    testedStockMonitor.pollMarket()

    then:
    verify(postRequestedFor(urlEqualTo("/alert"))
            .withRequestBody(containing("stockfan@test.local"))
            .withRequestBody(containing(monitoredStock
            + " is cheap enough")))
}
```

This creation packs quite some power into relatively few lines of code by testing the following: On behalf of a user identified by an e-mail address and a phone number, the stock monitor queries a service that provides a price quote that's attractive enough to trigger a notification. The service exposed as /alert is then invoked to notify the user somehow. The WireMock library allows invoking two fake REST endpoints in less than one and a half seconds and provides constructs for both stubbing and mocking. This test will work beautifully until the local firewall is reconfigured or it's executed in an environment that already runs another server on port 8080 (which is the current default).

Impact

Any nontrivial application hosts a multitude of opportunities to create tests that run almost as fast as unit tests but require a degree of environmental coupling. I hope that the aforementioned examples have been inspiring and given you a sense of what such a test may look like. The least common denominator of this chapter's tests is that they all start a server somehow. However, that server took relatively little time to start, so waiting has been acceptable. Still, I'd argue that running such tests as unit tests is a bad idea. Here are some reasons:

- **Slower developer feedback**—These tests run fast, but they're slower than unit tests. Impatient developers, used to quick feedback, may stop running them while writing code. This is not a good thing, especially if they abandon the habit of using tests to get feedback about their code.

- **Slower in a continuous integration (CI) environment**—CI servers are often slower than developer workstations, simply because there are more of them. What they lack in raw computing power, they tend to compensate for through availability. The difference in performance will be apparent when running the tests, which will become not-so-fast tests on weaker machines.

- **Shaky portability**—All the preceding examples could easily be affected by local permissions, disk space, firewall settings, or occupied sockets, which is why unit tests avoid certain constructs.

- **Confusing**—Fast medium tests tend to blur the line between different types of tests. Developers who are new on the team will wonder what goes where, and there will be endless discussions.

- **Sluggish unit test suite**—One in-memory database test takes one second. Ten such tests take two seconds.[4] Combine that with some other *almost* unit tests, and the unit test suite will start getting sluggish. Not sluggish enough to trigger any rework, but slow enough to annoy somebody on a bad day. If the sluggishness passes a certain threshold, the tests will no longer be executed. Alternatively, the developers will actually run the sluggish tests and task switch to Dilbert strips or Reddit while waiting for them to finish before checking in their code. Goodbye, flow.

Running tests that are almost unit tests along with actual unit tests isn't the end of the world, but they *do* make the test suite slower, more brittle, and more sensitive to environment settings. In time, such suites risk crumbling under their own weight as they grow, and they'll be abandoned eventually. That said, such tests are usually relatively simple to write and they may give great bang for the buck, although I strongly suggest that they be kept separate from tests that can never fail because of environmental issues.

Summary

Some tests run *almost* as fast as unit tests but do things unit tests shouldn't do and pay the price by environmental dependence. Unless monitored and eventually moved to another suite, they'll devour the unit test suite and make it slow, sensitive to the executing environment, and possibly brittle.

---

4. The first test takes one second because of initialization. The following nine tests don't suffer from this delay.

Chapter 12

TEST DOUBLES

In Chapter 9, "Dependencies," we learned how to expose and pass around collaborators to make dependencies explicit and break them. It's perfectly natural that program elements, most notably objects, somehow depend on each other, but such relations have to be controllable. In this chapter, the subject will be revisited and explored in greater detail. Dependencies can be controlled in several ways, depending on what part they play in a test. Sometimes collaborating objects should be ignored, which may not be as easy as it sounds. Sometimes they're of paramount importance and must be surveilled with utmost scrutiny.

Test double[1] is a general term for an object that replaces a collaborator. Different kinds of test doubles have different tasks, spanning from replacing the collaborator and making it return predefined values, to monitoring every single call to it. Five kinds of test doubles, with varying areas of use, will be described in this chapter: stubs, fakes, mock objects, spies, and dummies. The next chapter follows up by illustrating how frameworks are used to implement some of them.

Stubs

The simplest and most generic test of an object that depends on another object looks like what is shown in Figure 12.1.

This gives rise to an almost canonical test method:

```
[TestMethod]
public void CanonicalTest()
{
    var tested = new TestedObject(new Collaborator());
    Assert.AreEqual(?, tested.ComputeSomething());
}
```

---

1. For more in-depth descriptions and more rigorous definitions of the various types of test doubles, see *XUnit Test Patterns: Refactoring Test Code* by Gerard Meszaros (2007). In this chapter, I try to follow his nomenclature, but I do make some slight deviations and sometimes emphasize different things.

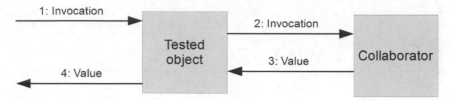

FIGURE 12.1   1: The test code calls the tested object. 2: The tested object invokes its collaborating object. 3: The collaborator performs a computation and returns a value. 4: The tested object uses that value and returns a result that can be derived from it.

The collaborator, conveniently implementing the `ICollaborator` interface, is passed in to the constructor of the tested object, as has been described in Chapter 9. However, we still can't tell what the value of the first argument of `AreEqual` should be (notice the question mark in place of a proper argument). The reason is that the implementation of `ComputeSomething` looks like this:

```
public int ComputeSomething()
{
    return 42 * collaborator.ComputeAndReturnValue();
}
```

This is the simplest case, where the tested object just calls its collaborator, which returns some value. That value is in turn refined somehow and returned to the calling test. From previous chapters we know that the value supplied by the collaborator is called indirect input. To keep the example simple, this value is just multiplied by a number.

To take control of a dependency like this, a *stub* is needed. The primary motivation behind stubbing is to control the tested object's indirect input. Because the collaborator is injected in the constructor of the tested object, creating a stub is very straightforward. All that's needed is an implementation that returns a hard-coded value.

```
class CollaboratorStub : ICollaborator
{
    public int ComputeAndReturnValue()
    {
        return 10;
    }
}
```

This stub can now be used instead of the real object and the test can be rewritten as follows:

```
[TestMethod]
public void CanonicalTestWithStub()
{
    var tested = new TestedObject(new CollaboratorStub());
    Assert.AreEqual(420, tested.ComputeSomething());
}
```

Stub Flexibility

A stub that returns a single value is the least complicated, but also the least intelligent kind. Sooner or later, another test will require a different value to be returned. This is a crossroads. From here one can either decide to implement a new stub that returns another hard-coded value or to extend the existing one:

```
class ParameterizedStub : ICollaborator
{
    private int value;
    public ParameterizedStub(int value)
    {
        this.value = value;
    }

    public int ComputeAndReturnValue()
    {
        return value;
    }
}
```

Once embarking on this journey, the possibilities are endless. For example, if a test requires an exception to be thrown, a tiny `if` will save the day:

```
class ParameterizedStub : ICollaborator
{
    private int value;
    public ParameterizedStub(int value)
    {
        this.value = value;
    }

    public int ComputeAndReturnValue()
    {
```

```
        if (value < 10)
        {
            throw new InvalidOperationException();
        }
        return value;
    }
}
```

However, there is a danger to this. Although we feel very clever as we implement increasingly complex stubs, we run the risk of mirroring business logic. Sooner or later the intelligent stub will contain simplified versions of real business rules, and when the original rules change, the stub will do more harm than good. It will confuse those who aren't familiar with the changes to the business rules and it will make maintaining and keeping the rules up to date harder. Conversely, spawning hordes of similar stubs just because a series of tests requires different values won't make the test suite particularly beautiful, or maintainable, for that matter. Using parameterized stubs is fine, but conditional or otherwise complex logic in them should be avoided. This guideline applies to stubs used in unit tests. When stubbing larger components or systems, it's often quite hard to avoid some kind of logic in the stub.

Stubbing to Get Rid of Side Effects

Apart from controlling indirect input, stubs may serve another purpose. Imagine a variation of the simple test scenario outlined previously, with the twist that this time the collaborator doesn't return anything. Instead, it starts doing things that turn the test into something other than a unit test, like writing or reading a file, establishing a network connection, or updating a database. Figure 12.2 summarizes this scenario.

Assuming that side effects aren't the focus of the test, we just need a way to get rid of them. To do that, all we need to do is to implement an "empty" stub that replaces the side effect–ridden code.

Fakes

In some cases, stubbing isn't enough. The behavior that would be stubbed away is required by the tested object. On the other hand, it comes with side effects and shenanigans that would break a unit test. In such cases, a *fake object* may be a reasonable trade-off. Fake objects are lightweight implementations of collaborators, and their primary purpose is to provide something that's self-consistent from the perspective of the caller.

In Figure 12.3, the tested object makes several calls to another object. These calls not only affect its state, but also result in side effects. Afterward, the object expects a

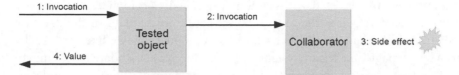

FIGURE 12.2 1: The test code calls the tested object. 2: The tested object invokes its collaborator. 3: The collaborator performs an operation that results in one or more unobservable side effects. 4: The tested object returns a value that's relevant to the test, but isn't based on the interaction with the collaborating object.

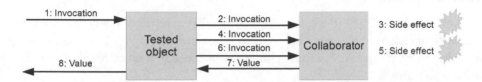

FIGURE 12.3 1: The test code calls the tested object. 2, 4: The tested object invokes its collaborator. 3, 5: The collaborator performs an operation that results in one or more unobservable side effects. 6: The tested object queries the collaborator. 7, 8: The result of that query is based on the internal state of the collaborator and is passed on to the caller of the tested object.

nontrivial result that is somehow based on those calls. A typical example fitting this structure would be a sequence of operations that first persist and manipulate data somehow and then query it. In an average business application, it could be this type of code:

```
public Invoice MakePurchase(Customer customer,
        Product product, Discount discount)
{
    var purchase = purchaseFacade.CreatePurchase(customer);
    purchaseFacade.AddProduct(purchase, product);
    var invoice = purchaseFacade.CreateInvoice(purchase);

    if (discount != null)
    {
        invoice.ApplyDiscount(discount);
    }
    return invoice;
}
```

`CreatePurchase`, `AddProduct`, and `CreateInvoice` all result in data being created and persisted somehow. My intention behind putting them in a "facade" was to simulate some nasty legacy persistence mechanism. Once all data related to making a purchase are persisted, a discount may optionally be applied. The `Apply-Discount` method refreshes the invoice object based on the data in the database and the supplied discount, and is thus equivalent to a query. Code like this usually contains a lot of magic in a legacy system and makes a great candidate for faking. In this example, `purchaseFacade` would be a fake implementation that would produce correct enough invoices, while avoiding persistence and all complicated business rules that usually govern the creation of such entities.

Mock Objects

Stubs provide indirect input in a controlled manner. Fakes replace collaborators with simpler self-consistent implementations. Given these, the missing piece of the puzzle is the ability to verify indirect output. This is the purpose of a *mock object*, or more commonly just "mock."

Mock objects are game changers in a way, as they shift a test's focus from *state* to *behavior*. Tests that focus on state end with assertions that check return values or somehow query the tested object's state. They typically look like this:

```
assertEquals(expectedValue, tested.computeSomething())
```

or

```
Assert.AreEqual(expectedValue, tested.Value).
```

Behavior-based tests are fundamentally different. Their goal is to verify that certain *interactions* have occurred between the mock object and the tested code or another collaborator. Whereas the two preceding assertions care about what a method returns and what value a property has, a behavior-based test making use of mock objects would care about whether `tested.computeSomething` has been called, and possibly how many times, and whether the `Value` property has been queried.

Verifying Indirect Output

Suppose that the tested object invokes a method on another object and gets nothing back; that is, it calls a `void` method. Furthermore, that method may produce one or more side effects that simply won't work with unit tests. Such a dependency could just be stubbed away, but in this case the goal of the test is to make sure that the collaborating object is actually called properly. To perform this kind of verification, mock objects are preprogrammed with expectations on the interactions to come (see Figure 12.4).

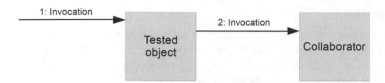

FIGURE 12.4   1: The test code calls the tested object. 2: The tested object invokes its collaborator, which may not return anything or possibly just produce a side effect.

This scenario illustrates the primary use of mock objects: verification of interactions. The simplest case is determining whether an interaction actually has occurred. A typical interaction test verifies the arguments to the mock objects to some degree, whereas less typical tests may focus on counting the number of times the interaction has happened.

Let's assume that we're modeling a shopping workflow, the kind that you go through when buying things online: You pick the items you want to buy, identify yourself, and finally you apply a discount code (if you have one) before checking out. In code, this sequence could be implemented like so:

```
new PurchaseWorkflow(new Books10PercentOffCampaign())
        .addItem(Inventory.getBookByTitle("Developer Testing"))
        .usingExistingCustomer(12345678)
        .enterDiscountCode("DEAL");
```

Now, suppose that we want to test how this purchase flow interacts with the object that represents a campaign.[2] We want to make sure that the campaign's `applyDiscount` method is indeed invoked and that its arguments are correct. Thus, a test using a mock object instead of a real campaign object verifies the indirect output of the `PurchaseWorkflow` class when applying a campaign discount.

The indirect output can be verified with a different amount of rigor, which will be illustrated by three mock objects that become more and more elaborate. In this chapter, these mock objects are implemented "by hand" to illustrate that there's nothing magic about interaction testing and that mocking frameworks aren't mandatory.

---

2. The campaign object implements a simple interface, `Campaign`, which contains one method—`applyDiscount`. When implemented, it's responsible for modifying the price of purchased items and updating the customer's bonus points. In the preceding code snippet, the name `Books10PercentOffCampaign` suggests that the campaign applies a discount to any purchased books.

On Upcoming Test Names

The test names in the upcoming examples are meant to emphasize the type of mock object used, rather than explaining what the test does. They clearly violate all guidelines on test naming, and you may only use this naming style if you're writing a book chapter on differences between different implementations of mock objects.

Scenario 1—Here we just want to verify that the `PurchaseWorkflow` class indeed calls a campaign's `applyDiscount` method.

```
@Test
public void useLenientMock() {
    LenientMock campaignMock = new LenientMock();
    new PurchaseWorkflow(campaignMock)
            .addItem(getBookByTitle("Developer Testing"))
            .usingExistingCustomer(1234567)
            .enterDiscountCode("DEAL");
    campaignMock.verify();
}
```

The corresponding mock object confirms the interaction without caring about the parameters passed to `applyDiscount`. Note that the `verify` method contains an assertion! This is the mock object's way of telling that it knows what to verify.

```
private class LenientMock implements Campaign {

    private boolean wasInvoked = false;

    @Override
    public void applyDiscount(Long customerNumber,
                              String discountCode,
                              Purchase purchase) {
        wasInvoked = true;
    }

    public void verify() {
        assertTrue(wasInvoked);
    }
}
```

Scenario 2—Here we want to verify that the interaction takes place and that the indirect output of `PurchaseWorkflow` is within reasonable bounds.

```
@Test
public void useAverageMock() {
    Purchase expectedPurchase
```

```
        = new Purchase(getBookByTitle("Refactoring"));
    AverageMock campaignMock = new AverageMock(expectedPurchase);
    new PurchaseWorkflow(campaignMock)
            .addItem(getBookByTitle("Refactoring"))
            .usingExistingCustomer(1234567)
            .enterDiscountCode("WEEKEND DEAL");
    campaignMock.verify();
}
```

The mock object verifies that the customer number is positive at least, that the campaign code is propagated, and that the workflow actually adds items to the purchase.

```
private class AverageMock implements Campaign {

    private Purchase expectedPurchase;
    private boolean wasInvoked;

    private AverageMock(Purchase expectedPurchase) {
        this.expectedPurchase = expectedPurchase;
    }

    @Override
    public void applyDiscount(long customerNumber, String discountCode,
                             Purchase purchase) {
        assertThat(customerNumber, greaterThan(0L));
        assertEquals("WEEKEND DEAL", discountCode);
        assertEquals(expectedPurchase, purchase);
        wasInvoked = true;
    }

    public void verify() {
        assertTrue(wasInvoked);
    }
}
```

Scenario 3—The final test performs rather rigorous checks on the parameters passed to `applyDiscount` and it counts the number of invocations.

```
@Test
public void useDemandingMock() {
    DemandingMock campaignMock = new DemandingMock();
    new PurchaseWorkflow(campaignMock)
            .usingExistingCustomer(12345678)
            .addItem(getTraining("TDD 101"))
```

```
            .addItem(getBookByTitle("TDD from scratch"))
            .enterDiscountCode("DISCOUNT_123X")
            .enterDiscountCode("DISCOUNT_234Y")
            .enterDiscountCode("DISCOUNT_999Z");
    campaignMock.verify();
}
```

This last mock has very precise expectations: `applyDiscount` should have been called exactly three times with customer numbers in the range [1000000, 9999999], the discount code matching a regular expression, and the purchase being approved by a custom argument matcher.[3]

```
private class DemandingMock implements Campaign {

    private int timesInvoked;

    @Override
    public void applyDiscount(long customerNumber, String discountCode,
                              Purchase purchase) {
        assertThat(customerNumber,
                allOf(greaterThanOrEqualTo(1000000L),
                        lessThanOrEqualTo(9999999L)));
        assertTrue(discountCode.matches("DISCOUNT_\\d{3,10}[X-Z]?"));
        assertThat(purchase, new PremiumPurchaseMatcher());
        timesInvoked++;
    }

    public void verify() {
        assertEquals(3, timesInvoked);
    }
}
```

Do these mock objects make sense? How useful are they? It depends. The mock from the first scenario just verifies whether `applyDiscount` has been invoked. This is a pure interaction test. If you trust everything else, this might suffice. The second mock adds some basic sanity checks. This makes sense if many things happen in the tested object before it produces its indirect output or if the quality of the code is low and you want to be extra defensive in your test. However, a test using this mock no longer only fails if the interaction doesn't happen, but may also fail for many other reasons. Finally, the third mock starts applying business rules to its verification, like the format of the customer number and discount code, and the composition of the

---

3. The source code of this matcher is in Appendix B.

purchase. Verification like this leads to brittle tests and usually indicates problems with the tested code or other tests. In this particular example, if the format of the customer number and discount code really were that important, then they probably would deserve their own classes. The last matcher would probably only be useful if the goal of the test was to verify indirect input supplied by another collaborator.

When using mock objects, it's very tempting to verify as much as possible and as strictly as possible. The general rule of thumb for maintainable tests is: **Don't**. Or rather, understand the trade-off between strict and thorough verification and the test's sensitivity to changes to the code. This topic will be covered in greater detail in the next chapter.

Verifying Indirect Input Transformations

A special case of verifying the tested object's indirect output is verifying how the indirect input from its collaborators is transformed. Although slightly pedantic, this distinction has been helpful to me many times, and I'd like to share it. Consider the case depicted in Figure 12.5.

The actual form may vary, but the important part is that the collaborator is called with a parameter that's important enough to be verified by the test but that cannot be set up directly by it. A possible case would be testing the update method of a thermometer.

```
public void update() {
    double temperature = sensor.getTemperature();

    if (displayMode == DisplayMode.CELSIUS) {
```

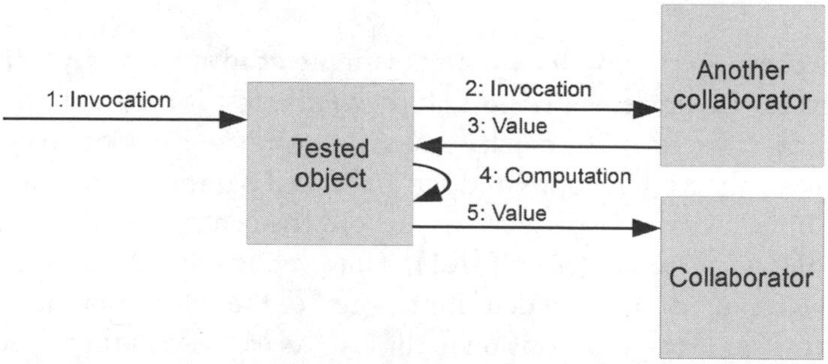

FIGURE 12.5   1: The test code calls the tested object. 2–3: The tested object invokes a collaborator (a test double or the actual implementation), which returns a value. 4: The value is processed somehow by the tested object. 5: The value returned by the other collaborator and processed by the tested object is used as a parameter when calling the collaborator that's of interest to the test.

```
        display.output(formatForDisplay(temperature));
    } else {
        display.output(formatForDisplay(
                celsiusToFahrenheit(temperature)));
    }
}

private double celsiusToFahrenheit(double celsius) {
    return celsius * 1.8 + 32;
}

private String formatForDisplay(double number) {
    return df.format(number) + " °" + displayMode.getSymbol();
}
```

The thermometer can be configured to display temperature in Fahrenheit or Celsius, but it has a sensor that reads the temperature in Celsius only. If the `update` method is to be tested, it'll need to take both temperature conversion and formatting into account, as the thermometer only displays one digit after the decimal point. The temperature returned by the sensor is the indirect input provided by another collaborator, whereas the formatting and temperature conversion are the computation.

Tests of `update` would most likely stub the sensor and verify the interaction with a mock display. Depending on how the tests were set up, this single inspection point would be able to tell both whether the temperature conversion is correct and whether the output is correctly formatted.

Spies

The distinction between *spies* and mock objects is quite academic, in my opinion. Whereas mock objects are implemented so that they *fail* a test if their expectations aren't met (I put various asserts in the mock objects in the previous section to emphasize this), spies *capture* their interactions and the associated parameters for later use. Mock objects are, in fact, spies too, because they record the behavior of the program element involved in the interaction (Martin 2014). However, the difference is that the mock *itself* uses the captured values to determine whether the interaction happened correctly, whereas the spy leaves this decision to the test. As we'll see in the next chapter, this doesn't necessarily apply to mocks created by a mocking framework. Spies constructed dynamically by frameworks get less coupled to the tested code than do mock objects, which reduces the likelihood of making tests brittle.

Time for an example. If the test making use of the "average" mock object were rewritten to use a spy instead, it would look like this:

```
@Test
public void demonstrateSpy() {
    Purchase expectedPurchase
            = new Purchase(getBookByTitle("Refactoring"));
    CampaignSpy campaignSpy = new CampaignSpy();

    new PurchaseWorkflow(campaignSpy)
            .addItem(Inventory.getBookByTitle("Refactoring"))
            .usingExistingCustomer(1234567)
            .enterDiscountCode("WEEKEND DEAL");

    assertThat(campaignSpy.customerNumber, greaterThan(0L));
    assertEquals("WEEKEND DEAL", campaignSpy.discountCode);
    assertEquals(expectedPurchase, campaignSpy.purchase);
}

private class CampaignSpy implements Campaign {

    public long customerNumber;
    public String discountCode;
    public Purchase purchase;

    @Override
    public void applyDiscount(long customerNumber,
                              String discountCode,
                              Purchase purchase) {
        this.customerNumber = customerNumber;
        this.discountCode = discountCode;
        this.purchase = purchase;
    }
}
```

The test looks strikingly similar to its mock counterpart, except for the placement of the assertions. In cases where I can't use a framework to create a mock object and I have to craft it by hand, I always resort to the spy-based approach, the reason being that it allows me to keep the assertions in the test.

Dummies

Dummy is the final term in the test double nomenclature. Dummies are values you don't care about from the perspective of the test. They're typically passed as arguments, although they can be injected or referenced statically at times. There's little science around dummies, but I'd like to point out two things about them. First, naming them appropriately often helps. If a test is all but trivial, its readability isn't increased by the presence of nulls, zeroes, or empty strings. It might be a matter of taste, but personally I prefer:

```
[TestMethod, ExpectedException(typeof(ArgumentOutOfRangeException))]
public void ShouldFailForTooYoungCustomers()
{
    int age = 10;
    string ignoredFirstName = "";
    string ignoredLastName = "";
    CustomerVerifier.Verify(age, ignoredFirstName,
    ignoredLastName);
}
```

when testing something like this . . .

```
public static void Verify(int age, string firstName, string lastName)
{
    if (age < 20)
    {
        throw new ArgumentOutOfRangeException("Minimum age is 20");
    }

    // Method continues...
    // Do something with the name parameters
```

. . . to the version following, or something similar with nulls instead of the empty strings.

```
[TestMethod, ExpectedException(typeof(ArgumentOutOfRangeException))]
public void ShouldFailForTooYoungCustomers()
{
    CustomerVerifier.Verify(10, "", "");
}
```

There is, of course, a middle ground, but it only works for strings:

```
CustomerVerifier.Verify(10, "NOT_USED", "NOT_USED");
```

Although one can guess that nulls and simple default values indicate a dummy, I still think it's worthwhile to highlight what's *not* important. This is a matter of programming language. If the language supports named arguments somehow, naming dummies is less of an issue. Because the example happens to be C#, which happens to support named arguments . . .

```
CustomerVerifier.Verify(age: 10, firstName: "NOT_USED",
          lastName: "NOT_USED");
```

Second, if you feel that you're using too many dummies and that it doesn't feel right, then your instincts probably serve you well. Overuse of dummies often indicates that the tested code probably does too much or that the test verifies something irrelevant, most likely the former.

Verify State or Behavior?

This chapter and the subsequent one often mention state/behavior testing or verification. There's an ongoing debate about which style is "better." Both styles have their advantages and disadvantages and, above all, uses.

State Verification

State verification is employed when the final outcome of interacting with the object of the test is best observed by examining a value or a data structure produced by that object. A state-based test performs one or more operations on the target object and then queries it and possibly some of its collaborators to assess whether the outcome of the operations was correct. In an object-oriented environment, the simplest case of state verification is invoking a mutator followed by an accessor (which many would consider "too simple to break"), whereupon the result is fed to an assertion.

```
given:
Car testedCar = new Car()

when:
testedCar.setSpeed(40)

then:
testedCar.getSpeed() == 40
```

Apart from confirming that the tested car has the ability to accelerate to 40 mph instantaneously (hmm), this example also shows that the speed is stored in the tested object and is thus part of its state. If such a state is made up of many variables' values, a state-based test may easily fall victim to checking too many seemingly unrelated values or digging too deeply into the tested object. Consider this:

```
given:
Car testedCar = new Car()

when:
```

```
testedCar.setSpeed(40)

then:
testedCar.getSpeed() == 40
testedCar.getGear() == 2
testedCar.getTachometer().getValue() == 2000
```

This could be a characterization test attempting to pin down an arguably odd creation, or it could be a test written by a developer who got seduced into adding a few more assertions[4] while at it. In either case, the car seems to have quite a few peepholes that may appear tempting for state-based peeking.

State verification feels most natural in cases where the tested operation returns something, and, if that something looks right, then the implementation that created it is judged to be correct.

Now, how about functions that don't affect any state? Is checking them state or behavior testing?

```
assertEquals(10, new Calculator().add(6, 4));
```

I would say neither, as would functional programming aficionados, but it turns out that verifying functions that don't mutate any state falls in the category of state-based testing. The reason is that the result of the operation is still best observed by inspecting data produced by that operation.

Behavior Verification

When the expected outcome of an operation cannot be observed by querying the object of the test, *behavior verification* is used instead. Most often behavior verification is synonymous with using mock objects verifying interactions. At times, the tested object may store much of its state in collaborating objects. In such cases, what would normally be a state-based test can turn into a test of behavior.

Behavior verification feels most natural when the tested object exposes no state; nothing is returned and few or no methods expose whatever state it may have. This is usually true for code that contains many command type of calls (as in Command-Query Separation; Fowler 2005). Hence, interaction tests are often encountered in larger systems made up of several layers, where some of the layers contain little logic or state and are mostly responsible for orchestrating calls to other layers and components, like in this `BillingService` class:

---

4. Although the framework used in this example, Spock, uses conditions rather than assertions.

```
public void ChargeCustomer(CustomerId customerId,
                           IList<Product> products)
{
    var customer = customerRepository.Find(customerId);
    var invoice = CreateInvoice(customer, products);
    invoiceRepository.Save(invoice);
    mailService.SendInvoice(customer, invoice);
}

private Invoice CreateInvoice(Customer customer, IList<Product> products)
{
    var invoice = new Invoice(customer.Id);

    // Do something interesting with products here...

    return invoice;
}
```

Unit-testing this method would amount to making sure that it indeed manages to call `SendInvoice` for the correct customer with an invoice that reflects the supplied products.

The Arguments

Those who argue against behavior testing will have a point when they say that such tests won't detect algorithmic errors. After all, checking that an algorithm has been called with certain parameters doesn't guarantee that it's been implemented correctly. The `SendInvoice` method in the last example could be completely wrong. It could send the invoice to a print shop using some batch file transfer mechanism instead of e-mailing it to the customer. If `mailService` were a mock object, this blunder would pass unnoticed.

Another case against behavior testing is about the tests knowing too much about the internals of the tested code, that is, being too tightly coupled. After all, if interactions are to be verified, the tests need to know about them. Should some of the interactions change, the tests will break. This argument is similar to that of poking too extensively into the internal representation of an object. It, too, may change. A way of making behavior-based tests more stable is to keep them coarse-grained. The test wants to know that `mailService` was indeed called, but it doesn't have to dissect the invoice passed to `SendInvoice` and verify that it's correct to the last bit.

Testing Behavior

The phrase "testing behavior" doesn't always refer to verifying interactions using a mock object. Instead, it refers to testing the actual behavior of a program element, which was defined as "the outcome produced by its functionality under certain preconditions" in an earlier chapter.

From this it follows that a program element's behavior may be to return something suitable for state verification, or to perform a number of invocations, which would be tested by verifying interactions. Phew.

Summary

Different kinds of test doubles are used when dealing with dependencies in unit tests:

- *Stubs* are used to control indirect input and sometimes to get rid of side effects.

- *Fakes* provide self-consistent implementations of collaborators, which in practice means that they're lightweight implementations.

- *Mock objects* are used to verify indirect output and occasionally indirect input from other collaborators.

- *Spies* record the interactions and their parameters for later checking.

- *Dummies* are values that are irrelevant to the test—usually arguments.

The discussion of stubs, fakes, and mocks brings into the foreground the distinction between state and behavior testing. State verification is about querying the tested object's (and possibly its collaborators') state after having invoked some of its operations. Behavior verification is about checking whether a certain interaction has occurred between a mock object and the tested object or other collaborators.

State-based tests are good for finding algorithmic errors, but they run the risk of being too invasive. Behavior-based tests won't find any algorithmic errors and are vulnerable to being too coupled to the implementation. Both types of tests can become brittle. State-based tests may look at too much state or dig too deeply into an object, whereas behavior-based tests may be too strict when verifying the interaction.

Chapter 13
MOCKING FRAMEWORKS

Today the number of cases in which we want to implement test doubles by hand is quite limited. *Mocking frameworks* have been evolving for several years and have reached full maturity by now. At the time of writing, they've gone through generations of evolution and have reached a point where they offer very rich functionality and truly simplify many aspects of interaction testing. A case in point is the fact that mocking frameworks, despite their names, not only construct mock objects, but also stubs and spies.[1] My experience is that this versatility often leads to confusing tests, where the role of the test double is ambiguous and unclear. That's why I emphasize the type of test double wherever possible. To avoid this confusion altogether, some people prefer the term *isolation frameworks*, because the name carries with it the promise that the frameworks may create different kinds of test doubles that isolate the code under test from its collaborators.

Frills aside, mocking frameworks provide three fundamental kinds of operations:

- Test double construction

- Expectations setup

- Interaction verification

Different mocking frameworks implement these operations in different ways, each of which has its strengths and weaknesses. Therefore, the first part of this chapter is about familiarizing you with the variations to give you a sense of what a mocking framework can do and what kind of code it will give rise to.

Constructing Test Doubles

Constructing test doubles is very simple in a modern mocking framework. In most cases it amounts to one line of code that says: "give me a test double of this class." The simplest test doubles are based on interfaces; the framework creates a concrete class that implements the interface.

---

1. Although the mocking framework may use the term *spy* differently from how it was described in the previous chapter.

```
var dependencyStub = new Mock<IDependency>();
```

The two mocking frameworks used most prevalently in the examples in this section don't even distinguish between stubs and mocks during the construction stage. This first example is based on Moq for C#. Using Java's Mockito, the construction would be almost identical.

```
Dependency dependencyStub = mock(Dependency.class);
```

A framework that *does* make the distinction between stubs and mocks is Spock, but the syntax is still quite similar:

```
def dependencyStub = Stub(Dependency)
```

That's it, if all we need is a stub that returns a simple default value, like 0 for numerical types and null for objects. The previous one-liners indeed produce working stubs, and at this point only the variable name offers a clue about the type of test double.

Mocking Framework Magic

Behind the scenes many of the frameworks make use of *dynamic proxies*. Proxies are objects that act as a surrogate for another object by exposing the same interface as the proxied object (Gamma et al. 1994). Often they delegate calls to the proxied object, but they don't have to. Callers are often not aware of whether they are talking to the actual object or the proxy. When proxies are created at runtime, they're dynamic.

Test double creation has advanced way beyond simple proxying and has, with time, been sugarcoated with extra features like

- Creating test doubles of concrete classes as opposed to interfaces only

- Having the test double implement multiple interfaces

- Annotation-driven creation

- Automatic test double injection

The list of nifty features varies among frameworks and changes and evolves constantly. Spend some time reading your favorite framework's documentation.[2]

---

2. This book doesn't contain any details about the mocking frameworks it uses. I don't want the contents to become obsolete because of some latest and greatest API changes.

Once a test double has been created, we need to decide whether we'll use it as a mock, a stub, or both. The third option isn't encountered that frequently, because it implies that the test double will serve as a provider of indirect input *and* as an observer of indirect output/interactions at the same time. In the majority of cases, this is something you don't want, though you may find yourself doing this when testing legacy code (which, unconstrained by things like Command-Query Separation or the Single Responsibility Principle, may pile interaction on interaction in long sequences).

Setting Expectations

An *expectation* is a statement that tells the test double how to respond to an invocation. Historically, setting up expectations was a crucial step in configuring a mock. Older mocking frameworks relied on first setting up, or "recording," a number of expectations, then having the test interact with the mock, and finally verifying that the expectations were fulfilled. Creating true mock objects, they immediately failed the test if they encountered an interaction with the mock that didn't match any expectations. Reusing one of the examples (the one using the "average" mock) from the previous chapter, an interaction test using a true mocking framework (jMock) would look like this:

```
Mockery context = new Mockery();

@Test
public void discountCodeIsAppliedInThePurchaseWorkflow() {
    final Campaign campaignMock = context.mock(Campaign.class);
    final Purchase expectedPurchase
            = new Purchase(getBookByTitle("Refactoring"));

    context.checking(new Expectations() {{
        oneOf(campaignMock).applyDiscount(
                with(greaterThan(0L)),
                with(equal("WEEKEND DEAL")),
                with(equal(expectedPurchase))));
    }});

    new PurchaseWorkflow(campaignMock)
            .addItem(getBookByTitle("Refactoring"))
            .usingExistingCustomer(1234567)
            .enterDiscountCode("WEEKEND DEAL");
    context.assertIsSatisfied();
}
```

This test would fail during the call to `applyDiscount` if the expectation weren't satisfied, that is, the parameters didn't match, and it would fail during the verification phase (`context.assertIsSatisfied()`) if the method wasn't called at all.

Mockito, Moq, and Spock all construct mocks that behave like spies (or nice mocks); that is, they just record the interactions and let them happen, which means that no predefined expectations are required. Instead, the interactions are verified at the end of the test. This will be apparent in the upcoming examples.

Strict and Nice Mocks

A mocking framework can produce up to three distinct flavors of mocks: normal, strict, and nice. The terminology varies a little between different frameworks, but basically, nice mocks won't make the test fail if they encounter an unexpected interaction, whereas strict and normal mocks will. Strict mocks want all interactions to happen exactly as specified by the expectations; otherwise, they make the test fail. Some frameworks also require that the interactions happen in a specific order with strict mocks.

Because this terminology is a bit fluid, you do want to look up the exact features and definitions in your framework's API documentation.

Stubbing

Expectations are typically associated with mocks, but I'll be using the word in a broader sense, which will allow me to speak of expectations as a means of configuring stubs. Being just a proxy created on the fly, a stub without any expectations only returns default values—in practice zero—for methods that return a primitive numerical data type, and nulls for methods that return objects (and maybe even empty collections for methods that return collections). Invocations of methods that don't return anything will just pass through. To become more usable, the stub needs to be told how to behave, which is equivalent to implementing logic in a hand-coded stub.

Methods that don't take any arguments are quite easy to set up. Using Moq, the setup would look like the following:

```
dependencyStub.Setup(d => d.ComputeAndReturnValue()).Returns(10);
```

And using Mockito, it would be almost identical:

```
when(dependencyStub.computeAndReturnValue()).thenReturn(10);
```

These expectations tell the stubs to return a fixed value and correspond to just implementing a single line method with a return statement.

When the method to be stubbed takes one or more arguments, we have to start thinking about what to do with them. Consider a single argument method. If "hand-crafted," it would look like this:

```
int ComputAndReturnAnotherValue(int arg)
{
    return 10;
}
```

The argument is ignored. To achieve this in a mocking framework, it needs to be instructed to do so, which is done by supplying a predicate that tells it how to react to method arguments. Such predicates are called *argument matchers*.[3] They can become almost arbitrarily complex, although they shouldn't, because complex nested matchers imply too many assumptions about a collaborator (thus making the test sensitive to changes to that collaborator) and make the test harder to read. Moq's matchers are static boolean methods in the It class.

```
dependencyStub.Setup(d => d.ComputeAndReturnAnotherValue(
    It.IsAny<int>())).Returns(10);
```

Mockito has its own methods for matching primitive data types and a simple interface to Hamcrest matchers for more demanding cases. This gives developers the freedom to implement any predicates they need.

```
when(dependencyStub.computeAndReturnValue(anyInt())).thenReturn(10);
```

Spock has the interesting capability to match any argument (or arguments), without even caring about the type, which is quite powerful when you just want to get your stub up and returning values.

```
dependencyStub.computeAndReturnValue(_) >> 10
```

The most common way of matching arguments is using the equals method. It's like saying: "if the method is called with an argument that is this value, then return that value." In fact, it's so common that it's implicit (in the frameworks used here at least). To achieve the equivalent of

```
int ComputAndReturnAnotherValue(int arg)
{
```

---

3. It's the same mechanism as that used by the AssertThat method and has been covered in Chapter 7, "Unit Testing."

```
    return arg == 42 ? 10 : 0;
}
```

no argument matcher is needed—the expectation is set up using the exact value. Note that zero, expected in all cases except when `arg` is 42, will be returned as a result of the stub's default behavior.

```
dependencyStub.Setup(d => d.ComputeAndReturnAnotherValue(42)).Returns(10);
```

Equality, or lack of implementation thereof, is probably the most common source of errors when using mocking frameworks. It's just like in the case of assertions. If we fail to implement the `equals` method in the classes we create, the test double will start behaving mysteriously. Will the assertion at the end of the next test succeed or fail?[4]

```
class Banana {
    public String color = "yellow";
}

interface Monkey {
    boolean likes(Banana banana);
}

@Test
public void monkeysLikeBananas() {
    Monkey monkeyStub = mock(Monkey.class);
    when(monkeyStub.likes(new Banana())).thenReturn(true);

    assertTrue(monkeyStub.likes(new Banana()));
}
```

Sometimes—although less often than you might think—you need the stub to return different values on consecutive calls. Mockito lets you stack `thenReturn` directly:

```
when(dependencyStub.computeAndReturnValue(42))
        .thenReturn(10).thenReturn(99);
```

Moq needs you to swap `Setup` for `SetupSequence` to allow this kind of stacking. When using Spock's stubbing facilities, you just need to specify a list of values to return.

---

4. Hint: Are two banana objects equal if equals isn't implemented?

```
dependencyStub.computeAndReturnValue(42) >>> [21, 45]
```

Last, but not least, you'd want stubs to throw exceptions to allow you to verify your waterproof error handling, right? Using Mockito's short-hand syntax, a stub that would throw an exception would be set up like so:

```
Dependency dependencyStub =
        when(mock(Dependency.class).computeAndReturnValue(42))
        .thenThrow(new IllegalArgumentException("42 isn't the answer!"))
        .getMock();
```

Moq's syntax resembles Mockito's original syntax (which you can find in the documentation).

```
var dependencyStub = new Mock<IDependency>();
dependencyStub.Setup(d => d.ComputeAndReturnAnotherValue(42))
        .Throws(new ArgumentException("42 isn't the answer!"));
```

And, for completeness—the Spock way:

```
def dependencyStub = Stub(Dependency)
dependencyStub.computeAndReturnValue(42) >>
    { throw new IllegalArgumentException("42 isn't the answer!") }
```

These are the basics of setting up expectations. One can construct infinitely complex custom constraints/matchers to set up stubs that reply very intelligently to a variety of invocations. However, just like with stubs implemented by hand (which were discussed in the previous chapter), keep it simple. Overly intelligent stubs are a sign of danger.

Verifying Interactions

The main purpose of a mock object is to verify interactions. A fundamental building block of all mocking frameworks is a *verify* operation. Whereas a test that focuses on state will end with an assertion method, a test that revolves around a mock object will end with a verification.

Verifications also use constraints or matchers to decide whether the parameters passed to the mock's method are correct enough to qualify the invocation as a successful interaction. Because matchers have been covered already, we'll go straight on to examples and revisit the discount scenarios from the previous chapter. Let's see how they would be implemented using the three mock frameworks presented in this chapter.

   Scenario 1—Here we just want to verify that the `PurchaseWorkflow` class indeed calls a campaign's `applyDiscount` method. Mockito is used in this example, whereas Moq and Spock equivalents have been put in Appendix B, "Source Code."

```java
@Test
public void useLenientMock() {
    Campaign campaignMock = mock(Campaign.class);
    new PurchaseWorkflow(campaignMock)
            .addItem(getBookByTitle("Developer Testing"))
            .usingExistingCustomer(1234567)
            .enterDiscountCode("DEAL");

    verify(campaignMock).applyDiscount(anyLong(),
            anyString(), any(Purchase.class));
}
```

   Scenario 2—Here we want to verify that the interaction takes place and that the indirect output of `PurchaseWorkflow` is within reasonable bounds. This time, it's Moq's time to shine, and Mockito and Spock have been deferred to Appendix B.

```csharp
[TestMethod]
public void UseAverageMock() {
    var campaignMock = new Mock<ICampaign>();
    Purchase expectedPurchase = new Purchase(
            Inventory.GetBookByTitle("Refactoring"));

    new PurchaseWorkflow(campaignMock.Object)
            .AddItem(Inventory.GetBookByTitle("Refactoring"))
            .UsingExistingCustomer(1234567)
            .EnterDiscountCode("WEEKEND DEAL");

    campaignMock.Verify(cm => cm.ApplyDiscount(
            It.IsInRange(1, long.MaxValue, Range.Inclusive),
            "WEEKEND DEAL",
            It.Is<Purchase>(p => p.Equals(expectedPurchase))));
}
```

Scenario 3—This last test performs rather rigorous checks on the parameters to `applyDiscount` and it counts the number of invocations. Spock is used to demonstrate this scenario (Moq and Mockito are in Appendix B yet again).[5]

```
def "use demanding mock"() {
    setup:
    def campaignMock = Mock(Campaign)

    when:
    new PurchaseWorkflow(campaignMock)
            .usingExistingCustomer(1234567)
            .addItem(getTraining("TDD for dummies (5 days)"))
            .addItem(getBookByTitle("TDD from scratch"))
            .enterDiscountCode("DISCOUNT_123X")
            .enterDiscountCode("DISCOUNT_234Y")
            .enterDiscountCode("DISCOUNT_999Z");

    then:
    3 * campaignMock.applyDiscount(
            { it >= 1000000L && it <= 9999999L },
            { it =~ "DISCOUNT_\\d{3,10}[X-Z]?" },
            { it.getPrice() > 1000 && it.getItemCount() < 5 })
}
```

These examples show some capabilities of modern (at the time of writing) mocking frameworks and illustrate how similar they are. Many features have been left out, especially the framework-specific gold plating. Spend time getting to know your framework! Once you've done that, read the next section that talks about misuse, overuse, and other pitfalls.

Misuse, Overuse, and Other Pitfalls

Mocking frameworks are potent tools that let you wield incredible power. However, power nearly always corrupts. This section is devoted to describing some common corruptions observed in tests in the wild.

---

5. I've dropped the `PremiumPurchaseMatcher` here in favor of closure-based matching, which is more idiomatic in Spock and Groovy.

Oververifying

Every time a verification is executed on a mock object, *the test gets coupled to the internal implementation of a program element*, thus becoming sensitive to changes and refactorings of that program element. Instead of remaining green during refactoring and acting as a safety net, it will turn red and break for seemingly mysterious reasons. This is, in fact, an argument in favor of spy-like or nice mocks. By *not* expecting every single detail about every single interaction, they make the tests less coupled to the internals of the tested code, and thus less sensitive to it changing. On the whole, verification of interactions had better be kept coarse grained.

Just as keeping the number of assertions down in a state-based test is usually a good thing, the same goes for verify statements. As a rule of thumb, a test involving a mock object should verify *only one interaction*, and that should be the focal point of the test. Thus, if it breaks, it will be obvious that something vital and important has stopped working. A corollary to this is that the test should employ as few mocks as possible—preferably only one. However, just as multiple assertions may verify one logical concept, so can verifying multiple interactions. Tests of typical orchestration methods will most likely need both several mocks and multiple verifications. Oververification comes in several forms, as the following sections explain.

Too Many Verifications

Again, using the analogy of state-based tests, a test that has many assertions is most likely a poor test because

- It can break for many reasons
- It's not apparent what it actually checks

The same goes for mock tests that verify too many interactions. When doing this, they get coupled to multiple program elements, which makes them even more sensitive to changes of those elements and makes error localization harder.

Tests that set up many expectations or engage in heavy verification may have a hard time communicating their intent. A test that verifies this, then that, and finally something else will probably just lock down the implementation while providing little value.

Too Precise Verifications

Mocking frameworks make it easy to count the number of interactions with a mock. We've seen an example of this in Scenario 3 a few paragraphs back. Verifying that one thing calls another means locking down the implementation and introducing brittleness. Adding constraints on how many times the call is allowed to be made is even worse. Beware!

A similar argument goes for mocks that are configured to expect interactions to occur in a specific order. Somewhere deep in the codebase, there may be a piece of code that truly benefits from having the order of interactions verified; however, in all other cases—an overwhelming majority—this is the equivalent of inviting a vampire into your home.

Verifying that No Calls Have Been Made

Apart from having ways of verifying how many times an invocation has been made, mocking frameworks also have the ability to verify that *no* interactions have happened with a specific mock. It means that the test says: "I swear and promise, cross my heart, that object A has never called object B during this test." When would that be helpful? Hopefully not too often! There's always the exception to the rule, when it would be absolutely crucial to verify that an invocation has never happened, but in a crushing majority of cases, this just pulls in irrelevant and confusing checks. A developer who's new on the team has no chance of knowing whether the must-never-happen verification is relevant or not. Also, drawing a line for when *not* doing such verifications once you've started is also very difficult. Finally, when developing code test first, would verifying that something doesn't happen before the code is even written feel intuitive? For me it wouldn't.[6]

Summary: How to Verify Expectations

This summary applies to both setting expectations and verifying them, depending on where the majority of the work is done by the framework.

- Verify expectations sparingly.
- Stay away from constructs that make them stricter than necessary.
- Avoid surgically sharp verifications. They just provide a false sense of safety and make changing code a pain because of all the tests that will break for the wrong reasons.

Mocking Concrete Classes

Of all the functionality that mocking frameworks provide, one stands out: whether the framework can mock concrete classes or not. If you're using such a framework, an alarm should go off every time you mock something that's not an interface. In essence it means that you're replacing a class that has a concrete working implementation with one "reimplemented" by the mock object.

---

6. One of the creators of Mockito has written an interesting blog post on a similar topic (Faber 2008).

Interfaces for Mocking

Although mocking at the interface level and providing a mock collaborator implementation feels quite intuitive, introducing artificial interfaces only for the sake of mocking usually doesn't. If this is an issue, take a step back and examine the design. Do your abstractions make sense? Are the relations between the program elements reasonable?

Mocking Value-holding Classes

The low threshold to creating mocks and stubs may lure developers into creating more of them than necessary. This, in turn, may lead to mocks in the wrong places and overly complex and brittle tests. The next example resembles something I've seen more than once in different codebases. Consider a trivial value-holding class like `Person`:

```
public class Person {
    private String firstName;
    private String lastName;
    private int age;

    // Accessors and mutators go here ...
}
```

Regardless of how an object of this class would be used in a test, a real object should be created, not a mock. Sadly, this is what you might see instead:

```
Person person = mock(Person.class)
when(person.getFirstName()).thenReturn("Charlie");
```

This doesn't only look bad. More objective arguments against doing this might include the following:

- Replacing simple working implementations with mocks or stubs may introduce bugs. After all, working code is replaced with a test double. The production code no longer gets tested in some contexts, because it's been replaced.

- Setting up expectations turns simple object initialization into something more complicated. Now you have to read the test thoroughly and sort the stubs into two categories: the important ones and the artificial ones.

- Purely state-based tests now start feeling like behavior-based tests because of the presence of the word "mock" in the initialization of the stub. There are worse problems, but why confuse things if you don't have to?

Mocks Returning Mocks

The Mockito documentation says that whenever a mock returns a mock, a fairy dies.[7] I believe it to be true. Returning a mock from another implies *transitive* digging in interactions between objects. Those who have written enough tests will have found the one case in 500 where this is just the thing you want to do, but in all remaining cases, please let the fairy live.

Summary

Creating stubs and mocks is easy with today's frameworks. They host functionality for test double creation, expectation setup, and interaction verification. *Constraints* or *argument matchers* are important building blocks, because they determine whether a stub will respond to a query and whether a mock counts an interaction as successful. Mocks come as nice, normal, and strict. Nice mocks tolerate unexpected interactions, whereas strict mocks don't, and additionally require that all expected interactions occur—sometimes in a specific order.

Mocking frameworks provide their own matchers, and adding new ones is easy. However, too complex matchers may know too much about the interactions they verify and thus make the tests unnecessarily rigid.

Mock tests can easily be overspecified. Overly restrictive verification doesn't automatically imply correctness, but is often a sign of poor code; things that should be tested somewhere else end up being matched during verification. On the whole, constantly be aware of the trade-off between depth of verification and coupling to the implementation.

Finally, mocking concrete classes and mocks returning mocks should sound your alarm bells.

---

7. http://docs.mockito.googlecode.com/hg/latest/org/mockito/Mockito.html#RETURNS_DEEP_STUBS

Chapter 14

TEST-DRIVEN DEVELOPMENT—
CLASSIC STYLE

Test-driven development (TDD) is the practice of driving the design of code with tests. In contrast to the traditional "write code – verify code" workflow, TDD mandates that the first task in any development undertaking be to write a test. Only then can the code that will make that test pass be written. If faithfully applied, no production code will ever come into existence unless it's preceded and accompanied by at least one test. This doesn't "auto-magically" guarantee correctness of the code, and many people would claim that TDD has nothing to do with testing. That said, test-driven code is, by definition, testable, and after reading the opening paragraphs of Chapter 4, "Testability from a Developer's Perspective," you know that such code stands a better chance of being tested—either by developers, who would add more tests to it to cover all equivalence partitions, edge cases, and possible error scenarios, or testers, who would be able to focus on an observable and controllable part of the system.

Test-driven development is performed in short cycles, each consisting of three phases—*red, green, refactor*. Red and green refer to the color of the bar (or any other visual indicator of failure or pass) displayed by many testing frameworks and IDEs when the test is executed. These are the steps of the workflow:

1. **Red**—Write a test. The test will fail because the functionality needed to make it pass doesn't exist. Often the test won't even compile, because it'll include references to program elements that haven't been created yet.

2. **Green**—Make the test pass. Take any shortcuts necessary, even if they make your eyes and heart bleed.

3. **Refactor**—Remove the badness introduced when making the test pass.

Working like this pushes us toward very short iterations—in the order of magnitude of minutes or even seconds—which consequently results in instantaneous feedback about the state of the code and our progress.

Actually, this is all there is to it, but test-driven development is one of those practices that are simple in theory but that explode into a bunch of questions and technicalities when applied in practice. To illustrate some of them, I'll use a TDD session that happens to demonstrate different practical aspects of the technique.

Test-driving a Simple Search Engine

In this session, I wanted to build a simple search engine. It would search for a word in a number of indexed documents and present the results ordered by the number of occurrences of that word in each document. Thus, when searching for the word *cat*, a document containing the word three times would be ranked higher than one containing it only once. This isn't the most sophisticated ranking scheme, but it should be sufficient for the example.

To make this an actual search engine[1] and not just a toy program that loops through files, I set the constraint that searching must be very fast,[2] whereas indexing may be arbitrarily slow. This specification allowed me to test-drive the search engine toward a certain design built on this simple idea:

- Each document has a unique ID.

- The index maps each word to a list of tuples containing the document ID and the number of times the word occurs in the document with that ID—word frequency.

- The list from the previous step is sorted on word frequency (see Figure 14.1). This enables ranking.

The design guided my choice of implementation at some points, and it allowed me to demonstrate how test-driving something toward specific requirements plays out. Language-wise, I chose Groovy written so that it would read like Java or C#. It gave me a powerful and very verbose `assert` method and a more compact notation around lists. All tests are written in JUnit; however, working with Groovy, I couldn't resist putting their Spock equivalents in Appendix B.

Options and Variations Ahead!

A word of caution! I intentionally didn't strive for a perfect example. There are plenty of those online. I could easily have "discovered" some things earlier, changed the order of tests, or written other tests altogether, but I wanted this session to be a typical TDD session with human decisions and shortcomings. Hence, this session doesn't reflect *the* way of test-driving a simple search engine, but *a* way. Everybody will do test-driven development differently depending on their strengths, weaknesses, preferences, experience, and familiarity with the problem.

---

1. For the sake of the example, I decided on an in-memory implementation, although the design would work for a disk-based solution as well with some adaptations.
2. "Very fast" means constant time with respect to the number of documents, that is, $O(1)$.

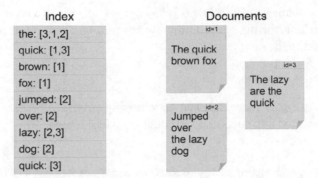

FIGURE 14.1   A simple index. The article "the" occurs in all three documents: twice in the third document and once in the other two. In the index, this is represented as "the: [3,1 2]," where the document with the most occurrences of "the" comes first—document 3. Note that there's a clash between documents 1 and 2 that both contain "the" once. It's been resolved by sorting the contending documents in ascending ID order.

Test 1: Discovering the API

For the first test, I chose the simplest search scenario I could think of—searching for a word in an empty index. I was quite confident that I could make this test pass without any problems.

```
@Test
void searchingWhenNoDocumentsAreIndexedGivesNothing() {
    SearchEngine searchEngine = new SearchEngine()
    assert [] == searchEngine.find("fox")
}
```

The test obviously didn't compile, because it referenced a class and a method that didn't exist. However, it forced me to express in code what a part of the API would look like—searching returns a list of something. Now, to make this test pass, I just added the class and a next-to-empty method.

```
class SearchEngine {
    List<Integer> find(String word) {
        return []
    }
}
```

At this point the objective was to make the test pass, even in a way hurtful to the eyes and the heart. I made it pass using a hard-coded empty list, and I had completed two out of the three elements of the TDD cycle—write a failing test and make it pass. Now it was time for refactoring. Alas, I didn't find anything worth refactoring at this point, so I moved on to the next test.

Test 2: Happy Path

Encouraged by my previous success, I went on to teasing out the full API of my search engine. Besides, I wanted it to succeed in producing its first match.

```
@Test
void searchingForADocumentsOnlyWordGivesThatDocumentsId() {
    SearchEngine searchEngine = new SearchEngine()
    searchEngine.addToIndex(1, "fox")
    assert [1] == searchEngine.find("fox")
}
```

Here I made a rather significant decision that would affect the entire example: I chose to represent the supposed documents as just strings. If this code were to live outside the pages of this example, it would most likely work on streams. In production, these streams would be file streams; in tests, they'd be in-memory streams feeding off strings. Acknowledging this, I decided that there was little to be learned from juggling streams and strings at this point, and it would just hurt the readability of the example code.

```
class SearchEngine {
    def index = []
    void addToIndex(int documentId, String contents) {
        index << 1
    }

    List<Integer> find(String word) {
        return index
    }
}
```

Another hard coding, and index was coming into existence. Progress! This "production" code didn't offer too many opportunities for refactoring. The test code, on the other hand, could be improved by removing the duplicated creation of the searchEngine object. Because I had the feeling that every test would start with this same line of code, I decided to move it to a test initializer method.

```
private SearchEngine searchEngine;
```

```
@Before
void setUp() {
    searchEngine = new SearchEngine()
}

@Test
void searchingWhenNoDocumentsAreIndexedGivesNothing() {
    assert [] == searchEngine.find("fox")
}

@Test
void searchingForADocumentsOnlyWordGivesThatDocumentsId() {
    searchEngine.addToIndex(1, "fox")
    assert [1] == searchEngine.find("fox")
}
```

Test 3: Searching in Multiple Documents

The hard coding bothered me and I wanted to get rid of it. After all, the code could only handle a very specific case. My intention was to make it more generic, which usually happens as more tests are added. I hoped that the next test would push the solution in that direction.

```
@Test
void allIndexedDocumentsAreSearched () {
    searchEngine.addToIndex(1, "fox")
    searchEngine.addToIndex(2, "dog")
    assert [2] == searchEngine.find("dog")
}
```

Changing the list to a map and adding the storing of a one-element list of document IDs in that map did the trick. The test passed.

```
class SearchEngine {
    def index = [:]
    void addToIndex(int documentId, String contents) {
        index[contents] = [documentId]
    }

    List<Integer> find(String word) {
        return index[word]
    }
}
```

I was just getting ready to move on, so I ran the entire test suite to make sure that I was on solid ground, and boom! It turned out that the first test was now failing. It complained about null being returned when a word wasn't present in the index. It was easy to fix. The lookup in the `find` method needed to return something reasonable if there were no matches, like an empty list.

```
List<Integer> find(String word) {
    return index.get(word, [])
}
```

Test 4: More Sophisticated Documents

It was time to make the "documents" more sophisticated by allowing them to contain more than one word. In this case, I decided that my intent with (as well as the semantic concept in) the test was best expressed using two assertions.

```
@Test
void documentsMayContainMoreThanOneWord() {
    searchEngine.addToIndex(1, "the quick brown fox")
    assert [1] == searchEngine.find("brown")
    assert [1] == searchEngine.find("fox")
}
```

I didn't even need to run this to know how miserably it would fail. There was no reading multiple words in the code, so failure was imminent. The good news was that it was easy to fix—just split the input up.

```
class SearchEngine {
    def index = [:]
    void addToIndex(int documentId, String contents) {
        contents.split(" ").each { word -> index[word] = [documentId] }
    }

    List<Integer> find(String word) {
        return index.get(word, [])
    }
}
```

Anything to refactor? Not really, but I wanted to help myself by spelling out what the index actually was, so I introduced the type: `Map<String, List<Integer>> index = [:]`.

Test 5: Finding Words in Multiple Documents

So far, searching only produced empty results or a single document ID. With the next test, I wanted the search engine to be able to find words in multiple documents.

```
@Test
void
searchingForAWordThatMatchesTwoDocumentsGivesBothDocumentsIds() {
    searchEngine.addToIndex(1, "fox")
    searchEngine.addToIndex(2, "fox")
    assert [1, 2] == searchEngine.find("fox")
}
```

This looked quite intimidating at first . . . anticlimax. Only one line of code needed changing. Resolving words to lists put me one step closer to the envisioned design.

```
class SearchEngine {
    Map<String, List<Integer>> index = [:]
    void addToIndex(int documentId, String contents) {
        contents.split(" ").each { word ->
            index.get(word, []) << documentId
        }
    }

    List<Integer> find(String word) {
        return index.get(word, [])
    }
}
```

After having written the code, I realized that the test had passed out of sheer luck. Nothing in the code implied any ordering of document IDs, so what I was getting back was a list that reflected the insertion order. Had I started by adding "fox" to the second document, the test would fail, because `find` would return [2, 1]. I had a number of options here, ranging from a custom matcher that would ignore list order to comparing the lists as sets, but I decided on the simplest one, which was to sort the output before comparing. I just changed the assertion to `assert [1, 2] == searchEngine.find("fox").sort()`

Test 6: Removing Duplicate Matches

Closing in on the intended design, I could start preparing for ranking. For it to work, the result of searching would have to consist of unique document IDs.

```
@Test
void multipleMatchesInADocumentProduceOneMatch () {
    searchEngine.addToIndex(1,
            "the quick brown fox jumped over the lazy dog")
    assert [1] == searchEngine.find("the")
}
```

How does one implement uniqueness? My first idea was that sets can't hold dupli-cates, so I quickly rushed ahead and changed the implementation of the index.

```
class SearchEngine {
    Map<String, Set<Integer>> index = [:]
    void addToIndex(int documentId, String contents) {
        contents.split(" ").each { word ->
            index.get(word, [] as Set) << documentId
        }
    }

    List<Integer> find(String word) {
        def results = []
        results.addAll(index.get(word, []))
        return results
    }
}
```

All tests passed! Now about refactoring . . . the transformation of a set into a list in find didn't turn out too beautiful. Should something be done about that? This was one of the most difficult moments in this session. The tests were all green, but based on the design, I knew that I wouldn't be able to make this work using sets.[3] Therefore, I decided to refactor, not so much in response to the current state of the code, but to prepare for the things to come. As a side effect, the find method became uncluttered again.

```
class SearchEngine {
    Map<String, List<Integer>> index = [:]
    void addToIndex(int documentId, String contents) {
        contents.split(" ").each { word ->
            def documentIds = index.get(word, [])
            if (!documentIds.find {i -> i == documentId} ) {
                documentIds << documentId
            }
```

_____

3. Not with my understanding of the problem at that stage anyway.

```
        }
    }

    List<Integer> find(String word) {
        return index.get(word, [])
    }
}
```

Instead of using a set, I implemented the uniqueness "by hand" by only adding a document ID to a word's list of document IDs if it wasn't already in that list. This proved to be helpful in the upcoming step.

Test 7: Introducing Ranking

Next, I went ahead with a larger step. I wanted the search engine to rank its matches.

```
@Test
void documentsAreSortedByWordFrequency() {
    searchEngine.addToIndex(1, "fox fox dog")
    searchEngine.addToIndex(2, "fox fox fox")
    searchEngine.addToIndex(3, "dog fox dog")
    assert [2, 1, 3] == searchEngine.find("fox")
    assert [3, 1] == searchEngine.find("dog")
}
```

This meant that the index had to store the number of times a word occurred in a given document. The underlying data structure needed changing again. Here I needed to stop. Even though I had just refactored the code in the previous step, I decided that I needed another refactoring[4]; I wanted my implementation of the index to support what I was about to do next. The good thing about this, though, was that it allowed me to demonstrate an important aspect of TDD: *Never refactor with a red bar.* Obediently, I @Ignored the failing test before proceeding.

Guided by my design idea, I knew roughly what to do. I wanted to store the word frequencies somehow. I didn't perceive the upcoming code change as entirely trivial, so I implemented the most naïve solution that I could think of: instead of just storing the document ID for each word, I started storing two values—the document ID and

---

4. In hindsight, this turned out to be more of an application of incremental design than refactoring, and not entirely in the spirit of purist TDD, because it was done in anticipation.

the number of times the current word has appeared in the document with that ID. I chose to call this class `WordFrequency`.[5]

```
class SearchEngine {
    Map<String, List<WordFrequency>> index = [:]
    void addToIndex(int documentId, String contents) {
        contents.split(" ").each { word ->
            def wordFrequencies = index.get(word, [])
            if (!wordFrequencies.find {wf -> wf.documentId == documentId})
            {
                wordFrequencies << new WordFrequency(documentId, 1)
            } else {
                def wordFrequency = wordFrequencies.find
                        { wf -> wf.documentId == documentId }
                wordFrequency.count++
            }
        }
    }

    List<Integer> find(String word) {
        return index.get(word, []).collect { wf -> wf.documentId }
    }
}

class WordFrequency {
    int documentId
    int count

    WordFrequency(int documentId, int count) {
        this.documentId = documentId
        this.count = count
    }
}
```

Now the code reflected the design idea completely. It was neither aesthetically pleasing nor efficient, but it worked! To implement ranking from this vantage point was easy—all I had to do was to re-enable the test and sort the list of word frequencies. I added the following line of code after the if-else in the `addToIndex` method:

---

5. A smaller step here would be to represent the pair as an array. However, I've never been a fan of arrays where the location of the element has a meaning, like it would here: `arr[0]` = `documentId`, `arr[1]` = `frequency`. It's just confusing.

```
wordFrequencies.sort { wf1, wf2 -> wf2.count <=> wf1.count }
```

Red, green, refactor. Now, here were opportunities. I started by removing the obvious duplication of `wordFrequencies.find`. Restructuring the code that added a new word frequency to the list of frequencies allowed me to simplify the `Word-Frequency` class's constructor by dropping the count parameter. Finally, I pulled out all of this code into a new method that I called `bumpWordFrequencyForDocument`.

```
void addToIndex(int documentId, String contents) {
    contents.split(" ").each { word ->
        def wordFrequencies = index.get(word, [])
        bumpWordFrequencyForDocument(wordFrequencies, documentId)
        wordFrequencies.sort { wf1, wf2 -> wf2.count <=> wf1.count }
    }
}


private void bumpWordFrequencyForDocument(List<WordFrequency> frequencies,
        int documentId) {
    def wordFrequency = frequencies.find
            { wf -> wf.documentId == documentId }
    if (!wordFrequency) {
        frequencies << (wordFrequency = new WordFrequency(documentId))
    }
    wordFrequency.count++
}
```

Next, I did something that some might call "premature optimization." Yes, a part of me really suffered inside because of the superfluous sorting that was taking place, though the main reason was that I wanted better readability. I moved away the sorting from the loop and put it into its own method (with some minor adjustments to the target of the sorting). This change made the `addToIndex` method quite small and readable. It also had the advantage of raising the level of abstraction of `addTo-Index`. Instead of dealing with rather atomic operations on maps and lists, it now started to communicate its intent quite clearly.

```
void addToIndex(int documentId, String contents) {
    contents.split(" ").each { word ->
        bumpWordFrequencyForDocument(index.get(word, []), documentId)
    }
    resortIndexOnWordFrequency()
}
private void bumpWordFrequencyForDocument(List<WordFrequency>
        frequencies, int documentId) {
```

```
    def wordFrequency = frequencies.find
            { wf -> wf.documentId == documentId }
    if (!wordFrequency) {
        frequencies << (wordFrequency = new WordFrequency(documentId))
    }
    wordFrequency.count++
}

private resortIndexOnWordFrequency() {
    index.each { k, wfs -> wfs.sort
            { wf1, wf2 -> wf2.count <=> wf1.count } }
}
```

Test 8: Ignoring Case

Now that I had implemented the intended design, I went for some finish. Making the search engine treat uppercase and lowercase equally was one such detail. This would keep the index to a manageable size and make lookups work in a reasonable way. Thus, the next test was about mixing cases and making sure that it didn't matter.

```
@Test
public void caseDoesNotMatter() {
    searchEngine.addToIndex(1, "FOX fox FoX");
    searchEngine.addToIndex(2, "foX FOx");
    searchEngine.addToIndex(3, "FoX");
    assert [1, 2, 3] == searchEngine.find("fox")
    assert [1, 2, 3] == searchEngine.find("FOX")
}
```

Making this pass wasn't very exciting. It was a matter of adding toUpper-Case() in two places. In my eyes it didn't break the code enough to mandate any refactoring.

```
void addToIndex(int documentId, String contents) {
    contents.split(" ").each { word ->
        bumpWordFrequencyForDocument(index.get(word.toUpperCase(), []),
                documentId)
    }
    resortIndexOnWordFrequency()
}

List<Integer> find(String word) {
    return index.get(word.toUpperCase(), []).collect {wf -> wf.documentId}
}
```

Test 9: Dealing with Punctuation Marks

As a last step, I decided to strip away some punctuation marks from the index. After all, they were guilty of introducing extraneous words into the index and messing up lookups. For example, "quick," and "quick;" were two separate index entries at this point due to the splitting at word boundaries.

```
@Test
public void punctuationMarksAreIgnored() {
    searchEngine.addToIndex(1, "quick, quick: quick.");
    searchEngine.addToIndex(2, "(brown) [brown] \"brown\" 'brown'");
    searchEngine.addToIndex(3, "fox; -fox fox? fox!");

    assert [1] == searchEngine.find("quick")
    assert [2] == searchEngine.find("brown")
    assert [3] == searchEngine.find("fox")
}
```

I let the test spell out what punctuation marks I cared about. Again, I went with what I thought was the obvious solution. After all, test-driven development isn't about taking tiny steps all the time. It's about being able to (Beck 2002).

```
void addToIndex(int documentId, String contents) {
    contents.replaceAll("[\\.,!\\?:;\\(\\)\\[\\]\\-\"']", "")
            .split(" ").each {
                    word -> bumpWordFrequencyForDocument(
                            index.get(word.toUpperCase(), []), documentId)
                    }
    resortIndexOnWordFrequency()
}
```

As soon as I had finished typing the regular expression for replacement, I saw the refactoring I needed to do, but first I ran all tests and was rewarded with the green bar. Now, what would the last refactoring of the session be? It struck me that I had added similar logic in two different places. I had placed conversion to uppercase after splitting the document into words, but for some reason, I had decided that the stripping of punctuation marks should be done before breaking the document up into words. Both of these operations are in fact preprocessing. I made that clear in code by extracting them into a method.

```
void addToIndex(int documentId, String contents) {
    preProcessDocument(contents).split(" ").each { word ->
        bumpWordFrequencyForDocument(index.get(word, []), documentId)
```

```
    }
    resortIndexOnWordFrequency()
}

private String preProcessDocument(String contents) {
    return contents.replaceAll("[\\.,!\\?:;\\(\\)\\[\\]\\-\"']", "")
            .toUpperCase()
}
```

This concludes this book's TDD session. Now I'll bring in some TDD theory to explain some decisions and turns I've made throughout it.

Note

All source code produced in this session can be found in Appendix B.

Order of Tests

Deciding in what order to write tests (and what tests to write) is often quite a challenge for developers new to test-driven development. Ironically, the order is rather important. Your sequence of tests should not only help you make progress, but also learn as much as possible and avoid the inherent risks of your implementation while doing it. Conversely, if you have no strategy for picking the next test to write, you're likely to start spinning around interesting or easy cases, or you run out of ideas. Next time, try writing your tests in the following order:

1. **Degenerate case**—Start with a test that operates on an "empty" value like zero, null, the empty string, or the like. It'll help to tease out the interface while ensuring that it can be passed very quickly.

2. **One or a few happy path tests**—Such a test/tests will lay the foundation for the implementation while remaining focused on the core functionality.

3. **Tests that provide new information or knowledge**—Don't dig in one spot. Try approaching the solution from different angles by writing tests that exercise different parts of it and that teach you something new about it.

4. **Error handling and negative tests**—These tests are crucial to correctness, but seldom to design. In many cases, they can safely be written last.

Red- to Green-bar Strategies

Turning a red bar into a green bar is also an art. The intuitive reflex is often to type what we believe is the correct solution. However, there are other ways, especially if we're not dead certain in which direction the solution is going. In his book *Test-driven Development by Example*, Kent Beck (2002) offers three strategies for turning a red bar into a green bar. The sample session includes them all.

- **Faking**—This is the simplest way to make a test pass. Just return or do whatever the particular test expects. If the test expects a specific value, then just hand it over. Tests that pass after faking usually break when the next test wants something that isn't a constant value or fixed behavior.

  This technique is easy to spot. Hard-coded values, especially in the early tests, are faked values. Remember the hard-coded lists in the first tests?

- **The obvious implementation**—Sometimes beating about the bush just isn't worth it. If we know what to type, then we should type it. The twist is that seemingly obvious implementations may yield a red bar.

  Using the obvious implementation usually implies taking slightly larger steps. I did it several times in the example. However, notice that I never took the technique to its limits by typing in the entire algorithm in one breath. Doing this would actually probably not work, because it would force me to implement every single detail correctly. Had I made a mistake doing it, I'd have to resort to development by debugging, which is kind of regressing to old, bad habits.

- **Triangulation**—Some algorithms can be teased out by providing a number of examples and then generalizing. This is called *triangulation* and has its roots in geometry. Reasonably, a single test may be made green by faking, whereas multiple tests with different parameters and expected results will push the code in the direction of a general algorithm. The catch with triangulation is that once the solution is teased out, some of the tests can be deleted, because they're redundant. This, however, would degenerate the scenario to something that could be solved using a nongeneral algorithm or even a constant.

Alternatives and Inspiration

In the beginning of this chapter, I made it sound like test-driven development is very simple. In a way it is, but as this chapter has shown, there's a lot of room for freedom and interpretation in the technique. In this light, I'd like to point out that the style of TDD I've used here is easy to learn for beginners, but it deviates slightly from what you may find in other books.

The greatest source of inspiration for my style of TDD is Kent Beck's book *Test-driven Development by Example* (2002). This is where the red-green bar patterns come from and where I've learned that the size of the steps we take is dependent on our level of security and comfort. The difference between my style and the style described in that book is around removal of duplication. In Beck's book, refactoring is about removing duplication. This is what *drives* the design. My refactorings sometimes address duplication, but more often they aim for conciseness and removal of particularly ugly code.

If you feel like getting more rigorous and keeping to small steps to make sure that no code whatsoever will come into existence without a test, I suggest that you read the chapter on TDD in Robert C. Martin's book *The Clean Coder* (2011) and his online material. His way of doing TDD results in all steps being as small as possible. He has also found a way to break TDD impasses in which you feel that you need to take a big step without the support of the tests. Read his work on the *Transformation Priority Premise* (Martin 2010).

Challenges

When adopting test-driven development, a team faces some challenges that it must overcome rather quickly. If most of the issues I'm about to describe aren't swiftly resolved, they turn the adoption into a painful process and a team trauma. Not convinced? Try this scenario and send me a penny for every line you've heard at work.

Imagine Monday morning. Positive Peter and Negative Nancy are just getting their morning coffee from the machine. Barry Boss bounces in . . .

Barry Boss: I went to this cool conference last week. They did TDD maaagic. So must we! It'll make us ten times as productive!

Positive Peter: Our team has been experimenting a little (without telling you), but our codebase hasn't been designed with testability in mind and is a mess. We need to make some structural changes to it first, or start on a new system.

Barry Boss: What would that cost me?

Positive Peter: Well, we've always been rushing toward the next release and accumulating technical debt without addressing it, so I'd say . . . a couple of weeks.

Barry Boss: What? Weeks without productivity! Start doing this TDD thing on the next project, which is due in eight months.

Positive Peter: (Sighs and starts walking away thinking about how to update his resume)

Negative Nancy: That's right! Our code is special. It's like no other code in the world. Our business rules are uniquely complex. Therefore, they cannot be unit tested, so trying this test-driving thing is doomed to fail. Others can do it, but their code isn't as mission critical as ours.

Barry Boss (in a solemn voice): Indeed. Our code is special and mission critical.

Negative Nancy (feeling victorious): And besides, even if we had tried this thing, it wouldn't have given us complete testing anyway!

This short dialog embodies four very common challenges facing a team that's on its way to adopt TDD.

Our Code Can't Be Tested

One of the most common challenges when introducing TDD is the demoralizing and often truly challenging presence of legacy code. Many who return from a two-day workshop on test-driven development aren't able to fathom how what they've learned in a controlled environment can be transferred to their system. They usually have a point.

Legacy code is code without tests, but more importantly, it's code that isn't designed with testability in mind. Such code tends to be riddled with temporal coupling and indirect input. It houses a multitude of monster methods,[6] and its components are intertwined in a bizarre web of dependencies that have spun out of control. Adding any kind of test to such code may be no small feat.

Basically, there are two ways of introducing test-driven development into a legacy codebase:

- Do it only on new classes, components, or subsystems—everything that can be designed from scratch and isn't tainted by the legacy code.

- Refactor the old code to make it testable enough so that it can be modified and extended in a test-driven fashion. A big-bang refactoring of the whole legacy codebase is pretty much always out of the question, so the work needs to proceed incrementally. Only the code that's closest to the functionality that needs changing or extending is refactored. Sometimes even that is too great

---

6. Monster method: A complicated method of high cyclomatic complexity with many areas of responsibility. Most likely, at least 100 lines long.

an undertaking. In such cases we can only opt for refactoring away one or a few antitestability constructs and postpone 100 percent TDD for another occasion. This is an incarnation of the Boy Scout Rule.[7]

Often, this challenge is of the chicken and the egg nature: in order to make code testable, we need to write enough tests to get a feeling for what testable code looks like. And conversely, in order to write tests, we need a testable codebase.

Our Code Is Special

This is a slight variation of "our code can't be tested" and is by far the most common argument against unit testing and test-driven development (in fact, any kind of quality measures performed by developers). It goes like this: *"Other businesses' code is testable by nature or simpler than ours. Therefore, they can test it. Our code, on the other hand, is **special** and can't be tested."*

This is simply not true. The only "special" thing about untestable code is that it's especially coupled, tangled, twisted, and intertwined. All of these properties are endangering a successful adoption of test-driven development, but the attitude and belief that the code *really is* special are even more damaging.

Test-driven Development Isn't Complete Testing

In my experience, this argument is brought up in organizations where there's a culture of spending lots of time thinking about perfect solutions in advance and trying to implement them, or doing nothing at all (i.e., a combination of analysis paralysis and an "all or nothing" attitude). It's also reinforced by strong QA departments that advocate separate testing phases and the unique and independent tester mind-set. In such organizations it doesn't "pay off" to do something that will inspire confidence at one level but may need complementary techniques (such as end-to-end testing) to provide a sufficient overall coverage and confidence. Furthermore, the fact that *developers* do some *"testing"* isn't mildly looked upon either.

This argument goes against the very fundamental premise behind this book, which is about developers doing as much as they can to ensure correctness. The fact that unit testing needs to be complemented by other activities aimed at ensuring quality shouldn't be controversial, but axiomatic. No single technique in itself is sufficient to guarantee that a complex system works correctly. That's why we rely on different aspects of developer testing, static analysis, continuous integration, code reviews

---

7. Boy Scouts are supposed to leave the campground cleaner than they found it. So should developers do with code.

and pair programming, sometimes formal methods, and eventually various types of manual testing. Test-driven development, with its emphasis on unit tests, provides a good foundation for many quality assurance activities.

Starting from Zero

Yet another challenge to adopting test-driven development is that the introduction exposes various deficiencies and shortcomings in the organization's way of working. Often, the problem isn't that the team or organization lacks the practice of test-driven development. Rather, it's that it lacks

- A suite of unit tests and the skills to develop it
- A CI environment that runs the tests
- Proficiency in testing frameworks and libraries
- Knowledge about what and how to test
- A codebase that's designed with testability in mind
- The culture and interest to care about these things

(By the way, did you notice that this book just happens to be about these topics?)

In such circumstances, taking the step toward test-driven development is an enormous challenge. Many practices have to be learned, revised, and improved at once.

Test First or Test Last?

Is code developed "test first" superior to code developed "test last" with good unit testing discipline? A question of this magnitude deserves a diplomatic answer: it depends.

Testability depends on controllability and observability, not on time and precedence. Knowing how to handle constructs that have an adverse impact on controllability and observability, we can safely write tests after having written the production code. For example, if we happen to remember that the presence of the new operator in the code we're about to write will probably result in indirect input, then we obviously need to externalize this creation by using injection, a factory method, a factory class, or some other construct that can be controlled by the test. If we think in terms of contracts with reasonable preconditions and postconditions, our interfaces will be just as good as if driven by tests. From this perspective, writing the test after the production code doesn't matter. To be perfectly clear: by "after," I mean *seconds or minutes* after, not weeks or months!

However . . .

Learning what testable code looks and feels like takes quite some time. Also learning it in theory may be hard; it's best experienced in practice. In this regard, starting with test-driven development offers a gentle and stepwise introduction. In addition, the practice helps in maintaining the discipline to get the tests written. Tests written supposedly after the production code may be forgotten or omitted in the heat of battle. This will never happen when working test first.

Then there's the issue of applying TDD to drive the design of the system, not the individual modules. Test-driving at this level competes with old-school design work. Yes, a developer experienced in producing good interaction protocols and interfaces is likely to get them right to some extent, but that might be a gamble with no feedback loops.

On the other hand . . .

Test-driven development requires being able to visualize both the solution and how to test the solution, which can be an obstacle with technologies that are new or unfamiliar to the developer.

To summarize, code following reasonable contracts written in a testable way may be just as "good" as code written using test-driven development. However, working test first definitely makes achieving testability, correctness, and good design a lot easier.

Summary

Test-driven development is a way of using tests to drive the design of the code. By writing the test before the code, we make the code decoupled and testable.

Test-driven development is performed in a three-phase cycle:

1. Write a failing test

2. Make it pass

3. Refactor

The refactoring stage is crucial to the technique's success, because this is where many principles of good design are applied. When adding tests, the following order of doing it usually helps:

1. Degenerate case

2. One or more happy path tests

3. Tests that provide more information

4. Negative tests

There are three ways of making tests pass:

- *Faking*—Returning the expected value hard-coded to fake a computation
- *The obvious implementation*—Using the obvious code that would solve the problem
- *Triangulation*—Teasing out the algorithm by providing example after example of different inputs and expected results

Common challenges when introducing test-driven development are

- *Our code can't be tested*—The misconception that legacy code is beyond redemption
- *Our code is special*—The misconception that the organization's code is more complex than others
- *Test-driven development isn't complete testing*—The misconception that test-driven development is useless because it must be complemented by other means of quality assurance
- *Starting from zero*—The lack of fundamental practices that precede test-driven development

There's nothing magical about code created using test-driven development. Such code can be crafted without writing tests first. However, doing this requires a lot of experience.

Chapter 15

TEST-DRIVEN DEVELOPMENT— MOCKIST STYLE

The kind of test-driven development that was presented in the prior chapter will get us far, but truth be told, there are situations in which it's hard to apply. Many developers work with large enterprise systems—often much larger than necessary due to overinflated design and accidental complexity—composed of several layers. Test-driving a new feature starting at the boundary of an enterprise system using the techniques we've seen so far is challenging, even for seasoned TDD practitioners. This type of complexity is also demoralizing to those who are just beginning to learn test-driven development.

A Different Approach

Let's say that we've been tasked with implementing a simple web service for registering new customers and their payment details. Such functionality is common enough in a typical customer-facing enterprise system. The overall requirements for this first version of the solution are that customers should be able to pay with direct bank transfers and the major credit cards (PayPal and Bitcoin will appear in version 2.0).

A quick session at the whiteboard reveals the design idea shown in Figure 15.1, guided by the system's existing architecture and design conventions.

Now, suppose that we want to test-drive a customer registration endpoint, which happens to be a RESTful web service that interacts with other services, which, in turn, call repositories[1] and client code that communicates with external parties. What would the `assertEquals` of the first test look like? What if the customer registration endpoint doesn't even return anything except for HTTP status codes? Fortunately, there is a solution.

The quick design session exposes a couple of components with different roles and responsibilities. Some of them may already exist in the current system; some may need adding. Nevertheless, the sketch tells us how the different objects should interact and collaborate. From here we can test-drive this design, and the various interactions between the objects, before getting to details such as persistence and external

---

1. As in "repository pattern" from domain-driven design.

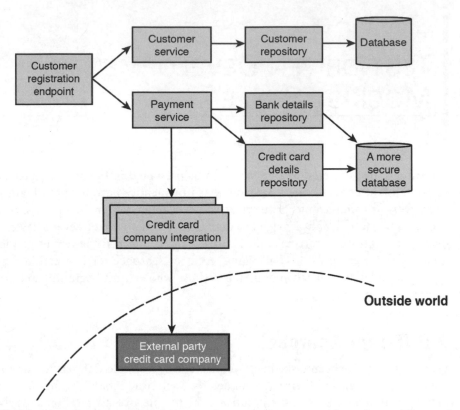

FIGURE 15.1 Components required to implement customer registration, while staying true to the system's architecture and design guidelines.

integrations. The sketch also hints that the majority of operations are what one would call "commands," that is, instructions to do something, not to return something. In other words, most of the design follows the "Tell, Don't Ask" principle (or Law of Demeter, if you will).

A situation like this is ideal for the *mockist* style of test-driven development, which focuses on interfaces and interactions and favors the use of mock objects to do so. It also encourages doing some design thinking before writing the tests.

Test-driving Customer Registration

In this style of test-driven development, we usually start as close to the system boundary or the user as possible. We then write a test that would tease out the interactions with the closest collaborators. Eager to get started, we avoid the technical complexity around making the customer registration service some kind of network-aware endpoint, and focus on its interface and interactions with its closest collaborators instead. Hence, the purpose of the first test is to drive these interactions.

```
@Test
public void personalAndCardDetailsAreSavedForCreditCardCustomers() {
    CustomerRegistrationEndpoint testedEndpoint
            = new CustomerRegistrationEndpoint();
    CustomerService customerServiceStub = mock(CustomerService.class);
    PaymentService paymentServiceMock = mock(PaymentService.class);
    testedEndpoint.setCustomerService(customerServiceStub);
    testedEndpoint.setPaymentService(paymentServiceMock);

    RegistrationDetails details = new RegistrationDetails();
    details.firstName = "Joe";
    details.lastName = "Jones";
    details.paymentType = "C";
    details.cardType = "VISA";
    details.cardNumber = "1111222233334444";
    details.cvv2 = "123";

    Customer customer = new Customer("Joe", "Jones");
    CustomerId newCustomerId = new CustomerId(12345);

    when(customerServiceStub.registerCustomer(customer))
            .thenReturn(newCustomerId);

    testedEndpoint.registerCustomer(details);

    CreditCardDetails cardDetails
            = new CreditCardDetails(CreditCardType.VISA,
                111122223334444L, 123);
    verify(paymentServiceMock)
            .registerCreditCard(newCustomerId, cardDetails);
}
```

This is a gigantic test (it took around 15 minutes to write). True, it could have been simpler, but because we already have a design idea, we don't need to strive for the simplest thing that could possibly work. Given some building blocks and a general feeling for the solution, aiming for an intuitive API feels more natural, to me at least.

In an actual system, some of the classes would already exist and there would be less work putting everything together, but nonetheless, the test would still require a lot of work. What can we deduce from this first test?

- **The method of invocation is established**—The tested method is called with an object of a class that only has public string fields. This indicates that we expect `RegistrationDetails` to be populated by a framework that converts XML or JSON into Java.

- **The interface to the collaborators is specified**—Both services have registration methods that operate on domain objects (`registerCustomer`, `register-CreditCard`). We've just determined how to call the collaborators.

- **Domain classes are revealed**—`CustomerId`, `CustomerDetails`, `CreditCardDetails`, and the `CreditCardType` enum. As said before, these classes may already be present in the system or may have just been discovered.

- **The order of interactions is specified**—Not only have we specified which objects to collaborate with, the test also tells us that we register the customer first to get a customer ID, which is required to register the payment method.

Missing Fields

Some fields have been left out from the registration details, like address, maybe date of birth, card holder's name, and card expiration date. In real code they would be there, but I wanted to keep the example short and relevant.

Now, notice that there's only one verification, so to make this test pass, we could just use the simplest of the red-green bar strategies—faking (Beck 2002).

```java
public class CustomerRegistrationEndpoint {
    private CustomerService customerService;
    private PaymentService paymentService;

    public void registerCustomer(RegistrationDetails details) {
        paymentService.registerCreditCard(new CustomerId(54321),
            new CreditCardDetails(CreditCardType.VISA,
                    1111222233334444L, 123));
    }

    public void setCustomerService(CustomerService customerService) {
        this.customerService = customerService;
    }

    public void setPaymentService(PaymentService  paymentService) {
        this.paymentService = paymentService;
    }
}
```

This code will make the test pass; the customer details are completely ignored and hard-coded credit card details are being registered. However, by initializing both the registration details and customer details to consistent reasonable values in the test, and by providing a stub of `CustomerService` that really uses them, I wanted to create some maneuvering room for the upcoming production code.

Using faking to make the test pass is fine, but if you trust your design and are comfortable with mock objects, I suggest nailing the entire chain of interactions in one sweep.[2] After all, this style of test-driven development is best suited for driving the interactions between objects, and a well-written test should provide enough groundwork for an obvious implementation (the second red-green bar strategy). In this case, it would be along these lines:

```
public void registerCustomer(RegistrationDetails details) {
    Customer customer = new Customer(details.firstName,
            details.lastName);
    CustomerId newCustomerId = customerService.registerCustomer(customer);
    paymentService.registerCreditCard(newCustomerId,
        new CreditCardDetails(CreditCardType.valueOf(details.cardType),
            Long.parseLong(details.cardNumber),
            Long.parseLong(details.cvv2)));
}
```

Not so scary, right? Nothing's faked and all values are being faithfully shuffled between the interacting objects. Still, this is pretty rough code. It contains no error handling, and the parsing looks crude[3] (which means that `CustomerRegistrationEndpoint` definitely needs some more tests). However, it *does* illustrate the interactions needed for registering a customer who pays with a credit card. In the refactoring stage, I'd probably move the creation of the `CreditCardDetails` domain object to a separate method to get rid of the parsing, which looks out of place because it's on a different level of abstraction than the rest of the code. What's more interesting is the next test!

What that would be is far from obvious. It could be one of these:

- A test of `CustomerRegistrationEndpoint` with a customer who wants to pay using direct bank transfers. This would detail more of the main flow.

- A test of `CustomerService` to discover the interaction with the customer repository.

---

2. This again is a way of saying that we can take larger steps while doing test-driven development if we feel secure.
3. So crude that one of my reviewers objected to even using the word *parsing*.

- A test of `PaymentService` to explore the invocation of the code that integrates with the credit card gateway and persists the result.

In the previous chapter, it was said that we should pick tests along the happy path or tests that provide us with more information and knowledge. At this point, testing registration of another payment type would provide little information. The design sketch tells us that no new collaborators would be introduced (both services are already used in the first test), so the test would be quite similar to the one for registering customers paying with credit cards. Although it wouldn't be wrong in any way to explore that alley, going forward with one of the other tests should be more enlightening.

Discovering what persistence of insensitive data in the database would look like seems easy enough, so a test of `CustomerService` it is.

```
@Test
public void validCustomerIsPersistedDuringRegistration() {
    CustomerServiceImpl testedService = new CustomerServiceImpl();
    CustomerRepository customerRepositoryMock
            = mock(CustomerRepository.class);
    testedService.setCustomerRepository(customerRepositoryMock);
    Customer customer = new Customer("Joe", "Jones");
    testedService.registerCustomer(customer);
    verify(customerRepositoryMock).save(customer);
}
```

This is a typical "pass-through" test; it verifies that one layer calls another layer. You'll be writing a lot of these in enterprise applications (which should really make you start thinking about design and architecture). Still, it takes us in the right direction. It brings the `CustomerServiceImpl`[4] class to life and defines the interaction between the service and the repository.

Because we're still concerned with credit card registrations, the next test would tease out a concrete implementation of `PaymentService`, which would be of a pass-through nature as well.

```
@Test
public void registerNewCardDetailsAndStoreSecureIdentifier() {
    final CustomerId customerId = new CustomerId(12345);
    PaymentServiceImpl testedService = new PaymentServiceImpl();
```

---

4. Many people consider naming classes ending with "Impl" to be an antipattern, and I agree. However, I'm not trying to present perfect code, but code that we've all seen time after time and that we can relate to.

```
CreditCardRepository cardRepositoryMock
        = mock(CreditCardRepository.class);
CreditCardGateway creditCardGatewayStub
        = mock(CreditCardGateway.class);

testedService.setCreditCardRepository(cardRepositoryMock);
testedService.setCreditCardGateway(CreditCardType.VISA,
        creditCardGatewayStub);

CreditCardDetails cardDetails
        = new CreditCardDetails(CreditCardType.VISA,
                1111222233334444L, 123);
when(creditCardGatewayStub.registerCreditCard("1111222233334444",
        "123")).thenReturn("FA04BC12");

testedService.registerCreditCard(customerId, cardDetails);

verify(cardRepositoryMock).save(
        new SecureCreditCardId(customerId, "FA04BC12"));
}
```

Being more complex than the test for `CustomerService`, this test forces us to start thinking about how data is represented. For example, the interface to the credit card gateway seems to be string oriented, whereas our code uses domain objects like `SecureCreditCardId`.

Adding More Tests

Had the example included more components, it would become quite apparent that I've been adding tests in a breadth-first manner. It's the most convenient approach in systems where the various layers pretty much just delegate calls to lower-layer components. But what do we do once we reach "fringe" classes like `Customer-Repository` (see Figure 15.2), the nameless integration client, a domain class, or a class that performs some computation?

We switch strategies! Testing such classes using mock objects makes little sense. If the fringe class performs persistence or calls a remote system, an integration test of some sort would probably be required.[5] Conversely, if it performs a computation, a normal state-based unit test will suffice.

---

5. Actually, we could write a mock test here as well, but it would have to be accompanied by an integration test.

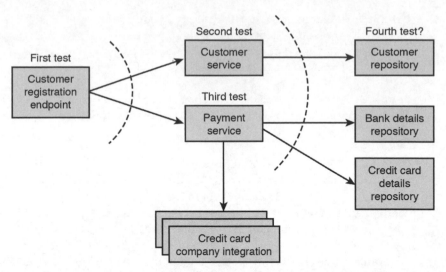

FIGURE 15.2   When using the mockist style in a layered system, we are in practice adding mock-based tests breadth first. Then, we switch strategy at the fringes.

Shunning Mockist TDD

In my opinion, many resources often make irrelevant comparisons between mockist and classic TDD, especially the older ones. Often, they talk about a purely algorithmic problem, try solving it using a mockist approach, and judge it inferior. Such resources also often use words like always and never. An argument could go like this: "A mockist TDD practitioner will always use mocks. When test-driving a sorting algorithm, he will verify that elements are swapped, but his test will never actually be able to tell whether the list has indeed been sorted."

There are drawbacks with interaction-based testing, and they've already been covered in Chapter 12, "Test Doubles." Used excessively, such tests will lock down the implementation, but used with care, such tests will help in discovering well-designed interactions. Therefore, use the style that's suitable for the problem at hand, and don't be afraid of switching between classic and mockist TDD.

Double-loop TDD

Developing code using only mock-based interaction tests should make you feel a little uneasy. At the end of the day, such tests won't determine whether the program works *as a whole.* It's great that the design has been driven by tests and that all interactions are verified, but does it all come together? Remember that each test only checks interactions between collaborators in adjacent layers.

The authors of the book *Growing Object-Oriented Software, Guided by Tests* describe a great solution to this (Freeman & Pryce 2009). Although they never use this term themselves, if I recall correctly, they propose *double-loop TDD*.

Another Feedback Loop

Double loop TDD adds, as the name would suggest, another feedback loop to the development cycle (see Figure 15.3). This is achieved by introducing an automated "acceptance test,"[6] which is created *before* writing the first unit test (targeting the object closest to the system boundary). The test is written so that it exercises the feature to be implemented end to end. By writing such a test, we get three benefits:

- It lets us verify that all interaction tests, and any other unit tests for that matter, add up to a working solution.

- It tells us when a larger chunk of functionality is *actually* finished.

- It forces us to deploy and invoke the new feature in a realistic way.

Depending on the type of application, "end-to-end" may mean different things. Anyhow, the purpose of the test is to execute the system from the outside so that all of it must be deployed somehow and so that the tested functionality will be accessed in the same way a user or another system would access it. Given the various deployment options and complexities of some application stacks, creating the first automated end-to-end acceptance test will be a challenge, because it will require the *entire* infrastructure to be in place before any production code is written. However, this places the new functionality in a context and allows verifying the technology stack and its components from the very beginning of the development effort. No more late-integration problems!

Do you remember the first example in this chapter, the customer registration endpoint? Testing it by an end-to-end test would have you do the following:

1. Start the framework or container that would provide a web service for performing the registration

2. Deploy/start the registration endpoint

3. Post registration details to the endpoint

---

6. I've put the words in quotes, because the test is technical and has little to do with user acceptance.

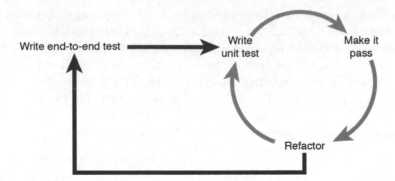

FIGURE 15.3   Double-loop TDD: The outer feedback loop consists of an end-to-end "acceptance test," and classic and mockist TDD provide the inner loop.

4. Verify the result

5. Shut everything down

Points 1, 2, and 5 are essential plumbing, although they force you to decide how to deploy the endpoint.[7] To get past point 3, you'd have to figure out whether the test should use a framework to invoke the service, or take a more "raw" approach, like a hand-crafted HTTP POST request. Point 4 is the interesting one. How would you verify the result? In an end-to-end test, querying the underlying database for the secure identifier would be cheating under normal circumstances. However, because it's a *secure* identifier, it might be the only way (unless the test grows even larger to include a call to the credit card gateway where the identifier is present). Such conundrums are the topic of Chapter 18, "Beyond Unit Testing."

Closing the Circle

Back in Chapter 2, "Testing Objectives, Styles, and Roles," I briefly mentioned BDD, acceptance test-driven development, and specification by example—three techniques all of which have one thing in common: they rely on automatic acceptance tests derived from examples developed together with the customer. Hence, viewing these techniques as double-loop TDD isn't controversial in any way.

---

7. This is no easy decision by any means. Many options have become available in recent years. First, you need to decide on whether to deploy to the cloud, a local virtual machine, or good old bare metal. Second, you may decide on using a virtual machine manager, like Vagrant. Third, you may go for a tool that does the provisioning, like Chef or Puppet, or to use lightweight virtualization. Docker is the de facto standard at the time of writing. Then there's the choice of bootstrapping the application . . .

Summary

Mockist TDD is an alternative approach to test-driven development (in contrast to "classic" TDD). This style primarily focuses on the *design of the system*, not the implementation of individual classes. As the name suggests, mock objects play a large role, as they are used to drive the interactions and to establish interfaces between objects.

   Double-loop TDD means that unit tests are preceded by automated end-to-end acceptance tests, which require the entire infrastructure and deployment process of the feature to be in place. Such tests will fail until the entire feature is implemented. Adding this safety net to test-driven development is particularly helpful if the majority of the tests are based on mock objects and it's hard to decide whether the sum of all interactions equals a correct implementation of the feature.

Chapter 16

DUPLICATION

Duplication is the root of many evils in software development and is particularly harmful for testability, which was broken down into observability, controllability, and smallness in Chapter 4, "Testability from a Developer's Perspective," where I claimed that duplicated code presented an additional challenge to testing. The argument was that there was no way to infer that if certain functionality was tested from one entry point in the application, it would behave the same if accessed from another.

Why Duplication Is Bad

From a test-aware developer's point of view, duplication is bad in several ways:

- **Duplication breeds duplication**—Now this may sound like a circular argument, but bear with me. Like many other bad programming practices, duplication is prone to the broken window syndrome.[1] It means that if there's no duplicated code in the system (no broken window), then everybody will think twice before becoming the first to go wild on the keyboard shortcuts for copy and paste. Conversely, if there are already heaps of duplicated code (the windows are broken), then breaking yet another window doesn't matter.

- **There's more of everything**—Duplication adds to the existing mass of code. In particular, programming by copy and paste results in more code to be browsed, covered by tests, compiled, and packaged. IDEs that index the code will also suffer performance-wise. More code results in more stress on the developer's short-term memory. Mental resources must be spent to keep track of what duplicated version of the code you're looking at and how many more there are.

- **Duplication introduces bugs**—There are special kinds of bugs that only arise from duplicating things that shouldn't be duplicated. Imagine a business rule, or any kind of behavior, being duplicated across three different program

---

1. Broken window theory (short and simplified): An abandoned building will start getting vandalized once one of its windows gets broken. The broken window signals that nobody cares and invites to doing more damage.

elements. Individually, these program elements may actually be covered by tests. Now, should the business rule change, a very keen and thorough developer is required. That developer must locate *all* duplicated implementations of that rule and change them. Not doing so, by leaving one implementation out, results in a dialog like the following between Ursula the user and our developer David:

Ursula: Didn't we lower the minimum age of customers from 20 to 18 last week?

David: Yes, we did. Look here. When registering on our site, I can enter 18 as age and get registered.

Ursula: True, and I've seen that we are sending promotions to such customers, but they don't appear in the CMS.

David (after browsing some code): Duh. I forgot to change *that* code.

Ursula: How about the reports then?

David: Let me check . . .

In my experience these conversations take place far too often. Usually, the outcome is that the level of confidence in the software, and eventually the developer's ability, drops. A user doesn't understand or care about the fact that the developer has scattered duplicates of functionality and business rules throughout the codebase and must maintain all of them.

- **Duplication messes up metrics**—Apart from monitoring test coverage, professional developers will use all sorts of metrics to gauge the quality of their code: number of constructs that often cause bugs, number of violations of coding conventions and guidelines, and cyclomatic complexity, to name a few. How does duplication mess this up? Consider a piece of code that contains some particularly nasty nesting, which triggers warnings about cyclomatic complexity. Duplicating this code will immediately double the number of warnings. True, more code has been added, but no new code has been written.

  Duplication, and in particular copy and paste programming, affects the reliability of various coverage metrics. What does 10 percent statement coverage mean for a codebase where at least half of the code has been duplicated by copy and paste programming? Fortunately, there's a corollary to this: the fastest way to increase test coverage is to remove duplicated code. Code goes away; the amount of code covered by tests goes up. Ta-da!

Metric Tip of the Day

It's been said in the preceding paragraph, but it's worth repeating—
The fastest way to increase test coverage is to delete code![2]

Taking Advantage of Duplication

Duplication can't be only bad, because nobody would duplicate anything if there were only downsides to it. What people usually pursue by duplicating is productivity. It can indeed be achieved, but not in the manner it's typically done.

Generally, programming by copying and pasting code is not a productive way of working. Sadly, some organizations have a culture of admiring the *quantity*[3] of code written—the person who produces the most code is the hero. I've seen developers produce around 1,000 lines of code per day by "reusing" existing code. This worked in the short run, as long as everything fit in one person's head, but the systems produced in this fashion had to be scrapped rather quickly, because they were impossible to maintain.

Then there are the exceptions. If you run a short online campaign each year that requires a few adjustments to the previous year's code, then maybe copying the entire site from last year will save some time. Similarly, if your mobile game app is expected to live for six months and never enter maintenance, maybe it'll pay off to assemble it from other existing game apps in a copy and paste manner. In short, developing noncritical systems with short life spans may benefit from slapping together existing pieces of code.

A more sustainable way to achieve productivity by allowing a degree of duplication would be to acknowledge that singularity, the opposite of duplication, introduces bottlenecks and coupling. If nothing is duplicated, then testability is outstanding from a singularity point of view. However, some hot spots in the code may lead to queues and quarrels, as multiple teams struggle to work in these areas simultaneously, while trying to ensure that they don't break anybody else's functionality. By relaxing the requirement on everything being totally singular and allowing parallel implementations, we can increase throughput. The trick is to either build a very loosely coupled system or partition it in such a way that this becomes natural and doesn't have too negative an impact on testability and consistency.

---

2. Then there's the exception to the rule, as one of my reviewers pointed out. He followed this tip once, and he removed the only code that had unit tests.
3. I'd wager that such organizations' admiration of *quality* is proportionally inverse.

Mechanical Duplication

There are several ways to introduce duplication into code and stress a developer's short-term memory. *Mechanical duplication* is my fancy term for copy and paste programming, which may be performed in adjacent sections of the source code or across different modules. The outcome is still the same: suddenly two or more instances of the same code must be maintained. The results of working with these copies may range from irritation and bugs (as in the case of Ursula and David) to confusion and misunderstanding. In the following pages, some examples of such duplication are provided, along with examples of typical bugs.

About the Upcoming Examples

The upcoming examples attempt to capture the soul and essence of legacy code to better illustrate the various duplications. Therefore, they contain calls to deprecated methods, old idioms, and generally funky logic.

Copy and Paste

This is the canonical form of the copy and paste operation. One or several lines of source code have been duplicated. This is usually easily cured using "extract method" refactoring. In the following example, depicting an average insertion method, the developer felt compelled to copy the dubious validation logic to the update method as well.

```
public void create(Customer customer) {
    if (customer.getGender() == Gender.UNKNOWN
            || customer.getDateOfBirth() == null) {
        throw new IllegalArgumentException(customer
            + " not fully initialized");
    }

    // More logic here ...
}


public void update(Customer customer) {
    if (customer.getGender() == Gender.UNKNOWN
            || customer.getDateOfBirth() == null) {
        throw new IllegalArgumentException(customer
            + " not fully initialized");
    }

    // More logic here ...
}
```

The obvious opportunity to introduce bugs here lies in changing one instance of the duplicated code and not the other. Such simple bugs would normally be caught by unit tests, but systems where this kind of duplication is practiced usually don't impress when it comes to unit test coverage.

Block Copy and Paste

This duplication refers to identical blocks of code occurring in several places in the code. This phenomenon could also be described as the inverse of the "extract method" of refactoring—in-lining. There's no clear line between a normal copy and paste and a block one, but if you get annoyed by blocks of similar code, then it's probably the latter.

I decided to give this construct its own name after having seen classes with manually written SQL queries that mapped the result set to objects in identical ways over and over again. And while copying a few lines of code somewhere once in a while may be forgivable, duplicating entire blocks never will be.

Building on the previous example, extending the validation logic to include age would raise my block duplication warning flag:

```
public void create(Customer customer) {
    if (customer.getGender() == Gender.UNKNOWN
            || customer.getDateOfBirth() == null) {
        throw new IllegalArgumentException(customer
            + " not fully initialized");
    }

    LocalDate now = new LocalDate();
    Period period = new Period(customer.getDateOfBirth(),
            now, PeriodType.yearMonthDay());
    if (period.getYears() < 18) {
        throw new IllegalArgumentException(customer + " is underage");
    }

    // Equally scary logic for saving would go here...

}
public void update(Customer customer) {
    if (customer.getGender() == Gender.UNKNOWN
            || customer.getDateOfBirth() == null) {
        throw new IllegalArgumentException(customer
            + " not fully initialized");
    }

    LocalDate now = new LocalDate();
```

```
    Period period = new Period(customer.getDateOfBirth(),
            now, PeriodType.yearMonthDay());
    if (period.getYears() < 18) {
        throw new IllegalArgumentException(customer + " is underage");
    }

    // More logic here...
}
```

Large blocks not only increase the chance of diverging implementations, but are also tiring to read (both in source code and in a book).

Constructor Copy and Paste

Constructor copy and paste means that constructors are duplicated instead of calling each other. Depending on the language, this may be an issue, or it may not. Because of the way constructors tend to look, this gives rise to a particularly ugly kind of copy and paste duplication and thus deserves a name of its own.

```
public NetworkInterface(Inet4Address ipAddress,
                        NetMask netMask,
                        Inet4Address broadcast,
                        Inet4Address defaultRoute) {
    this.ipAddress = ipAddress;
    this.netMask = netMask;
    this.broadcast = broadcast;
    this.defaultRoute = defaultRoute;
}

public NetworkInterface(Inet6Address ipV6Address,
                        NetMaskIpV6 ipV6NetMask,
                        Inet6Address ipV6DefaultRoute) {
    this.ipV6Address = ipV6Address;
    this.ipV6NetMask = ipV6NetMask;
    this.ipV6DefaultRoute = ipV6DefaultRoute;
}

public NetworkInterface(Inet4Address ipAddress,
                        NetMask netMask,
                        Inet4Address broadcast,
                        Inet4Address defaultRoute,
                        Inet6Address ipV6Address,
                        NetMaskIpV6 ipV6NetMask,
                        Inet6Address ipV6DefaultRoute) {
```

```
        this.ipAddress = ipAddress;
        this.netMask = netMask;
        this.broadcast = broadcast;
        this.defaultRoute = defaultRoute;
        this.ipV6Address = ipV6Address;
        this.ipV6NetMask = ipV6NetMask;
        this.ipV6DefaultRoute = ipV6DefaultRoute;
    }
```

The more assignments in the duplicated constructors and the more constructors, the greater the chance of forgetting an assignment in one of them.

Method Duplication

This could also be called "method copy and paste." It means that a method has been copied from one context to another. In object-oriented systems, the most obvious context would be a class. However, a context may also be a namespace, module, or project.

Typically, "utility" methods become victims of this flavor of duplication. The method in the following example is one such. It's actually a reconstruction of something I once found in a codebase in eight different classes.

```
public static long diffTime(Date t1, Date t2) {
    if (t1.getDate() != t2.getDate()) {
        throw new IllegalArgumentException(
            "Dates must be equal for comparison to work");
    }
    return (t2.getHours() - t1.getHours()) * 60;
}
```

The obvious problem here is divergence, and the danger lies in the methods having the same name, while behaving differently. It's not hard to imagine that someone would try to "repair" the diffTime method to look like this . . .

```
public static long diffTime_revised(Date t1, Date t2) {
    if (t1.getDate() != t2.getDate()) {
        throw new IllegalArgumentException(
                "Dates must be equal for comparison to work");
    }
    return (t2.getHours() * 60 + t2.getMinutes())
            - (t1.getHours() * 60 + t1.getMinutes());
}
```

. . . in seven out of eight places in the code. Imagine the kind of bugs this would give rise to and how the end users would perceive the system's behavior.

Knowledge Duplication

In contrast to mechanical duplication's stamping of the same lines of code across the system, *knowledge duplication* is the result of deliberate design decisions. It may be the kind of duplication needed to achieve decoupling, independence, or maneuvering space for redesign and rewriting. Unfortunately, it may also be a result of ignorance and conflict, in which case the effects are the same as those of mechanical duplication, but on a larger scale.

Knowledge duplication is about reintroducing existing concepts and functionality, but doing so not by copying existing code, but by writing new code. Such code may use different names and abstractions, look different, be more testable, or just better, but it still duplicates existing functionality. This has consequences for both development and testing.

In codebases with true collective code ownership and teams taking turns working on different parts of the system depending on their current focus, developers must both know about all instances and versions of the duplicated functionality and actively choose how to act on this knowledge. Do they change or add things in one instance or both? Do they try to delete one instance? Where do they write unit tests? Not knowing of all the duplicates also has its costs, the obvious one being the risk of introducing yet another one.

Testing of systems with a high degree of mental duplication also becomes harder, especially from a black box perspective. Not knowing how many "solutions" there are behind common functionality and implementation of business rules, more testing is required—like in the copy and paste example in Chapter 4.

Next follow some variations of knowledge duplication, starting with the simple cases and progressing to the more sophisticated ones.

Similar Functionality in Different Methods

In a larger system that's been around for a while, it's inevitable that there'll be methods that duplicate each other's behavior. The overlapping won't be complete, because if it were, it would just be mechanical duplication. It's more likely to be around 50 to 90 percent. In addition, the methods will probably live in separate contexts and have different names that don't necessarily sound similar. Different developers, development styles, and architectural trends will have had that effect. Therefore, it shouldn't be surprising to find both a `Customer.payInvoice()` method and a `PaymentUtils.billCustomer()` method doing roughly the same thing in the same system.

There are several reasons why such methods may come into being. Some are good, some are bad.

- **Deliberate partitioning**—The system has been partitioned in a way that allows certain duplication to make teams working in parts that mostly don't overlap independent of each other.

- **Choice**—The developer knew that there was a method that did something similar to what he needed to accomplish but chose to ignore it because there were design guidelines or a new architecture that required another solution. (This is where methods should get deprecated.)

- **Ignorance**—The developer wasn't aware of the fact that there was a method that accomplished the task at hand (probably because it was poorly named and lived in an unintuitive context, or simply because it was the developer's first day on the job), so he[4] created a new one.

- **Fear**—The developer needed something that behaved like an existing method, but only in four out of five cases. Dreading to break existing code, he didn't refactor the original method and introduced a new one instead.

- **Laziness**—Again, the developer needed something that behaved like an existing method most of the time, but not always. Instead of adapting the existing method to handle more cases, he crafted a similar duplicate.

- **Conflict**—A bunch of developers couldn't agree on the best way of implementing something, so as an act of passive aggression one of them wrote a new method that behaved exactly the way he thought it should.

When it comes to duplicated methods, my advice is this: keep the duplication that's been introduced on purpose. Sometimes some detective work may be required to determine whether that's the case. Get rid of the methods introduced by ignorance, laziness, fear, or conflict, if you happen to touch that code, as they only add more broken windows.

Similar Functionality in Different Classes

Just as methods may get created with overlapping functionality, so can classes. My experience is that this is less common, probably because classes are based on nouns and are easier to find. Of course, once competing classes entrench themselves in a

---

4. "He" refers to "he or she," but is used for readability.

system, they're even harder to get rid of than overlapping methods. Classes leave a larger footprint and may get deeply entangled via their methods.

The reasons for creating competing and overlapping classes are the same as those for creating duplicated methods, but they lean more toward ignorance and deliberate design choices. If a concept has a totally alien name in an older part of a system, then surely a new developer might create a new class for it with a more intuitive name.

Competing Implementations

This duplication lies in solving a similar problem differently in the same system. It's easiest to spot on the architectural or design level. For example

- Module A uses this logging framework, and module B uses that logging framework.

- Module C relies on handwritten SQL, whereas module D uses an O/R mapper.

- Module E uses a date library, whereas date computations have been implemented from scratch in module F.

- Module G performs client-side validation, whereas server-side validation is preferred by module H.

This list easily grows. From the developer's point of view, this switching can be interesting, dreary, or just a fact of life. However, I'd argue that it has a certain impact on testing. Would you test a system that you knew was built using an O/R mapper differently from one that relied on handwritten SQL?

Using different frameworks or idioms across the system doesn't automatically have to decrease testability. Here maintainability and consistency are more of an issue. If the system is really loosely coupled and there's a deliberate strategy that says that teams get to pick their own stacks, then roll with it. If the system is more of a monolith containing four generations of logging frameworks, three unit testing frameworks, five web frameworks, and two dependency injection frameworks, obviously starting a conscious effort to reduce this fragmentation will benefit maintainability, performance, and most likely testability as well.

Competing Domain Models

This is the last and final form of knowledge duplication. It's encountered in larger systems that have been around for more than just a few years. They've grown and evolved in directions that nobody could foresee at the time of their creation. Ten years later, they no longer support the business model or the needs of their users. Still, they keep a decade of data hostage, and there's no way that they're going to be rewritten.

In such cases starting afresh with a new domain model, new concepts, new technology, and new everything may save the system and allow the business to function without any interruptions. This comes at the cost of the ultimate duplication of knowledge: everybody working with the system—at least from the internal point of view—must be aware of what model they're working with. So when a new business rule is introduced, care must be taken to implement it in either both models or just the new one while deprecating or deleting functionality in the old one.

Naturally, both models and their related concepts will require different kinds of testing, because they'll have been built by different people using different technologies, which, no doubt, will make them have their own different quirks.

My advice on competing domain model duplication is that it shouldn't drag on forever. The process of transition between domain models is a slow one—in large systems in particular—and you don't want to be stuck in the middle. Being there has certain distinct disadvantages. In terms of testability, you're most likely in a place where you have to maintain two stacks of testing tools, and you have to be on your toes when it comes to requirements: Which model supports which functionality? Development-wise, all good things happen in the new code (both the production and test code), and morale plummets when working with the old code. Bad morale is seldom good for correctness. Therefore, make the transition as swift as possible.

Summary

From a testability point of view, duplication is the developer's and the tester's enemy. It makes the codebase larger and more difficult to navigate, it breeds more duplication, it leads to specific kinds of bugs that are about changing something in x out of y places—and forgetting about the remaining $y - x$ instances—and it messes up metrics. Allowing a certain degree of duplication may increase a development organization's throughput, though, as bottlenecks may be removed.

Duplication can be divided into *mechanical* and *knowledge*. The former is the result of copying and pasting code in various ways and is easy to fix. The latter is about overlapping and competing concepts, and can be very challenging to get rid of if unwanted, because it may reside in the very core of the system's architecture. Knowledge duplication may be fueled by ignorance, fear, laziness, conflict, or a combination thereof. It may also be a result of deliberate actions taken to reduce a team's need for synchronization around hot spots in the code.

Chapter 17

WORKING WITH TEST CODE

Apart from following principles of good design, just like production code, test code has an extra area responsibility—to explain and to describe what the production code is supposed to be doing. Also, just as with production code, some people may feel uncomfortable deleting it. This chapter contains some pointers about how to work with existing test code, how to improve it, and when to delete it.

Commenting Tests

Should test code be commented? That depends. On one hand, the quality of the test code should be on par with the quality of the production code. It should be well structured, follow all the principles of good design, and test names should be accurate and descriptive (and so should the variable names) (Tarnowski 2010). On the other hand, some tests will still be difficult to understand, even though they live in nicely named methods with clean code and good variable names. In certain cases, cause-and-effect relations cannot be deduced from good intent-revealing names alone. Sometimes a specific combination of input and state will trigger a business rule that's hard to describe without using some well-placed comments. However, these cases should be quite rare; if the production code is so cryptic that its *test code* must be commented to explain the business rules, then some lights should go red.

Strategies for Comment Avoidance

Whenever your fingers start to itch to write a comment in your test code, take a deep breath and think about whether you're actually trying to compensate for some problem in the code. Before resorting to comments, try the following strategies.

Adjust the Test's Name

Try conveying what's specific about the test and its expected outcome. The nature of the test should be apparent from the name. Experiment with the naming conventions from Chapter 7, "Unit Testing," and don't be afraid to challenge them if it increases readability and makes the intent more clear.

Use Variables and Constants to Clarify the Test

Code should never contain magic numbers. In test code, there's another dimension—well-named variables can carry just that additional piece of information needed to explain the test's workings and intention.

Instead of:

```
@Test
public void simpleMisspellingsAreTolerated() {
    ParsedAddress address = addressParser.parse("Sesame streat 123", 1);
    assertEquals("Sesame street", address.streetName);
}
```

Write:

```
@Test
public void simpleMisspellingsAreTolerated() {
    String misspelledStreetAddress = "Sesame streat 123";
    int toleratedNumberOfErrors = 1;
    ParsedAddress address = addressParser.
            parse(misspelledStreetAddress,toleratedNumberOfErrors);
    assertEquals("Sesame street", address.streetName);
}
```

Use Asserts with Messages

As a third line of defense, use assertion methods that allow specifying a message that will be displayed if the assertion fails. By including an extra message, we're packing more information into the code and not into the comments.

Instead of:

```
// Verify that an IP address has been allocated
assertNotNull(IpAllocator.allocate());
```

Write:

```
assertNotNull("Failed to allocate IP address", IpAllocator.allocate());
```

Needless to say, this can result in bloat as well. Adding obvious messages to assertions just clutters the code, so pick your battles. Your general rule should be to use neither comments nor assertion messages.

If you still really need an assertion message, make the test fail just to see what the combined message looks like. Watch the phrasing to make sure that it's informative and that the string supplied by you concatenated with that of the assertion doesn't produce a confusing message. For example, this message

```
assertNotNull("IP address", IpAllocator.allocate());
```

produces the following output:

```
java.lang.AssertionError: IP address
```

This isn't helpful at all, and a better message would be needed to actually help you understand why the assertion failed. As a final note, don't get fancy with these messages; plaintext only. No clever logic to construct the message string.

Use Factories or Builders

Data setup, especially of similar-looking data, usually yields comments that explain the differences. Just as introducing explanatory variables and constants helps to increase readability, using factory methods/classes or builders also removes the need for comments.

Instead of:

```
@Test
public void productsInHistoryWithTotalPriceLessThan100_
        NoFreeShipping() {
    Customer customer = new Customer(1, "Mary", "King");
    Purchase purchase = new Purchase();
    // Not eligible for free shipping.
    purchase.addProduct(new Product(1, "Product", new Money(99)));
    customer.getPurchaseHistory().add(purchase);
    assertFalse(customer.hasFreeShipping());
}

@Test
public void productsInHistoryWithTotalPriceGreaterThan100_
        GetFreeShipping() {
    Customer customer = new Customer(1, "Mary", "King");
    Purchase purchase = new Purchase();
    // This time the customer has passed the threshold
    // for free shipping by exceeding $100.
    purchase.addProduct(new Product(1,"Product", new Money(150)));
    customer.getPurchaseHistory().add(purchase);
    assertTrue(customer.hasFreeShipping());
}
```

Write:

```
@Test
public void productsInHistoryWithTotalPriceLessThan100_NoFreeShipping() {
    Customer customerWithoutFreeShipping
            = customerWithTotalPurchaseAmount(99);
    assertFalse(customerWithoutFreeShipping.hasFreeShipping());
}

@Test
public void productsInHistoryWithTotalPriceGreaterThan100_GetFreeShipping() {
    Customer customerWithFreeShipping
            = customerWithTotalPurchaseAmount(150);
    assertTrue(customerWithFreeShipping.hasFreeShipping());
}

private Customer customerWithTotalPurchaseAmount(double amount) {
    Customer customer = new Customer(1, "Mary", "King");
    Purchase purchase = new Purchase();
    purchase.addProduct(new Product(1,"Product", new Money(amount)));
    customer.getPurchaseHistory().add(purchase);
    return customer;
}
```

Factory methods, factory classes, and builders have certain effects on test code. Occasional factory methods sprinkled throughout the codebase tend to introduce duplication. Many tests will want to construct central objects or data structures in a simple way, and you'll end up with 10 different factory methods doing pretty much the same thing. This, if not sooner, is a good time to refactor the code and create *one* factory or builder that will be used by all tests. On the other hand, such helper classes may introduce coupling between previously unrelated tests. This shouldn't be a problem, but rather an opportunity to think about the design of the test code and some more refactoring.

Split Up Test Classes

Although we should strive to keep classes small, some nontrivial classes will require quite a few tests. These tests may focus on different behavior and use different libraries. A typical example is the test class in which half of the tests use mock objects, whereas the other half don't. This usually leads to apologetic comments in the setup code and in the tests:

```
public class PaymentServiceTest {
```

```
private PaymentService testedService;
private PaymentRepository paymentRepositoryStub;

@Before
public void setUp() {
    testedService = new PaymentService();

    // The checksum and batch tests won't need
    // this, but this mock won't break them.
    paymentRepositoryStub = mock(PaymentRepository.class);
    testedService.setPaymentRepository(paymentRepositoryStub);
}
```

Even if this isn't the case and the problem isn't in the comments, splitting a test class that mixes state tests with interaction tests into at least two test classes is usually a step toward better maintainability.

Deleting Tests

Test code being regular code, it should be quite apparent when to refactor, redesign, or *delete* tests. There's nothing about test code that gives it permission to ignore design principles and patterns or to disregard guidelines such as those in the book *Clean Code* (Martin 2008) or the like. If this were true of test code out there, this entire section would be superfluous. However, this is not the case, and in my personal experience, there's something about deleting test code that sparks arguments that wouldn't be brought up in a conversation about "regular" code. With this in mind, I'm wrapping up with some pointers about when to delete test code.

Prime Candidates for Deletion

Go ahead and delete tests in the following situations:

- **Tests that haven't kept up with refactoring**—Every large codebase contains some tests that haven't caught up with ongoing or recent refactoring. The code exercised there has been refactored many times and its semantics and purpose have changed, but the tests have only been adjusted to compile and pass, without any reflection on their true purpose. Such tests tend to look like gibberish and should be removed or rewritten.

- **Developer learning tests**—Tests written by developers who have just started writing unit tests often make good candidates for deletion, especially the ones that test nothing. Such tests may come into existence when the developer who wrote them was absorbed in ending the test with some kind of assertion and forgot about actually testing anything useful. Such tests just confuse and must go.

- **Tests that don't compile**—In some extreme cases that unfortunately exist, some tests don't even compile. This may not even be perceived as a problem, because teams/organizations in which this happens usually don't compile and run their tests anyway. Such tests should be deleted. Making them compile is often not worth the effort, because the compiled result will probably fall into one of the preceding categories anyway.

- **Tests that are commented out**—Do you keep code that's commented out? Then why keep tests that are?

- **Redundant tests**—When two tests verify the same thing they are, by definition, redundant. Tests are usually not created redundant, but they become redundant after rounds of refactoring and redesign. Compared to the earlier points, this isn't the worst that can happen to you. However, redundant tests add to the overall number of tests and create a false feeling of safety. A bigger concern is the fact that multiple tests may start failing because of a single bug. Having many redundant tests in the codebase also encourages the existence of tests that "test everything"—that is, that verify irrelevant state or interactions because they can. After all, oververification is just another type of redundancy. Needless to say, such tests are often useless for defect localization. For these reasons, I really recommend that redundancy among tests be reduced, which may imply refactoring, rewriting, or removing tests.

Possible Candidates for Deletion

Consider deleting tests in these situations:

- **Ignored tests**—Using a test framework's *ignore* feature may be a way of saying that the functionality needed to make the test pass isn't in place yet (which shouldn't really happen in the case of unit tests), or it could be a fancy way of commenting out tests that don't pass. Keep your ignored tests under observation, and delete them if they stay that way for too long.

- **Tests using an older framework**—Migrating between testing frameworks or mocking frameworks isn't that big a deal. Technology evolves. However, as you migrate, make sure that you adjust your tests accordingly. If not, consider deleting some of them. For maintenance reasons, you don't want to be in a situation where you're running two unit testing frameworks and three different mocking frameworks in the same codebase (this has actually happened to me). The difficulty lies in keeping the syntax and various quirks and oddities of the different frameworks in your head. Also, that's demanding a lot from developers that enter your team. So, if a dozen unit tests use EasyMock[1] whereas several thousand rely on Mockito,[2] either fix the ones that chain you to EasyMock or delete them (and drop EasyMock from the project entirely) to achieve consistency.

- **Outgrown tests**—This is an interesting category of tests. These are tests that were once useful, but that have been replaced by more useful tests. This is often true of tests that were created when using triangulation (described in the chapter on test-driven development). When trying to triangulate the solution, a number of tests come into existence, and once the algorithm is found, they may no longer be needed. They're not really 100 percent redundant, but they feel awkward. Some people prefer to delete such tests.

Why It's Important to Delete Tests

Apart from following software engineering practices, I can see several strong arguments in favor of deleting tests, one being *transparency and truthfulness*. Codebases that contain thousands of tests feel quite safe to refactor. However, if half of the tests belong in the "prime candidates for deletion" category, does it feel equally safe to refactor? At the end of the day, we want to be truthful to ourselves about the quality of the test code, and keeping tests that add no value is neither transparent nor truthful. Another reason is *providing a good example*. Although this shouldn't be a valid reason, it's unfortunately still a fact that a fair number of developers still feel uncomfortable around test code. By keeping only tests that are well written, up to date, and meaningful, we provide developers new to testing with good examples. Finally, there's *simplicity*. I've made a similar argument in Chapter 16, "Duplication." If there's less of everything, including dead or irrelevant test code, we have a bigger chance of developing a true understanding of our system and we won't waste time thrashing around in its dark corners.

Summary

Test code follows the same conventions as production code and should be of equal quality. Use comments sparingly and only in cases where a well-written test may not illuminate some intricacies of the tested code.

Before commenting test code, try these strategies:

---

1. Which is an older mocking framework.
2. Which is newer than EasyMock.

- Adjust the test's name
- Use variables and constants to clarify the test
- Use asserts with messages
- Use factories or builders
- Split up test classes

Delete tests that

- Haven't kept up with refactoring
- Have been written by developers who were learning and that verify nothing
- Don't compile
- Are commented out
- Are redundant

Consider deleting tests that

- Make use of the testing framework's *ignore* functionality
- Are coupled to a framework that isn't used widely throughout the codebase or that has been abandoned in favor of a newer framework
- Once provided learning and information, but have been replaced by more accurate or otherwise more suitable tests

Chapter 18
BEYOND UNIT TESTING

As you grow accustomed to writing unit tests, you'll most likely appreciate the security and feedback they provide, and you'll want the same for bigger building blocks and their interactions.

Until now, many topics have been illustrated with unit tests. It's quite natural, because they constitute the basis of developer testing and embody many of the principles behind more complex tests. Besides, they can be kept small and to the point, which is rather helpful when explaining a concept or technique. If you get the low-level unit tests right, shifting toward higher-level tests, like integration tests or end-to-end tests, is relatively easy. Still, there are some differences and pitfalls worth mentioning.

This closing chapter will get you started on the journey toward advanced developer testing, for unit tests are but the first step. A word of caution: the topics covered in the following few pages can easily fill an entire book. I've tried my best to cherry-pick and highlight things that I consider important and helpful to the reader at this point to the best of my ability.

Tests that Aren't Unit Tests

The different test levels were described in Chapter 3, "The Testing Vocabulary." A significant portion of that chapter was spent explaining that the tests at each level aren't easy to define and that there's much room for interpretation and variation. Unit tests are no exception, but tests that aren't unit tests are even harder to classify. Such tests may do everything that unit tests should stay clear of, and this opens up endless possibilities. This section contains examples of tests that aren't unit tests and fall somewhere between and including integration tests and end-to-end tests.[1] Some of them contain details that are meant to be thought provoking on purpose. While reading them, I want you to think about whether they would provide any value in your current context.

---

1. Maybe settling for Medium and Large tests isn't such a bad idea . . .

Tests Enclosed in Transactions

Tests enclosed in transactions are among the simpler integration tests. Their purpose is to exercise persistence operations that involve writes without messing up the database,[2] which is why they typically appear around DAOs, repositories, or any other abstractions that wrap persistence. Each test starts a transaction, performs whatever operation that results in a write, checks the result, and rolls back the transaction. For obvious reasons, the transaction is also rolled back if an error occurs during the test. The transaction management can be implemented "by hand" or by a framework. Note that such tests differ from those running against in-memory databases in that they care about the state in which they leave the database. Tests that run in transactions are typically employed if an in-memory database can't be used, which isn't an uncommon scenario. The real database may use another SQL dialect and provide some crucial vendor-specific functionality. It may also have different performance characteristics or differ with respect to some other quality attribute.

Here's an example of what a test like this would look like if implemented using Java's Spring framework. In the following code, I've lumped together all address fields into one `shippingAddress` to keep the example brief.

```
@ContextConfiguration(classes = {TestContextConfiguration.class})
public class CustomerRepositoryTest extends
        AbstractTransactionalJUnit4SpringContextTests {

    @Autowired
    private CustomerRepository customerRepository;

    @Test
    public void readBackStoredCustomer() {
        long newCustomerId = customerRepository.nextIdentity();
        Customer customer = new Customer(newCustomerId, "John", "Smith",
                "john@smith.com", "100 Main St., Phoenix AZ 85236");
        customerRepository.save(customer);

        Customer savedCustomer =
                customerRepository.findById(newCustomerId);
        assertThat(savedCustomer, equalsIgnoringCreationDate(customer));
    }
}
```

---

2. Technically, such tests work for message queues or any other artifacts that support transactions, but let's keep to the most common case.

This test is quite benign. It verifies that a customer saved using the `Customer-Repository` class can be read back by the same repository. If a persistence framework is used, such tests give relatively little return on investment, because they're mostly testing that framework. They start making sense if the persistence operations are implemented by hand (which they were here using `JdbcTemplate`). I can witness first-hand that even something as trivial as saving a few fields in a straightforward table is prone to error because of misplaced commas and missing values in constructors. My personal failures aside, tests like this really start to shine when they exercise logic that's hard to test in other ways—methods that call stored procedures, database triggers, or persistence abstractions that hide business logic. All of this can happen within the confinement of a transaction and traces of it disappear upon rollback. The magic happens when the `AbstractTransactionalJUnit4Spring-ContextTests` class is given a transaction manager and data source that references the test database. Setting this up is the responsibility of the `TestContextConfiguration` class.

```
@Configuration
@ComponentScan("repository")
public class TestContextConfiguration {

    @Bean
    public PlatformTransactionManager transactionManager(
            DataSource dataSource) {
        return new DataSourceTransactionManager(dataSource);
    }

    @Bean
    public DataSource dataSource() {
        DriverManagerDataSource dataSource
                = new DriverManagerDataSource();
        dataSource.setDriverClassName("com.mysql.jdbc.Driver");
        dataSource.setUrl("jdbc:mysql://192.168.0.128/testdb");
        dataSource.setUsername("tester");
        dataSource.setPassword("secret");
        return dataSource;
    }
}
```

Short as it is, the test *does* rely on a database being available. On the whole, the actual complexity of such tests usually lies in how the database is set up and what kind of data it contains. This particular test is simple, because it doesn't require any data to be present in the database before it's executed. In an actual integration test suite, such tests would be in the minority, and many tests would start by populating tables or require that the database contain some base dataset.

Either way, the build that would run the integration test suite would be responsible for orchestrating both the execution of the tests and the availability of the database. Depending on the infrastructure and database type, this may be relatively easy or quite challenging.

Tests that Exercise a Service or a Component

It's not entirely uncommon for systems to be composed of building blocks that go by the name of components or services. Such building blocks hopefully have one area of responsibility and are readily accessible through some kind of public interface. Technologies like COM, RMI, EJB, or web services (REST or SOAP) come to mind. Tests that interact with such components must be able to orchestrate their start-up and then access them somehow. This often involves starting a server or some kind of platform that hosts the tested component or service.

These tests are common in projects where the team works with acceptance test-driven development or specification by example, because they target business functionality without bringing in the complexity of UI logic. The following test echoes the functionality of the previous example, but this time the customer is created by calling a RESTful web service.

```
@SpringApplicationConfiguration(TestContextConfiguration.class)
@WebIntegrationTest
class CustomerServiceTest extends Specification {

    @Autowired
    private CustomerTestRepository customerTestRepository;
    private RestTemplate restTemplate = new TestRestTemplate()

    def "Create a new customer"() {

        given:
        customerTestRepository.deleteAll()

        when:
        def newCustomer = new Customer(firstName: "John",
                lastName: "Smith",
                email: "john@smith.com",
                shippingAddress: "100 Main St., Phoenix AZ 85236")
        URI location = restTemplate.postForLocation(
                "http://localhost:8080/customers", newCustomer)
```

```
        then:
        location.path =~ /.*\/customers\/\d+$/

        and:
        customerTestRepository.customerCount() == 1
    }
}

class Customer {
    String firstName
    String lastName
    String email
    String shippingAddress
}
```

Here I almost feel like cheating. Again, I've used the Spring framework to start an entire server running a RESTful service by using one line of code—@WebIntegration-Test. On the other hand, wrestling with server start-up and service deployment isn't the key focus here. Instead, let me direct your attention to the fact that this test makes use of a repository[3] tailored specifically for testing to delete all customers and to count them. The implementation details of the deleteAll method aren't important. Its purpose is to delete all customers and their data (customers being the aggregate roots), so that observing creation of a new customer is easy.

When it comes to invoking the actual web service, the test is satisfied if the HTTP response contains a Location header that seems to be containing the URL of a new customer resource. In this case, the location is verified using a regular expression. Other alternatives would be inspecting the body of the response (as it could contain a representation of the new customer resource), the HTTP response code, walk the extra mile and GET the new customer resource, or pull the customer out from the database. What would be the right thing to do? Bear with me through some more examples, and we'll revisit this issue. (Although the short answer is: "it depends.")

Tests that Interact with Other Systems

Few applications are homogeneous, self-contained monoliths these days. Often, part of a system's functionality is supplied by another system or a third party. Therefore, it's not surprising that there'll be tests that exercise functionality spanning several systems. Such tests may further be divided into two categories: the ones that operate

---

3. Of course, it doesn't have to be domain-driven design like a repository. A good old DAO or a helper class that digs around in the database will do.

against an external party's sandbox or test environment, and the ones that fake the system they interact with. Both types come with their advantages and disadvantages.

Some types of services are best operated by vendors who have the know-how and compliant environments. Payment gateways are a typical example. Not only is processing of online payments most likely *not* the problem you want to solve, but storing card holder details also mandates compliance with a security standard called PCI DSS,[4] which is rather cumbersome to implement. Therefore, it's quite natural to turn to a third-party payment gateway provider and use their API to process payments. The vendor will most likely provide a test environment—a sandbox—against which you can test your integration. The sandbox will be very similar to the production environment, but will run on test data and be totally safe to interact with.

Tests that span across hops to external parties have to be prepared for interacting with environments they can't control. In practice it means that such tests may fail if the vendor's sandbox is down, and that they have to adapt to the quirks and mechanics of the third party's test environment and API. In other words, they run with limited controllability.

If the vendor's API is well designed, both using it and testing it shouldn't be hard. Therefore, both the production code and test code may look quite harmless. Have a look at this test that incorporates PayPal and executes a credit card payment to their test sandbox system.

```
def test_pay_with_visa_using_valid_payment_information
  address = Address.new({:first_name => "John",
    :last_name => "Smith",
    :street => "100 Main St.", :city => "Phoenix",
    :zip => "85236", :state=> "AZ"})

  visa_card = CreditCard.new('4417119669820331', 1, 2020, 874)
  tested_method = PayPalPaymentMethod.new
  payment_id = tested_method.make_card_payment(5.55, visa_card, address)
  assert_match(/^PAY\-[\w\d]+/, payment_id)
end
```

The test looks benevolent, and the code it tests isn't much scarier:

```
def make_card_payment(amount, credit_card, payer_address)
  payment = Payment.new({
    # ~20 LOC that construct a payment request from the arguments
  })
  if payment.create
```

---

4. https://www.pcisecuritystandards.org/pci_security/

```
        payment.id
    else
        raise PaymentError, payment.error
    end
end
```

However, PayPal's API abstracts away a sequence of two calls to a REST endpoint. The first call retrieves an authorization token, whereas the second performs the actual payment. In conclusion, the third-party API does all the heavy lifting.

In its present form, the test verifies that the request is constructed in a way that's acceptable to the endpoint and that the system that runs the test can establish a connection to PayPal's sandbox. Although it makes a succinct example, I'd probably make use of its mechanics differently on a real project. Either I'd turn this into a test that would ensure that PayPal's API is called correctly—I'd have the tested code return more than the ID and I'd check the response more thoroughly. Such a test would protect from inadvertent changes to the `PayPalPaymentMethod` class and the less likely scenario of PayPal changing its API. Or, I'd let this be the last phase of an end-to-end test that would exercise an entire workflow ending with a PayPal payment. In either case, the point is that nontrivial systems often need to contain tests that are at the mercy of a third party and network connectivity with the outside world. To further prove the point, I can reveal that this test timed out a few times while I was trying it out.

Not all integrations will involve third-party systems beyond your control. Some of the systems your application talks to will be other systems built in-house or third-party software executed on premises. If a test touches code that invokes this kind of external dependencies, they'll have to be controlled somehow. Hence, the openness of the protocol/API used for the integration will be of critical importance to the success of such tests. If the protocol is open enough, the external system can be replaced by something that the test can control. For instance, once I set out to emulate a physical network switch in software to test code that provisioned it. In this case it was plaintext over Telnet, so all I needed to do was write a server that responded to textual commands.

When replacing an entire system with a test double, the wording becomes important. It's most likely going to be a fake in the terminology presented in the chapter on test doubles, but it may equally well be a stub or a mock. If the interesting behavior is confined to the tested component, the test double used to substitute the external system will most likely be a stub. On the other hand, if it's more important to verify how the tested component interacts with the external system, the test double will obviously be implemented so that it records the interactions or behaves like a mock.

Tests Running through the User Interface

These tests exercise the system by interacting with it as an actual user would do—by entering data and clicking around in the user interface. They rely on libraries that control the user interface somehow. Web applications and mobile applications are natural candidates for such tests, although there are libraries for automating fat clients as well.

Tests that run through the UI are typically system tests or end-to-end tests (although nothing prevents them from testing *just* the UI). Operating at the highest level, they need pretty much the entire system to be up and running, likewise any connections to external systems. If such tests are the only way to verify some critical functionality, which may be the case in legacy systems, my suggestion is to at least put some effort into getting rid of integrations with external systems by replacing them with some kind of test double. Conversely, if the system is robust enough to allow testing complex workflows and long-running transactions through the user interface, then the tests should resemble actual execution as much as possible. That way, they'll replace tedious manual tests, at least.

Few tests have as bad a reputation as UI tests; they're often considered flaky and expensive to maintain. In many cases, it might be true; however, most of the time, the issue of stability can be solved. In my experience, UI-based tests fail for two major reasons:

1. **They're not good at dealing with asynchronicity and variable delays**—Web pages or mobile apps that rely on some external data take time to load. The actual time will depend mostly on network latency and the load on the server and the client (the browser or app). To deal with this variability, the test needs to examine the state of the application periodically to determine whether it has finished loading/updating, instead of just sleeping for a fixed period.[5] The same goes for handling asynchronous updates.

2. **They don't control the data**—Implementing UI tests without having them control the data in the system is a futile endeavor. The typical failure case is the test tries to access a specific entity through the interface, but that particular entity has been deleted or rendered unusable to the test somehow. Just

---

5. See the documentation of WebDriver's `WebDriverWait` class to get a feeling for how such waiting can be achieved (https://seleniumhq.github.io/selenium/docs/api/java/org/openqa/selenium/support/ui/WebDriverWait.html).

imagine a test that tries to find a customer that doesn't exist, or a test that attempts to log in to the application using a blocked account. Such tests usually don't have the word "stable" written all over them.

This next test exercises an entire online purchase workflow on a fictitious web site that markets and sells a book about WebDriver testing. It relies solely on the output of the user interface to determine whether it succeeds. It simulates a user's journey through four web pages: a start page and three pages where the user selects the number of books to buy, enters the shipping address, and finally the payment details. Halfway throughout, the test checks that the price was computed correctly, and at the end it looks for a confirmation message in the page and compares the presented shipping address with the address details it provided.

```
[TestInitialize]
private IWebDriver webDriver;

public void SetUp()
{
    webDriver = DriverFactory.NewHtmlUnitDriver();
    webDriver.Url = "http://localhost:8080";
}
[TestMethod]
public void OrderThreeBooks()
{
    const int PricePerBook = 15;
    string name = "John Smith";
    string streetAddress = "100 Main St.";
    string city = "Phoenix";
    string state = "AZ";
    string zip = "85236";

    var mainPage = new MainPage(webDriver);
    var selectNumberOfBooksPage = mainPage.ClickBuyNowButton();
    selectNumberOfBooksPage.SelectNumberOfBooks(Quantity.Three);
    var addressDetailsPage =
            selectNumberOfBooksPage.ClickAddressDetailsButton();
    addressDetailsPage.EnterFullName(name);
    addressDetailsPage.EnterStreetAddress(streetAddress);
    addressDetailsPage.EnterCity(city);
    addressDetailsPage.EnterState(state);
```

```
    addressDetailsPage.EnterZip(zip);
    var paymentDetailsPage = addressDetailsPage.ClickPaymentButton();

    var expectedTotalPrice = (int)Quantity.Three * PricePerBook;
    Assert.AreEqual(expectedTotalPrice, paymentDetailsPage.TotalPrice);

    paymentDetailsPage.EnterCardNumber("4417119669820331");
    paymentDetailsPage.EnterCVV2("874");
    paymentDetailsPage.SelectExpirationMonth(Month.January);
    paymentDetailsPage.EnterExpirationYear("2020");
    var confirmationPage = paymentDetailsPage.ClickPayButton();

    Assert.IsTrue(confirmationPage.PaymentSuccessFul);
    string expectedAddress = String.Format("{0}\n{1}\n{2}, {3} {4}",
            name, streetAddress, city, state, zip);
    Assert.AreEqual(expectedAddress, confirmationPage.Address);
}

[TestCleanup]
public void CleanUp()
{
    webDriver.Quit();
}
```

Being a WebDriver-based test, it relies heavily on *Page Objects*—abstractions of a web page's graphical elements and services. The Page Objects hide the gruesome details of plowing through a page's HTML markup to find individual elements and interact with them. If implemented with some care, they can also shield a test from the complexity of asynchronous communication, as well as changes to a page's layout. Notice that the test knows nothing about what the pages look like, only what input fields they contain.

The tricky part here is that the test really requires the entire system to be up, as well as integration with a credit card payment provider. This would typically be ensured by the build process. By the way, do notice that this test doesn't set up any data, which would be rather untypical in reality.

Fast and Stable WebDriver Tests

I've included an interesting detail in this test: the use of `HtmlUnitDriver`.[a] This particular driver makes the test run "headless", that is, without using any browser. This has several advantages:

- Tests can be executed in console-only environments, like CI servers that don't run a window system.
- Tests execute much faster, because they don't have to wait for a browser to render the pages.
- The speed of such tests forces them to be written so that they handle asynchronous behavior and potential race conditions during page loads correctly, as they'll no longer be masked behind rendering delays. In short, such tests will be stable!

The only downside is compatibility differences between the drivers. Obviously, a headless driver and its JavaScript engine will perform a little differently from a browser, but this seldom kills the show.

[a] The `DriverFactory` class that creates the driver is in Appendix B..

Tests that Invoke a System

Not all systems are accessed via a web interface, a mobile app, or the cloud. There are still systems out there that are accessed from a command shell. Unless the system contains some kind of interface that blocks while waiting for the user to press some keys, it can be tested by spawning the process we want to test and interacting with it through the three streams—stdin (standard input), stdout (standard output), and stderr (standard error). This is actually how you would test the classic "Hello World" program.

Nowadays, few systems are executed like this (at least compared to the number of mobile apps, web applications, or normal windowed applications). However, the techniques for spawning processes and controlling their input and output are still relevant in more complicated tests that may require that a system command be executed in the middle of the test.

The next test demonstrates what it looks like when the Builder pattern is used to produce complex data before running a test and what a test that spawns a process (identified by the `export.bin` system property) and interacts with the file system might typically do.

```
def setup() {
    outputDirectory = new File(System.properties['java.io.tmpdir'],
            "outgoing")
    if (outputDirectory.exists()) {
        FileSystemUtils.deleteRecursively(outputDirectory)
    }
    if (!outputDirectory.mkdir()) {
        throw new IllegalStateException(
                "Couldn't create output directory")
    }
}

def "Only new orders are exported to address files"() {

    def ordersToExport = 2
    def ordersToIgnore = 1

    given: "Two new orders and one cancelled"
    def firstCustomer = new CustomerBuilder()
            .withStreetAddress("42 Sesame Street").build()
    def firstCustomersOrder = new OrderBuilder(firstCustomer).
            build()
    def secondCustomer = new CustomerBuilder()
            .withStreetAddress("21 Jump Street").build()
    def secondCustomersOrder = new OrderBuilder(secondCustomer).build()
    def thirdCustomer = new CustomerBuilder()
            .withStreetAddress("1428 Elm Street").build()
    def ignoredOrder = new OrderBuilder(thirdCustomer)
            .withState(Order.State.CANCELLED).build()

    customerRepository.add(firstCustomer, secondCustomer,
thirdCustomer)
    orderRepository.add(firstCustomersOrder, secondCustomersOrder,
            ignoredOrder)

    when: "Executing the export"
    def process = "${System.properties['export.bin']} ${outputDirectory}"
            .execute()

    then: "The export succeeds"
    def output = process.in.readLines()
    output[0] == "Exporting to ${outputDirectory}..."
    output[1] == "${ordersToExport} order(s) exported, "
            + "${ordersToIgnore} order(s) ignored"
```

```
        and: "Two files are created"
        outputDirectory.list().length == 2
}
```

And There's More

The examples presented so far witness the variations that are possible when leaving the confines of unit testing. Still, I haven't included any examples of proper end-to-end tests that would start multiple servers (like a frontend and a backend or some micro-services), run different applications and exercise long-running transactions.

To keep the size of this chapter reasonable, I've also refrained from wrapping any of the examples in a BDD framework (like Cucumber, FitNesse, or Concordion) to get nice documentation, demonstrating model-based testing (using something like NModel or GraphWalker), or showing a test that relies on image recognition (Sikuli comes to mind).[6] Mobile applications, with their device quirks and challenges unique to running in mobile networks and with limited battery power, also didn't make this chapter. Furthermore, to keep the scope manageable, I've kept the examples within the domain of typical business applications.

Characteristics of Tests that Aren't Unit Tests

By virtue of their many moving parts, more complex tests get their own characteristics. Needless to say, they also require more time and effort to both create and maintain. Still, if implemented well, they'll save a tremendous amount of time that would otherwise be spent on regression testing, not to mention the additional confidence that they provide.

The different characteristics of larger tests place new requirements on both the development team and its closest stakeholders. Working with nontrivial tests requires a specific mind-set from each and every one on the team. Everybody must buy into that there's an infrastructure that needs to be looked after. On green-field projects, such an infrastructure can be built relatively easily, using lightweight virtualization and frameworks that abstract away much of the plumbing (like I did in some of the examples).

Older systems may require considerably more work, which, although truly rewarding once some of the decade-long pains have been alleviated, will eat a significant chunk of the development team's time, especially at the beginning of the journey. Therefore, it's of critical importance that both managers and stakeholders who have a say in the team's prioritization, such as product owners or the like, understand that not all of the team's efforts will result in pixels on the screen. The developers

---

6. Appendix A contains links to all aforementioned tools.

doing the actual maintenance of the suite should also agree that testing beyond unit testing is valuable and must be allowed to take time.

So, in addition to understanding that a test infrastructure is required, a team venturing into the fields of integration testing, system testing, workflow testing, or end-to-end testing must also be prepared to tackle such tests' quality attributes and behavior, which will be different from that of unit tests.

Testing Brown-Field Business Applications

Systems that have been running for a while—say 5 to 15 years—usually don't run the latest and greatest application stacks and libraries. Neither have they been designed with reproducible deployment in mind. This poses an additional challenge to running tests that require a working system, because such a system may not be possible to deploy. Here's a list of things that usually need doing to get a brown-field business application to a state where it's easy to expose it to integration or end-to-end testing:

- The one and only master database, which nobody dares to touch, needs to be broken down and its (re)creation automated so that instances of it, running with a minimal set of reference data, can be started at will in various test environments.

- The database needs to be versioned and changes to it handled automatically and consistently, so that deploying changes is painless and all environments run against similar databases.

- Server and container configuration need to be understood and standardized, so that setting up new instances is easy.

- Other parts of the infrastructure, like messaging middleware, load balancers, or log servers, may need tuning and cloning, so that they, too, become disposable and easy to spawn when needed.

- The preceding activities usually result in an overhaul of the deployment process and finally its automation.

- Last but not least, the system may need some rewrites so that its configurability improves and so that it can start in different environments and on different infrastructures.

These are all activities that fall in the domain of continuous delivery and DevOps, so I'll leave in-depth treatment to other sources. However, do notice that it's the need for testing that pushes a team in that direction.

Complexity

The further away from low-level tests on individual program elements, the greater the complexity. Higher-level tests contain more of everything. Often, they rely on a non-trivial build that performs orchestration of various resources, and they may require entire libraries to perform some specific aspects of their functionality. Selenium Web-Driver, which I made use of in the fourth example, is one such library, and mastering it fully is a science in itself. So is setting up test data by repopulating databases and constructing test-specific entity graphs or stubbing out entire systems, to name some prevalent drivers of complexity. There are more.

This inherent complexity also affects the composition and competency profile of the development team. To cope with tests that alter and rely on the environment and infrastructure, the developers must be no strangers to command-line magic, database administration, virtualization, and server/container configuration. This a rather relevant factor when recruiting new team members.

Also, given the many moving parts of complex tests, it's of vital importance that they be well written and that the test suite has an architecture that supports it. A haphazard, shantytown test suite may easily devour much-needed development time or even topple the project. Therefore, working with high-level tests, or at least setting up the structure of the test suite, is best left to the more senior members of team.

Stability

Tests that are more complex than unit tests tend to get much less stable. In the various preceding examples, we've seen that they're affected by things like the file system, server and application state, database contents, and network connectivity. In other words, they come with environmental preconditions. There are two generic ways to fulfill such preconditions: code for them or nuke and pave. These strategies aren't mutually exclusive and it's quite context dependent when to use either or both.

Coding for stability means that the tests contain code that checks whether the environment is sane. Such checks may include examining the file system, inspecting the data in the database, or verifying that a server is up and starting it if it isn't. Such actions are typically performed in the test initializer methods. The most fundamental checks, such as verifying that a directory exists or that a database connection is available, don't need to be performed for every test, so putting them in initializers that run once per test class (or module) or even less frequently is a good idea, as it also has a positive impact on performance.

Nuking and paving comes from a different angle. Instead of putting effort into verifying the environment, we reach a known state by resetting it; servers are restarted, databases emptied and loaded with known data, directories removed and re-created. The context sets the limits for what and how to reset. This is often where provisioning and virtualization come in. If sufficiently many or sufficiently complex resources need to be reset, it may actually be simpler to fire up a fresh virtualized environment containing ready-to-go versions of such resources. Lightweight virtualization[7] offers a middle ground—the application and its dependencies run in a container, which isn't that demanding on the underlying operating system. To get to a known state, only the container needs to be restarted (as opposed to restarting individual resources).

Error Localization

The more elaborate the test, the harder it is to achieve good error localization. The reason is the decrease in observability, which is more or less unavoidable for tests of increasing complexity. To be precise, the observability may still be quite adequate, but the program logic needed to make sense of what's actually happening may not. More things can go wrong in a large heterogeneous application stack, and a computer may have a hard time deciding what did. For example, let's think of a few reasons for why a test of a web application may fail:

- The web server hosting the web application is down.

- The application has been incorrectly deployed.

- A firewall is blocking access to the web server.

- Heavy load on the web server prevents the application from responding in time.

- The web server is missing some configuration or resource the application requests at runtime.

- The application misses some data.

- The application actually contains a good, old-fashioned bug.

Most of these error conditions will make the web browser output an HTTP error code, some kind of error message, or more frequently than we'd care to admit, a stack trace. This gives a human user with some knowledge of networking and web applications a fighting chance to make an educated guess about the cause of the problem. An automated test, on the other hand, would have a very hard time truly understanding what went wrong. It would need to interpret HTTP codes, parse error messages (or even worse, stack traces), and cope with time-outs and dropped connections to arrive at some sort of verdict.

Building intelligent automated error interpretation is something I'd really advise against. Sure, you can program arbitrarily complex diagnostics of the environment's and application's state and health, but should you? No! Any test that does this will be

---

7. Docker being the most popular choice at the time of writing.

bloated with extra code, and if you push this to your test infrastructure, it, too, will become very complex. Tests with many moving parts will fail for reasons that may be hard to understand, at least programmatically. Instead, aim for the second best thing: take your time inspecting what went wrong in the high-level test, and write a lower-level test, preferably a unit test that catches the bug. Conversely, if the problem lies in the environment, investing some time in improving its stability by means of a better setup, virtualization, or a better build process will generate higher pay-off than complex logic in individual tests.

Performance

Tests outside the domain of unit tests tend to pay the price in performance. Integration tests against small databases on fast networks may run relatively fast, whereas tests that run through the user interface may become painfully slow, especially if they start with lengthy data setup and then get caught doing round trips through all layers of the system. Tests working on larger batches of data will perform accordingly.

These differences in execution speed prompt us to divide tests into suites and hierarchies. There's no point in running slow tests unless the faster ones succeed first. Slower tests also run the risk of not being executed frequently enough, so keeping down the execution time of both the individual tests and the whole test suite will require deliberate effort: pruning redundant tests, making slow tests run faster (by reducing their footprint on the system), or by parallelizing the suite.

The following facets of performance don't affect unit tests (apart from CPU performance), but they need to be taken into account when working with more complex tests and larger test suites:

- **Network performance**—More complex tests will exercise several tiers, such as databases and software running on different servers. Network throughput and latency shouldn't come in their way.

- **Storage performance**—Nuking and paving resources or repopulating databases is disk intensive, especially in virtualized environments. Whatever the storage solution, it may become a bottleneck.

- **CPU performance**—Higher-level tests generally tend to be I/O bound. However, sluggish CI servers or slow shared resources may easily cripple many of them.

Environmental Dependence

The bigger a chunk of functionality a test exercises, the greater the chance that this functionality will rely on components that in turn rely on the environment. Although you can always strive to build platform-agnostic and highly configurable software, in truth, the average application usually makes assumptions about its execution environment. What kind of database does it use? Is it a relational database, a document database, or a key-value store? Does it rely on some vendor-specific functionality? What services does the application's server or container provide? Is some kind of messaging technology involved, and how? What external resources does the application access, and where are they located?

Even if you deploy the application to the cloud, you'll still make assumptions based on the quirks and capabilities of the particular cloud's stack, unless the application is very small or trivial.

All of this has a bearing on the tests. The more complex the execution environment, the more effort has to be put into making such an environment easily available for testing. Then there's the cost. It's cheap to have a CI server running a couple of agents capable of executing just unit tests; it's a matter of virtualizing a simple setup. At the other extreme are systems that contain a mainframe, a licensed database, and a full stack with various integrations in between. End-to-end testing in such an environment will be both complicated and costly.

Environmental dependence has direct impact on the breakdown of a team's work. Although a seasoned developer will crank out unit tests in tandem with production code without even thinking about it, addressing the aforementioned issues takes time, deliberate actions, and an understanding that writing tests that are more complex than unit tests introduces new tasks and responsibilities.

Target Audience

Whereas unit tests live in symbiosis with the source code and are the developers' pets, tests that are further away from the code have the potential of attracting a broader target audience. System and end-to-end tests (and integration tests to some extent) verify behavior that nontechnical stakeholders understand. Stakeholders who care about features and progress may feel very reassured by a human-readable suite of tests that exercise functionality they can grasp. After all, who wouldn't feel at least somewhat secure if it were possible to determine whether the system supports business rules like "when buying at least three books, the shopper is given a 20 percent discount in the next campaign" or "direct bank payments with incorrect check digits are sent to an error queue for manual inspection" at the click of a button? To get there, you have two options:

- You commit to implementing specification by example, acceptance test-driven development (ATTD), or behavior-driven development (BDD), all of which have been described earlier.

- You start by writing tests for important functionality that the stakeholders care about and execute them using a BDD framework, which will produce documentation[8] readable by anybody within the organization (provided that some effort has been put into authoring understandable tests).

Using the second approach is less collaborative and doesn't give many of the benefits of working in a BDD-like manner, but in certain settings it may be a good way of selling the advantages of automated acceptance testing to a broader audience.

Either way, the key is to present the tests and their results in such a way that everybody in the organization can comprehend them. If managers, the CTO, and, in a perfect world, the CEO understands the advantages of developers automating verification of critical functionality, you're more likely to get the support you need.

Pointers and Practices

Now that we've looked at some examples and characteristics of more advanced tests, it's time to distill the findings into some pointers and practices.

Test Independence

More complex tests should be independent of their surroundings and other tests, just like unit tests. This rule of thumb comes with some caveats. Tests that require the system or parts thereof to be available while they're running will often be dependent on the build that runs them. CI servers, with their plugins and scripts, are better suited for orchestrating resources like databases, queues, or any other kind of middleware or servers than home-grown utility classes in the test codebase.

Although this approach saves the tests from tinkering with peripheral, low-level dependencies, it introduces certain coupling between the tests and the context in which they run. In some of the examples, I avoided this to a degree by using Spring Boot, but for older systems this won't be an option.

Then there's the issue of temporal coupling between tests. For tests that revolve around some data's life cycle, it may feel tempting to build a sequenced test suite:

- First run tests that create data.

- Then run tests that poke around in that data (query, update, etc.).

- Finally, run tests that delete data.

---

8. In the language of specification by example, this would be "living documentation."

I strongly advise against this. This approach makes the build complex and brittle, and kills test isolation and independence. Then again, there are situations in which this may be the only working approach. We had to do this once on a project where we didn't own the test database. We could neither empty it (because other teams relied on it) nor insert tuples when we needed to, so this was the only way. On the whole, the approach worked, but we paid the price in complexity.

Setup

A higher-level test's setup is quite different from a unit test's. It's usually lengthier, more elaborate, and may poke in several application layers. The exact steps will obviously be different for a business application that requires a lot of state in persistent storage and a game that needs an interesting environment to verify some aspect of its mechanics.

As said in the section on test independence, part of the setup may be performed by the build that runs the tests, and it will hopefully ensure that the right environment is available when the test executes. From there, it's the test's responsibility to produce the state it requires. Here are some tips.

Rely on Start-up, Not Cleanup

It may seem intuitive that a test that pollutes the environment somehow, by creating a bunch of files and directories or data in some kind of database, should clean up after itself. To do so, it may use its cleanup method, but this approach is best viewed as a random act of kindness. If a test wants to stay decoupled from other tests, it should *never* rely on another test's cleanup to create its state. Instead, it should set everything up *before* executing, thus making itself independent of other tests and explicit about its preconditions.

Start with as Little State as Possible

If I'm writing a test that makes use of some kind of database,[9] I go to lengths to ensure that it only contains the bare minimum of state—data—needed by the tested functionality to execute. A test usually needs two kinds of data: reference data and possibly some entity data. Setting up reference data, for example, valid postal codes, country codes, product descriptions, various titles, or i18n strings, is the responsibility of the part of the build that creates the database. Unless something very interesting is happening to the reference data, the tests should rely on it being there and not concern themselves with its setup. As for entity data required for the test to run, see the next point.

---

9. The kind doesn't matter; relational, key-value, graph, etc.

By running tests with empty databases (or files, or queues), we gain certain advantages. One is speed. Empty or next-to-empty things are fast. Adding a record to an empty table or file will most likely not trigger indexing, rebalancing, garbage collection, or the like. Another advantage is simplicity. If the test needs to fetch something from a table or document that has only one record, it doesn't even have to know how to find it; it just has to fetch that single record. I made use of this in the second example, where I just counted the number of tuples. A third advantage is that the data footprint is easier to debug. Not that we want that, but should the imperfections of reality force us to check the contents of a database or file during a debugging session, it's going to be a much more pleasant experience if there's only one tuple to examine.

Invest in Data Helpers

Many tests may need a fair amount of entity data before being able to exercise the functionality they're checking. The archetype is the application that requires the user (test) to log in before being able to do anything interesting. User credentials are entity data,[10] which needs to be there at the beginning of each test. There are two ways to create such data: use the system's services, or construct it using a parallel implementation—a test utility package for creating data. Business applications tend to contain many services that create their typical entities, such as customers, orders, or invoices. So, if the test wants to verify that changing a customer's address works as expected,[11] it'll start by calling the component/service that creates a new customer. The first and second examples in this chapter illustrate what such a service might look like. The advantage of this is that existing functionality is used (and thus reused and tested yet another time). The disadvantages are that

- The service may not be readily available to the test, which may be running at another level of abstraction or lack access to the infrastructure needed to invoke the service

- If the setup necessitates the use of many different services, it quickly becomes cumbersome and awkward

- The service is unable to create entities with certain properties

In such cases, using a parallel implementation in the form of a library of builders or factories may be more advantageous. This is the same approach as described

---

10. Although some people may consider them "static" entity data and handle them like reference data.
11. It's irrelevant whether this is done at the persistence abstraction level, UI level, or somewhere between.

in Chapter 9, "Dependencies," with the constraint that the created object is an entity that can be persisted. In fact, this is the technique I prefer to reusing existing services.

As always, there are trade-offs to be made. The obvious disadvantage of utilities for creating data is that they add extra code. Depending on whether they reuse the existing entity model or not, they may get coupled to the database. Suddenly changing something in the database requires an update to the entity model *and* the utilities. In addition, independent implementations may create invalid data. They may forget to apply a business rule or piece of validation logic, thus bringing to life entities that would never have been created by the system. Finally, builders and factories may get quite complicated. And yes, they need unit testing . . .

On the plus side, they make it easy to create arbitrary variations of data. Entities produced by test factories or builders may reflect state that would be hard to reach. For example, consider a builder that's able to create a customer whose password has expired. Such a customer may not even be possible to create using the application's existing services (and that's a good thing), because expiration is most likely a result of actual time passing. In this case, a snippet like this would save the day:

```
var customerForPasswordUpdate
        = customerBuilder.withExpiredCredentials().build();
```

They can also contain logic that allows setting up very complex state. Finally, I'd say that a good implementation of data helpers will make the test very readable, verbose, and explicit.

Verification

Whereas unit tests should strive to fail for a single reason, more complex tests may be a bit more forgiving in that regard. Because they take longer to execute, a considerable amount of time may be saved if they're allowed to check several different things per test. The examples at the beginning of this chapter illustrated this in an almost provocative manner.

Personally, I think it's perfectly fine that more complex tests contain more assertions and that these assertions may operate on different layers or components, as long as they're related to the same concept. If an order confirmation service returns a status code, updates something in the database, and sends an e-mail, checking all three may be the right thing to do, especially if no other tests do it. Likewise, if we test a sequence of operations, adding a few guard assertions and intermediate checks here and there does more good than harm. That said, authors of tests that have a lot going on must always be mindful of the balance between error localization, test readability/maintainability, and the execution time of the test suite. Just because we can touch half of our system's features with one gigantic test doesn't mean that we should.

Use of Test Doubles

In the context of system and integration tests, test doubles will most likely be stand-ins for larger components or even entire systems. The PayPal example showed what an integration with an external system might look like. Pretty much every nontrivial system will have a number of such integrations, and they'll need replacing with some kind of test doubles.

On the positive side, configuring alternative endpoints for many types of integrations should be relatively easy. In most cases, this is a matter of changing a URL, especially if the application is designed with some testability in mind. Conversely, providing fake or mock implementations of external systems that contain lots of critical functionality may be complicated, time consuming, and not very effective. Because the majority of the systems our in-house application talks to won't come with well-documented sandboxes, we'll need to implement lightweight versions of them ourselves. Just like with any redundancy and duplication, we run the risk of implementing behavior that differs from that of the original system or component. In addition, these test doubles will need testing, and they need to evolve along with the systems that they replace. You probably see where I'm going with this. Whether this is worth doing is one of many important decisions a team needs to make.

Deciding on a Developer Testing Strategy

Teams that have committed to developer testing will sooner or later have to agree on a *developer testing strategy*. As the test suite grows to include tests that operate on different levels of abstraction and in different scopes, so does the need for detailing the boundaries and responsibilities of each type of test and, above all, deciding on what tests to invest in and to what extent. Depending on the team's situation and its system's characteristics, some types of tests will be critical, whereas some will be a waste of time. The expected lifetime of the system, anticipated future functionality, and current mix of tests also influence the contents of the testing strategy. As do the software stack and the system's age. The strategy itself doesn't have to be something formal chiseled into stone, but whatever the format, it needs to capture the team's decisions and guidelines on managing its combined testing.

A model that may provide a good starting point in the team's discussions is the *test automation pyramid* (Cohn 2009). This classic has been adapted and revised many times, but at the core it consists of a three-tier pyramid with unit tests at the bottom, "service" tests in the middle (tests that target functionality at the component or service level without using the user interface), and UI tests at the top. Some common adaptations are splitting the service test tier into two or three tiers to detail the difference between integration tests and component/service/API tests, or adding manual tests at the very top of the pyramid (see Figure 18.1).

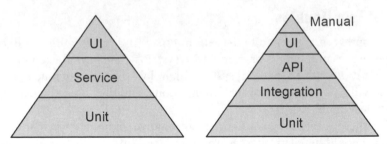

FIGURE 18.1   To the left: the classic test automation pyramid. To the right: one of many adaptations.

Because a pyramid's base is much larger than its top, the model implies that there are many more unit tests than UI tests, the motivation being that the latter tend to be brittle, expensive to write, and time consuming. The number of service tests lies somewhere between those two. This model may help a team visualize the test types it uses. An ambitious team that performs both integration testing and testing at the API level and has some smoke tests that go through the user interface may depict this as a four-tier pyramid (the bottom tier being the unit tests).

I've never seen anybody put any hard figures on the pyramid's tiers in real life, but obviously there will be a ratio between the various types of tests. My experience is that the system's age is the biggest influencing factor behind this ratio. On a green-field project, a team with a testing strategy along the lines of "all new code is developed test-first and we use acceptance test-driven development" will produce tests with a ratio that corresponds closely to what the automation test pyramid suggests. Such a team will obviously have many unit tests, a fair number of tests at the middle tier—such tests will be driven by the executable specifications—and a smaller number of, or maybe even no, tests that work through the user interface.

Conversely, a team that sets out to rejuvenate a convoluted intertwined legacy system may not even be able to visualize its tests using a pyramid. (Or using an inverted one perhaps.) For example, testing legacy systems where no attention has been paid to testability with unit tests ranges from unfeasible to unpractical and expensive. Retroactively adding unit tests takes a lot of time and often requires major refactoring that may break untested functionality, while providing little benefits within the nearest time frame. Instead, the team may be better off securing the critical functionality via tests that operate through the user interface (while learning how to make such tests stable, easy to write, and relatively fast) before thinking about how to address the issue of limited unit test coverage and what types of service-level tests would make sense. Teams in that position tend to adopt the stance: "develop new code with unit tests and refactor/redesign the old code when you're touching it to modify it."

These are some of the bigger issues the developer testing strategy needs to address, but there will be smaller ones too, which still need to be handled to avoid diverging implementations and misunderstandings. Here are some questions that may be helpful in reaching such an understanding:

- Which tests give bang for the buck and which don't?

- What types of tests are we running and how do they overlap?

- What types of tests are we avoiding (and why)?

- How large should a test preferably be? (Size depends on the level of abstraction too.)

- How many layers is a single test allowed to touch?

- Do we optimize for speed of execution or test simplicity?

- How do we handle test data and its setup?

- How do we approach integrations with external systems?

- What testing frameworks and libraries do we use?

- What trade-offs are we willing to make in the spirit of working with legacy code?

These are but examples, and I'm sure that your team can come up with many more questions of this sort. Answering them will help you define the context and boundaries for your tests, and no doubt a developer testing strategy will emerge. Make it available on an information radiator, and revisit and revise at intervals or when something interesting happens to the test suite or the system.

Summary

Tests that aren't unit tests—more complex tests—include integration tests, system tests, and end-to-end tests. In Google's simplified terminology this would be Medium and Large tests.

For typical business applications, these are fairly common types of complex tests:

- Tests enclosed in transactions

- Tests that exercise a service or a component

- Tests that interact with external systems

- Tests running through the UI

- Tests that invoke a system

These test categories aren't mutually exclusive.

Nonunit tests will be more complex, and we need to pay extra attention to their stability, error localization, speed, and environmental dependence. They still need to execute independently, and their setup will be more elaborate. To maintain their independence of other tests, they should set the environment to a clean state before running as opposed to cleaning up afterward. Execution time may be saved if they perform verification at multiple points or across different components. When dealing with integrations with other systems, high-level tests may require that entire systems be replaced by test doubles.

Furthermore, the presence of more advanced tests requires that the team decides on a developer testing strategy, which will guide the use of more complex tests and the evolution of the combined test suite.

Chapter 19

TEST IDEAS AND HEURISTICS

In this final chapter, I gather advice and pointers about what to actually test in a compact format. Bits and pieces of this information are scattered throughout the book, but they usually appear in their own contexts, where other things may be the key focus. Here's the big picture. Hopefully, this material will help you to cherry-pick and prioritize your tests, because there's always time pressure on real projects, and "testing everything" is practically impossible.

High-level Considerations

There are many decisions a team and the individual developers need to make when choosing what to focus on when writing tests. This section should provide some fuel for discussions about where to start and what to do, as well as some ideas about test design.

Test Effectiveness

Depending on the state of the system, a certain type of test may be more effective than another.

- **Unit tests**, with or without the practice of test-driven development, are a must when writing new code professionally, that is, being paid to do it with other people in a way that makes it maintainable in the future. Their presence ensures that the code is testable and they serve as a specification.

- **Component/service tests** will cover a lot of functionality, including correctness of the persistence mechanism in systems that have isolable components with well-defined responsibilities.

- **End-to-end** or **system tests** (possibly integration tests) may prove more effective, that is, provide coverage of critical functionality and catch regressions sooner, when dealing with older systems with convoluted code that's hard or time consuming to unit-test or that lacks any distinguishable components.

Test Recipe

A test recipe[1] helps you to pick what to test, and is especially helpful when working with unit tests (because they contain the highest amount of detail). The three test recipes in this section are phrased differently and maybe one of them will tickle your fancy in particular. If so, I encourage you to pursue the original source to get an accurate and exhaustive description of the recipe in question.

Recipe #1 (Vance 2013)

- Test the happy path
- Test alternative paths, that is, useful variations of the normal behavior
- Test the error paths
- Test data permutations
  - Boundary conditions
  - Data-driven execution
  - Runtime and dynamic binding
- Test the defects

Recipe #2 (Langr, Hunt, &Thomas 2015)

Right BICEP:

- Are the results **right**?
- **B**oundary conditions
- **I**nverse relationships
- **C**ross-check using other sources of truth
- **E**rror conditions
- **P**erformance characteristics

Recipe #3 (Beck 2002)

For code that you have written, test

- Conditionals
- Loops

---

1. I've borrowed this term from Stephen Vance's book *Quality Code: Software Testing Principles, Practices, and Patterns.*

- Operations
- Polymorphism

Level of Abstraction and Detail

Consider the level of abstraction at which your next test will operate and the amount of detail it needs to be concerned with. What language does the test use?

- **Unit tests** (and possibly integration tests) should cover all low-level mechanics, like different variations of input, boundary values, data-driven testing, input validation, and exhaustive branch coverage. Such tests may use technical terminology in the test code, but they should still attempt to test behavior that's meaningful from a user's point of view.

- **System** or **end-to-end tests** should exercise the bigger picture and make sure that the system works as a whole. Such tests shouldn't concern themselves with details and variations. They should span scenarios or use cases and use the language of the business.

Archetype

What format does the test follow, and how many cases does it cover?

- **Single example**—The test exercises some specific behavior and expects a specific correct answer.
  - *Variant:* **Scenario**—The test mimics a user's interaction with the system.
- **Tabular/data-driven**—The test exercises the same logic using many different values and expected results.
  - *Variant:* **Theory**—The test runs different combinations of preselected input values and verifies that the results satisfy some general statement(s).
  - *Variant:* **State transition**—The test is one of several tests that exercise an area of the system that's best modeled as a state machine.
- **Generative**—The test generates the parameters to the tested code, possibly many times.

Source of Truth

How does the test know that the result is correct?

- **Single value**—A single value is the only correct answer.
- **Range**—The correct value is within a known range or interval.

- **Set**—There are multiple correct values, and they correspond to a set of finite size.

- **Predicate**—Whether the value is correct can be determined by a function that says yes or no.

- **Cross-check**—An alternative implementation can be used to determine whether the value is correct.

- **Inverse function**—Applying an inverse function to the result produced by the tested code produces the input.

Low-level Considerations

This section contains things to be mindful of when working with some common elements of a program. The list is by no means exhaustive, but if you remember these points, your tests should cover a good majority of cases.

Zero-one-many

Make sure that the tests cover the following:

- **0 instances**—Empty collections/arrays, loops/conditional blocks that are never entered, possibly nulls, etc.

- **1 instance**—Collections/arrays with one element, queries that return a single tuple, loops that execute once, etc.

- **Multiple instances**—Collections/arrays with multiple elements, queries that return several tuples, loops that execute a number of times, etc.

Nulls

Stick `null/nil/undef` wherever you can if the type/array/collection permits it to see what happens.

Ranges

For a range $m-n$, check the behavior at the following:

- $m - 1$
- m
- n
- $n + 1$

Collections

Consider the following:

- Empty
- With one element
- With multiple elements
- Containing duplicates
- Alternative ordering of elements

Exceptions and Errors

Think about the following:

- Exception type (class)
- Exception message
- Nested exception
- Other exception parameters
- Check all error codes (for code that you've written)

Numbers

Keep in mind the following:

- Zero
- Negative
- Overflow of primitive types
- Floating point precision
- Other representations (like hexadecimal, octal, or scientific)
- Commas, periods, and spaces when represented as strings for parsing

Strings

Don't let this surprise you:

- Empty string (blank)

- One space
- Several spaces
- Special characters like \n, \r, \t, etc.
- Heading/trailing whitespace or special characters
- HTML entities
- Non-ASCII characters
- Encoding
- Overflow of fixed-size string buffers

Dates

Be mindful of the following:

- Different formats
- Number of days in each month
- Leap years
- Time zones
- Daylight saving time
- Accuracy (does a date have a time component?)
- Timestamp formats

Summary

When considering what test to implement next and how, think about the following:

- What type of test will be the most effective?
- Is there a recipe to guide the choice of the next test? What does it suggest?
- What level of abstraction will the test operate at?
- What's its style (archetype)?
- What source of truth will it use?

Common data types and abstractions all come with their specific gotchas that need to be addressed when authoring tests.

Appendix A
TOOLS AND LIBRARIES

Advanced Combinatorial Testing System (ACTS), http://csrc.nist.gov/groups/SNS/acts/documents/comparison-report.html

ALLPAIRS Test Case Generation Tool, http://www.satisfice.com/tools.shtml

AssertJ, http://joel-costigliola.github.io/assertj/index.html

Capybara, https://github.com/jnicklas/capybara

Checker Framework, http://types.cs.washington.edu/checker-framework/

Chef, https://www.chef.io/

Cofoja: Contracts for Java, https://code.google.com/p/cofoja/

Concordion, http://concordion.org/

Cucumber, https://github.com/cucumber

Docker, https://www.docker.com/

Dumbster Email Testing, http://quintanasoft.com/dumbster/

EasyMock, http://easymock.org/

FitNesse, http://fitnesse.org/

Fluent Assertions, http://www.fluentassertions.com/

GraphWalker, http://graphwalker.github.io/

Guava: Google Core Libraries for Java 1.6+, https://github.com/google/guava

HSQLDB, http://hsqldb.org/

HtmlUnit, http://htmlunit.sourceforge.net/

Jasmine, http://jasmine.github.io/

Jetty, http://www.eclipse.org/jetty/

jMock, http://www.jmock.org/

JUnit, http://junit.org/

junit-quickcheck, https://github.com/pholser/junit-quickcheck

Mocha, https://mochajs.org/

Mockito, https://github.com/mockito/mockito

Moq, https://github.com/Moq/moq4

netDumbster, http://netdumbster.codeplex.com/

NModel, https://nmodel.codeplex.com/

NUnit, http://nunit.org/

PowerMock, https://github.com/jayway/powermock

Puppet, https://puppet.com/

QuickCheck, https://bitbucket.org/blob79/quickcheck/

RSpec, http://rspec.info/

Sikuli, http://www.sikuli.org/

Spec#, http://research.microsoft.com/en-us/projects/specsharp/

Specflow, http://www.specflow.org/

Spock Framework, https://github.com/spockframework/spock

Spring Boot, http://projects.spring.io/spring-boot/

Timecop, https://github.com/travisjeffery/timecop

Vagrant, https://www.vagrantup.com/

WireMock, http://wiremock.org/

xUnit.net, https://github.com/xunit/xunit

Appendix B
Source Code

Test Doubles

LISTING B.1 PremiumPurchaseMatcher: A custom matcher that matches specific business rules.

```java
import org.hamcrest.Description;
import org.hamcrest.TypeSafeMatcher;

public class PremiumPurchaseMatcher extends TypeSafeMatcher<Purchase> {

    @Override
    public boolean matchesSafely(Purchase purchase) {
        return purchase.getPrice() > 1000 && purchase.getItemCount() < 5;
    }

    @Override
    public void describeTo(Description desc) {
        desc.appendText("A purchase with the " +
                "total price > 1000 and fewer than 5 items");
    }
}
```

Data-driven and Combinatorial Testing

LISTING B.2 A JUnit-based implementation of a parameterized test.

```java
@RunWith(Parameterized.class)
public class PremiumAgeIntervalsTest {

    @Parameter(value = 0)
    public double expectedPremiumFactor;

    @Parameter(value = 1)
    public int age;

    @Parameter(value = 2)
```

```java
    public Gender gender;

    @Parameters(name = "Case {index}: Expected {0} for {1} year old {2}s")
    public static Collection<Object[]> data() {
        return Arrays.asList(new Object[][]{
                {1.75, 18, Gender.MALE},
                {1.75, 23, Gender.MALE},
                {1.0, 24, Gender.MALE},
                {1.0, 59, Gender.MALE},
                {1.35, 60, Gender.MALE},
                {1.575, 18, Gender.FEMALE},
                {1.575, 23, Gender.FEMALE},
                {0.9, 24, Gender.FEMALE},
                {0.9, 59, Gender.FEMALE},
                {1.215, 60, Gender.FEMALE}}
        );
    }

    @Test
    public void verifyPremiumFactor() {
        assertEquals(expectedPremiumFactor, new PremiumRuleEngine()
                .getPremiumFactor(age, gender), 0.0);
    }
}
```

LISTING B.3 Theory test with custom `ParameterSupplier`. This test uses both a user-defined parameter supplier and `@TestedOn` (which is the only supplier that comes with JUnit).

```java
import org.junit.experimental.theories.Theories;
import org.junit.experimental.theories.Theory;
import org.junit.experimental.theories.suppliers.TestedOn;
import org.junit.runner.RunWith;
import util.supplier.AllGenders;

import static org.hamcrest.Matchers.*;
import static org.junit.Assert.assertThat;
import static org.junit.Assume.assumeThat;

@RunWith(Theories.class)
public class PremiumFactorsWithinRangeTestUsingTestedOn {

    @Theory
    public void premiumFactorsAreBetween0_5and2_0(
            @AllGenders Gender gender,
```

```
@TestedOn(ints = {17, 18, 19, 23, 24, 25,
            59, 60, 61, 100, 101}) int age) {

    assumeThat(age, greaterThanOrEqualTo(18));
    assumeThat(age, lessThanOrEqualTo(100));
    assumeThat(gender, isOneOf(Gender.FEMALE, Gender.MALE));

    double premiumFactor
            = new PremiumRuleEngine().getPremiumFactor(age, gender);
    assertThat(premiumFactor,
            is(both(greaterThan(0.5)).and(lessThan(2.0))));
    }
}
```

LISTING B.4   Parameter supplier implementation.

```
import domain.Gender;
import org.junit.experimental.theories.ParameterSignature;
import org.junit.experimental.theories.ParameterSupplier;
import org.junit.experimental.theories.PotentialAssignment;

import java.util.Arrays;
import java.util.List;

import static org.junit.experimental.theories.PotentialAssignment.forValue;

public class GenderSupplier extends ParameterSupplier {
    @Override
    public List<PotentialAssignment> getValueSources(
            ParameterSignature sig) {
        return Arrays.asList(
                forValue("gender", Gender.MALE),
                forValue("gender", Gender.FEMALE),
                forValue("gender", Gender.UNKNOWN));
    }
}
```

LISTING B.5   Parameter supplier annotation.

```
import org.junit.experimental.theories.ParametersSuppliedBy;

import java.lang.annotation.Retention;
import java.lang.annotation.RetentionPolicy;

@Retention(RetentionPolicy.RUNTIME)
```

```
@ParametersSuppliedBy(GenderSupplier.class)
public @interface AllGenders {
}
```

Test-driven Development

JUnit Version

LISTING B.6   The nine tests from the sample TDD session.

```
@Test
void searchingWhenNoDocumentsAreIndexedGivesNothing() {
    assert [] == searchEngine.find("fox")
}

@Test
void searchingForADocumentsOnlyWordGivesThatDocumentsId() {
    searchEngine.addToIndex(1, "fox")
    assert [1] == searchEngine.find("fox")
}

@Test
void allIndexedDocumentsAreSearched () {
    searchEngine.addToIndex(1, "fox")
    searchEngine.addToIndex(2, "dog")
    assert [2] == searchEngine.find("dog")
}

@Test
void documentsMayContainMoreThanOneWord() {
    searchEngine.addToIndex(1, "the quick brown fox")
    assert [1] == searchEngine.find("brown")
    assert [1] == searchEngine.find("fox")
}

@Test
void
searchingForAWordThatMatchesTwoDocumentsGivesBothDocumentsIds() {
    searchEngine.addToIndex(1, "fox")
    searchEngine.addToIndex(2, "fox")
    assert [1, 2] == searchEngine.find("fox").sort()
}

@Test
void multipleMatchesInADocumentProduceOneMatch () {
```

```
    searchEngine.addToIndex(1,
            "the quick brown fox jumped over the lazy dog")
    assert [1] == searchEngine.find("the")
}

@Test
void documentsAreSortedByWordFrequency() {
    searchEngine.addToIndex(1, "fox fox dog")
    searchEngine.addToIndex(2, "fox fox fox")
    searchEngine.addToIndex(3, "dog fox dog")
    assert [2, 1, 3] == searchEngine.find("fox")
    assert [3, 1] == searchEngine.find("dog")
}

@Test
void caseDoesNotMatter() {
    searchEngine.addToIndex(1, "FOX fox FoX");
    searchEngine.addToIndex(2, "foX FOx");
    searchEngine.addToIndex(3, "FoX");
    assert [1, 2, 3] == searchEngine.find("fox")
    assert [1, 2, 3] == searchEngine.find("FOX")
}

@Test
void punctuationMarksAreIgnored() {
    searchEngine.addToIndex(1, "quick, quick: quick.");
    searchEngine.addToIndex(2, "(brown) [brown] \"brown\" 'brown'");
    searchEngine.addToIndex(3, "fox; -fox fox? fox!");

    assert [1] == searchEngine.find("quick")
    assert [2] == searchEngine.find("brown")
    assert [3] == searchEngine.find("fox")
}
```

LISTING B.7 The `SearchEngine` **class.**

```
class SearchEngine {
    Map<String, List<WordFrequency>> index = [:]

    void addToIndex(int documentId, String contents) {
        preProcessDocument(contents).split(" ").each { word ->
            bumpWordFrequencyForDocument(index.get(word, []), documentId)
        }
        resortIndexOnWordFrequency()
    }
```

```
    private String preProcessDocument(String contents) {
        return contents.replaceAll("[\\.,!\\?:;\\(\\))\\[\\]\\-\"']","")
                .toUpperCase()
    }

    private void bumpWordFrequencyForDocument(List<WordFrequency>
            frequencies, int documentId) {
        def wordFrequency = frequencies.find
                { wf -> wf.documentId == documentId }
        if (!wordFrequency) {
            frequencies << (wordFrequency = new WordFrequency(documentId))
        }
        wordFrequency.count++
    }

    private resortIndexOnWordFrequency() {
        index.each { k, wfs -> wfs.sort
                { wf1, wf2 -> wf2.count <=> wf1.count } }
    }

    List<Integer> find(String word) {
        return index.get(word.toUpperCase(), [])
                .collect { wf -> wf.documentId }
    }
}
```

LISTING B.8   The `WordFrequency` **class.**

```
class WordFrequency {
    int documentId
    int count

    WordFrequency(int documentId) {
        this.documentId = documentId
    }
}
```

Spock Version

LISTING B.9   The nine tests from the sample TDD session, using Spock this time.

```
def "searching when no documents are indexed gives nothing"() {
    expect:
    searchEngine.find("fox") == []
}

def "searching for a document's only word gives that document's id"() {
```

```
    setup:
    searchEngine.addToIndex(1, "fox")

    expect:
    searchEngine.find("fox") == [1]
}

def "all indexed documents are searched"() {
    setup:
    searchEngine.addToIndex(1, "fox")
    searchEngine.addToIndex(2, "dog")

    expect:
    searchEngine.find("dog") == [2]
}

def "documents may contain more than one word"() {
    setup:
    searchEngine.addToIndex(1, "the quick brown fox")

    expect:
    searchEngine.find(word) == [documentId]

    // Slightly more strict than the JUnit version.
    where:
    word << ["the", "quick", "brown", "fox"]
    documentId << [1, 1, 1, 1]
}

def "searching for a word that matches two documents gives both documents' ids"() {
    setup:
    searchEngine.addToIndex(1, "fox")
    searchEngine.addToIndex(2, "fox")

    expect:
    searchEngine.find("fox").sort() == [1, 2]
}

def "multiple matches in a document produce one match"() {
    setup:
    searchEngine.addToIndex(1,
            "the quick brown fox jumped over the lazy dog")

    expect:
    searchEngine.find("the") == [1]
```

```
}

def "documents are sorted by word frequency"() {
    setup:
    searchEngine.addToIndex(1, "fox fox dog")
    searchEngine.addToIndex(2, "fox fox fox")
    searchEngine.addToIndex(3, "dog fox dog")

    expect:
    searchEngine.find("fox") == [2, 1, 3]
    searchEngine.find("dog") == [3, 1]
}

def "case doesn't matter"() {
    setup:
    searchEngine.addToIndex(1, "FOX fox FoX");
    searchEngine.addToIndex(2, "foX FOx");
    searchEngine.addToIndex(3, "FoX");

    expect:
    searchEngine.find("fox") == [1, 2, 3]
    searchEngine.find("FOX") == [1, 2, 3]
}

def "punctuation marks are ignored"() {
    setup:
    searchEngine.addToIndex(1, "quick, quick: quick.");
    searchEngine.addToIndex(2, "(brown) [brown] \"brown\" 'brown'");
    searchEngine.addToIndex(3, "fox; -fox fox? fox!");

    expect:
    searchEngine.find("quick") == [1]
    searchEngine.find("brown") == [2]
    searchEngine.find("fox") == [3]
}
```

Beyond Unit Testing

LISTING B.10 The `DriverFactory` class. Such classes hide the specifics of constructing various types of drivers from the tests. They're obviously more complicated in real test suites, but even this simple implementation hides the use of a directory (which would be configurable) and the fact that `HtmlUnitDriver` runs through the `RemoteWebDriver`.

```csharp
public class DriverFactory
{
    public static IWebDriver NewChromeDriver()
    {
        return new ChromeDriver(@"d:\drivers");
    }

    public static IWebDriver NewHtmlUnitDriver()
    {
        return new
            RemoteWebDriver(DesiredCapabilities.HtmlUnitWithJavaScript());
    }
}
```

BIBLIOGRAPHY

Adzic, Gojko. 2011. *Specification by Example: How Successful Teams Deliver the Right Software*. New York, NY: Manning Publications.

Adzic, Gojko. 2013. "Let's Break the Agile Testing Quadrants." http://gojko.net/2013/10/21/lets-break-the-agile-testing-quadrants/.

Alspaugh, Thomas A. 2015. "Kinds of Software Quality ("Ilities")." http://www.thomasalspaugh.org/pub/fnd/ility.html.

Bach, James. 2013. "Testing and Checking Refined." http://www.satisfice.com/blog/archives/856.

Bach, James. 2015. "Heuristics of Software Testability." http://www.satisfice.com/tools/testable.pdf.

Bath, Graham and McKay, Judy. 2008. *The Software Test Engineer's Handbook: A Study Guide for the ISTQB Test Analyst and Technical Analyst Advanced Level Certificates*. Santa Barbara, CA: Rocky Nook.

Beck, Kent. 2002. *Test-driven Development: By Example*. Boston, MA: Addison-Wesley.

Beck, Kent and Andres, Cynthia. 2004. *Extreme Programming Explained: Embrace Change, 2nd ed*. Boston, MA: Addison-Wesley.

Bolton, Michael. 2007. "Pairwise Testing (version 1.5, November, 2007)." http://www.developsense.com/pairwiseTesting.html.

Bolton, Michael. 2014. "The REAL Agile Testing Quadrants (As We Believe They Should Have Always Been)." http://www.slideshare.net/EuroSTARConference/306284037-2014-06dublinrst-agiletesting.

Borysowich, Craig. 2007. "Design Principles: Fan-In vs Fan-Out." http://it.toolbox.com/blogs/enterprise-solutions/design-principles-fanin-vs-fanout-16088.

Cimperman, Bob. 2006. *UAT Defined: A Guide to Practical User Acceptance Testing*. New York, NY: Addison-Wesley.

Claessen, Koen and Hughes, John. 2016. "QuickCheck - Automatic Specification-based Testing." http://www.cse.chalmers.se/~rjmh/QuickCheck/.

Cohn, Mike. 2009. *Succeeding with Agile: Software Development Using Scrum*. Upper Saddle River, NJ: Addison-Wesley.

Duvall, Paul M., Matyas, Steve, and Glover, Andrew. 2007. *Continuous Integration: Improving Software Quality and Reducing Risk*. Upper Saddle River, NJ: Addison-Wesley.

Evans, Eric. 2003. *Domain-Driven Design: Tackling Complexity in the Heart of Software*. Boston, MA: Addison-Wesley.

Faber, Szczepan. 2008. "Should I Worry about the Unexpected?" http://monkeyisland .pl/2008/07/12/should-i-worry-about-the-unexpected/.

Feathers, Michael C. 2004. *Working Effectively with Legacy Code*. Upper Saddle River, NJ: Prentice Hall.

Foote, Brian and Yoder, Joseph. 1999. "Big Ball of Mud." http://www.laputan.org/ mud/.

Fowler, Martin. 1999. *Refactoring: Improving the Design of Existing Code*. Boston, MA: Addison-Wesley.

Fowler, Martin. 2004. "JUnit New Instance." http://martinfowler.com/bliki/ JunitNewInstance.html.

Fowler, Martin. 2005. "Command Query Separation." http://martinfowler.com/bliki/ CommandQuerySeparation.html.

Fowler, Martin. 2007. "Mocks Aren't Stubs." http://martinfowler.com/articles/ mocksArentStubs.html.

Fowler, Martin, 2014. "Unit Test." http://martinfowler.com/bliki/UnitTest.html.

Freeman, Steve and Pryce, Nat. 2009. *Growing Object-Oriented Software, Guided by Tests*. Upper Saddle River, NJ: Addison-Wesley.

Gamma, Erich, Helm, Richard, Johnson, Ralph, and Vlissides, John. 1994. *Design Patterns: Elements of Reusable Object-Oriented Software*. Upper Saddle River, NJ: Addison-Wesley.

Gregory, Janet and Crispin, Lisa. 2008. *Agile Testing: A Practical Guide for Testers and Agile Teams*. Upper Saddle River, NJ: Addison-Wesley.

Gregory, Janet and Crispin, Lisa. 2014. *More Agile Testing: Learning Journeys for the Whole Team*. Upper Saddle River, NJ: Addison-Wesley.

Hendrickson, Elisabeth, Lyndsay, James, and Emery, Dale. 2006. "Test Heuristics Cheat Sheet, Data Type Attacks & Web Tests." http://testobsessed.com/wp-content/uploads/2011/04/testheuristicscheatsheetv1.pdf.

Humble, Jez and Farley, David. 2010. *Continuous Delivery: Reliable Software Releases through Build, Test, and Deployment Automation*, Upper Saddle River, NJ: Addison-Wesley.

Hunt, Andrew and Thomas, David. 1999. *Pragmatic Programmer: From Journeyman to Master.* Reading, PA: Addison-Wesley.

Hunt, Andrew and Thomas, David. 2003. *Pragmatic Unit Testing: In Java with JUnit.* Raleigh, NC: The Pragmatic Programmers.

International Software Qualifications Board (ISTQB). 2011. "Foundation Level Syllabus." http://www.istqb.org/downloads/finish/16/15.html.

Java Community Process (JCP). 2006. "JSR 305: Annotations for Software Defect Detection." https://jcp.org/en/jsr/detail?id=305.

JetBrains. 2016. "Code Quality Analysis - Code Annotations." https://www.jetbrains.com/resharper/features/code_analysis.html#Annotated_Framework.

Kaner, Cem, Bach, James, and Pettichord, Brat. 2001. *Lessons Learned in Software Testing: A Context-Driven Approach.* New York, NY: Wiley.

Kuhn, D. Richard, Kacker, Ranghu N., and Lei, Yu. 2010. "Practical Combinatorial Testing" *NIST Special Publication 800-142.* http://nvlpubs.nist.gov/nistpubs/Legacy/SP/nistspecialpublication800-142.pdf.

Kumar, Ajitesh, 2014. "7 Popular Unit Test Naming Conventions." https://dzone.com/articles/7-popular-unit-test-naming.

Langr, Jeff, Hunt, Andy, and Thomas, Dave. 2015. *Pragmatic Unit Testing in Java 8 with JUnit*, Dallas: The Pragmatic Programmers.

Marick, Brian. 2003. "My Agile Testing Project." http://www.exampler.com/old-blog/2003/08/21/#agile-testing-project-1.

Martin, Robert C. 2002. *Agile Software Development: Principles, Patterns, and Practices.* Upper Saddle River, NJ: Prentice Hall.

Martin, Robert C. 2008. *Clean Code: A Handbook of Agile Software Craftsmanship.* Upper Saddle River, NJ: Prentice Hall.

Martin, Robert C. 2010. "The Transformation Priority Premise. " http://blog.8thlight.com/uncle-bob/2013/05/27/TheTransformationPriorityPremise.html.

Martin, Robert C. 2011. *The Clean Coder: A Code of Conduct for Professional Programmers*. Upper Saddle River, NJ: Prentice Hall.

Martin, Robert C. 2014. "The Little Mocker." http://blog.8thlight.com/uncle-bob/2014/05/14/TheLittleMocker.html.

Meszaros, Gerard. 2007. *XUnit Test Patterns: Refactoring Test Code*. Upper Saddle River, NJ: Addison-Wesley.

Meszaros, Gerard. 2011. *XUnit Test Patterns*, http://xunitpatterns.com.

Meyer, Bertrand. 1997. *Object-Oriented Software Construction, 2nd ed*. New York, NY: Prentice Hall.

Microsoft Corporation. 2013. "Code Contracts User Manual (August 14, 2013)." http://research.microsoft.com/en-us/projects/contracts/userdoc.pdf.

Microsoft. 2016a. "Isolating Code Under Test with Microsoft Fakes." http://msdn.microsoft.com/en-us/library/hh549175.aspx.

Microsoft. 2016b. "Refactoring into Pure Functions." http://msdn.microsoft.com/en-us/library/bb669139.aspx.

North, Dan. 2006. "Introducing BDD." http://dannorth.net/introducing-bdd.

Oracle, 2013, "*The Java Language Specification: Java SE 7 Edition* - section 14.10." http://docs.oracle.com/javase/specs/jls/se7/html/jls-14.html#jls-14.10.

Osherove, Roy. 2005. "Naming Standards for Unit Tests." http://osherove.com/blog/2005/4/3/naming-standards-for-unit-tests.html.

Osherove, Roy. 2009. *The Art of Unit Testing: With Examples in .NET*. Greenwich, CT: Manning Publications.

OWASP, 2013. "OWASP Top 10—2013: The Ten Most Critical Web Application Security Risks." http://owasptop10.googlecode.com/files/OWASP%20Top%2010%20-%202013.pdf.

Palermo, Jeff. 2006. "Guidelines for Test-Driven Development." http://msdn.microsoft.com/en-us/library/aa730844(v=vs.80).aspx.

Poppendieck, Mary and Poppendieck, Tom. 2006. *Implementing Lean Software Development: From Concept to Cash*. Upper Saddle River, NJ: Addison-Wesley.

Pugh, Ken. 2011. *Lean-Agile Acceptance Test-Driven Development: Better Software Through Collaboration*. Upper Saddle River, NJ: Addison-Wesley.

RiSE (Microsoft). 2015. "Code Contracts for .NET." http://visualstudiogallery.msdn.microsoft.com/1ec7db13-3363-46c9-851f-1ce455f66970.

Ritchie, Stephen D. 2011. *Pro .Net Best Practices*. Berkeley, CA: Apress.

Saff, David and Boshernitsan, Marat. 2006. "The Practice of Theories: Adding "For-all" Statements to "There-Exists" Tests." http://shareandenjoy.saff.net/tdd-specifications.pdf.

Skeet, Jon. 2010. "Code Contracts in C#." http://www.infoq.com/articles/code-contracts-csharp.

Stallings, William and Brown, Lawrence. 2007. *Computer Security - Principles and Practice*. Upper Saddle River, NJ: Prentice Hall.

Stewart, Simon. 2010. "Test Sizes." http://googletesting.blogspot.se/2010/12/test-sizes.html.

Sutherland, Jeff and Schwaber, Ken. 2013. "The Scrum Guide (July 2013)." http://www.scrumguides.org.

Tarnowski, Alexander. 2010. "Why Must Test Code Be Better than Production Code." *Agile Record* 4:24–25.

Vance, Stephen. 2013. *Quality Code: Software Testing Principles, Practices, and Patterns*. Upper Saddle River, NJ: Addison-Wesley.

Weinberg, Gerald M. 1998. *The Psychology of Computer Programming*. New York, NY: Dorset House.

Woodward, Martin R. and Al-Khanjari, Zuhoor A. 2000. "Testability, Fault Size and the Domain-to-Range Ratio: An Eternal Triangle." *ACM SIGSOFT Software Engineering Notes* 25(5):168–172.

INDEX

A

Abstraction, level of
    high-level considerations for testing, 273
    programming language/frameworks
      impacting, 53–54
Acceptance test-driven development (ATDD),
    15–17
Acceptance tests
    end-to-end, as double-loop TDD, 221–222
    functional testing via, 27
    overview of, 26
    of services/components, 248–249
Accessor, in state verification, 173–174
Act, in Triple A test structure, 88–89
Actions
    in decision tables, 115
    in state transition model, 113–114
Activities, developer testing, 2–5
ACTS (Advanced Combinatorial Testing
    System) tool, pairwise testing, 149
Age checks, data types and testability, 72–76
Agile testing
    BDD, ATDD, and specification by
      example, 15–17
    summary, 19
    understanding, 13–15
Agile Testing Quadrants, 32–33
Algorithmic errors, in behavior testing,
    175–176
Almost unit tests
    examples, 152
    impact of, 156–157
    overview of, 151–152
    summary, 157
    test-specific mail servers, 153–154
    using in-memory databases, 152–153
    using lightweight containers, 154–155
    of web services, 155–156

APIs (application programming interfaces)
    in components, 24
    deciding on developer testing strategy, 268
    discovering for simple search engine,
      193–194
    domain-specific languages for, 42
    error/exception handling for public, 63
    testing web services, 155–156
    in tests using in-memory databases, 152
    using/testing vendor payment gateways,
      250–251
Archetype, considerations for testing, 273
Argument matchers, stubs in mocking
    framework, 181–182
Arguments
    contracts, 61
    stubs in mocking framework, 181–182
Arrange-Act-Assert, Triple A test structure,
    88–89
Assert, in Triple A test structure, 88–89
`AssertEquals` method
    as assertion method, 89, 106
    data-driven and combinatorial testing,
      136–137, 280
    generative testing, 143
    implementing mockist style TDD, 213–214
    mock objects, 164, 167–168
    spies, 171
    working with test code, 238
Assertions
    assumptions vs., 141
    constraints and matchers, 94–99
    contract verification, 62–63
    of equality, 93–94
    exceptions to one per test, 90–92
    fluent, 96–97